MODERN INFORMATION SYSTEMS

Edited by **Christos Kalloniatis**

Modern Information Systems
Edited by Christos Kalloniatis

Published by InTech
Janeza Trdine 9, 51000 Rijeka, Croatia

Publishing Process Manager Romina Skomersic

Technical Editor Teodora Smiljanic

Cover Designer InTech Design Team

Additional hard copies can be obtained from orders@intechopen.com

Modern Information Systems, Edited by Christos Kalloniatis
p. cm.
ISBN 978-953-51-0647-0

For EU product safety concerns:
IN TECH d.o.o., Prolaz Marije Krucifikse Kozulić 3, 51000 Rijeka, Croatia,
info@intechopen.com or visit our website at intechopen.com.

Meet the editor

Dr Christos Kalloniatis holds a B.Sc. in Informatics from the Department of Informatics of the Technological Educational Institute of Athens, an M.Sc. in Computer Science from the Department of Computer Science of the University of Essex, UK ,and a Ph.D. in Informatics from the Department of Cultural Technology and Communication of the University of the Aegean. Currently, he is a lecturer at the Department of Cultural Technology and Communication of the University of the Aegean. His current research interests include: Security and privacy in Information Systems, software engineering models and tools and cloud computing. He is an author of several refereed papers in international scientific journals and conference proceedings. He is a member of several program committees of national and international conferences related to Information Security and Privacy and software engineering and is also a reviewer in several scientific journals. He is a member of the Greek Computer Society and has served as a member on the ACM and the IEEE. He is married and lives in Mytilene, the capital of Lesvos Island, in Greece.

Contents

Preface

Nowadays, Information and Communication Systems Technologies are rapidly expanding in order to fulfill the increased needs of our demanding modern Information Society. More and more fundings are invested every year for the development of new, innovative and technologically advanced Information Systems that will be efficient enough to satisfy users' requirements and be adaptive enough so as to cooperate with the cutting-edge aspects of IT and mobile technologies.

The development of modern information systems is a demanding task. New technologies and tools are designed, implemented and presented in the market on a daily bases. Users' needs change dramatically fast and the IT industry copes to reach the level of efficiency and adaptability for its systems in order to be competitive and up-to-date. All this fast moving phenomenon leads to the realization of modern information systems with great characteristics and functionalities implemented for specific areas of interest. These systems provide high efficiency, cutting-edge characteristics and their implementation is based on novel and highly efficient techniques derived from well-known research areas.

Therefore, this book aims to present a number of innovative and recently developed information systems. It is titled "Modern Information Systems" and includes 8 chapters. This book may assist researchers on studying the innovative functions of modern systems in various areas like health, telematics, knowledge management, etc. It can also assist young students in capturing the new research tendencies of the information systems' development.

Christos Kalloniatis
Department of Cultural Technology and Communication,
University of the Aegean,
Greece

1

Use of Descriptive Statistical Indicators for Aggregating Environmental Data in Multi-Scale European Databases

Panos Panagos, Yusuf Yigini and Luca Montanarella
Joint Research Centre of the European Commission,
Institute for Environment and Sustainability,
Italy

1. Introduction

1.1 Policy context

There is a strong need for accurate and spatially referenced information regarding policy making and model linkage. This need has been expressed by land users, and policy and decision makers in order to estimate spatially and locally the impacts of European policy (like the Common Agricultural Policy) and/or global changes on economic agents and consequently on natural resources (Cantelaube et al., 2012).

The proposal for a framework Directive (COM (2006) 232) (EC, 2006) sets out common principles for protecting soils across the EU. Within this common framework, the EU Member States will be in a position to decide how best to protect soil and how use it in a sustainable way on their own territory. In this policy document, European Commission identifies 8 soil threats: soil erosion, soil organic carbon decline, salinisation, landslides, soil compaction, biodiversity and soil contamination. The policy document explains why EU action is needed to ensure a high level of soil protection, and what kind of measures must be taken. As the soil threats have been described in the proposed Soil Thematic Strategy for Soil Protection (COM (2006) 231), there is a need to address them and relative issues at various scales; from local/province scale, to regional/national scale, and at the end to continental/global scale. The modeling platform should be constructed in such a way that knowledge and information can be passed along the spatial scales causing the minimum loss of information. Particular interest will be given to outputs from the aggregation model such as organic carbon decline, soil erosion and soil.

The INSPIRE Directive (INSPIRE, 2007) aims at making relevant geographic information available and structurally interoperable for the purpose of formulation, implementation, monitoring and evaluation of Community policy-making related to the environment. To that end, data specifications for various themes are to be developed. The Soil theme is listed in Annex III of the INSPIRE Directive.

Soil organic data are requested for models relating to climate change. The role of soil in this debate, in particular peat, as a store of carbon and its role in managing terrestrial fluxes of carbon dioxide (CO_2), has become prominent. Soil contains about twice as much organic carbon as aboveground vegetation. Soil organic carbon stocks in the EU-27 are estimated to be around 75 billion tonnes of carbon (Jones et al., 2005).

Soil data and information are highly relevant for the development, implementation and assessment of a number of EU policy areas: agriculture, soil protection, bio-energy, water protection, nature protection, development policy, health and sustainable development. All those policy areas request soil data in various scales depending on the application.

Regarding research purposes, according to the data logs in European Soil Data Centre (Panagos et al., 2012), the users deploy ESDAC data mainly (but not exclusively) for modeling purposes (35%). Most of the modelling exercises request the input data to be transferred in a specific scale in order to fit the modeling purposes. Most of the modeling is performed in small scales covering few square kilometres; however, during the last years the modeling exercises performed in national or European level is increasing due to high demand for environmental indicators performance.

1.2 Multi-scale European Soil Information System (MEUSIS)

Implementation of the INSPIRE directive should emerge the development of a Multi-scale European Soil Information System (MEUSIS), from the data producer up to the final user, responding to the various needs at different scales. In order to achieve this, a common standard for the collection of harmonized soil information will have to be implemented. As a response to this requirement, MEUSIS is proposed as a harmonized hierarchical Grid (Raster) data system which constitutes an ideal framework for the building of a nested system of soil data. This reference grid is based on implementing rules facilitating data interoperability.

The final result of these developments should be the operation of a harmonized soil information system for Europe streamlining the flow of information from the data producer at a local scale to the data users at the more general Regional, National, European and Global scales. Such a system should facilitate the derivation of data needed for the regular reporting about the state of European soils by European Commission authorities.

However, soil geography, soil qualities and soil degradation processes are highly variable in Europe. Soil data sets from different countries have been often created using different nomenclatures and measuring techniques, which is at the origin of current difficulties with comparability of soil data. The availability of soil data is also extremely variable in Europe. Individual Member States have taken different initiatives on soil protection aimed at those soil degradation processes they considered to be a priority.

Traditionally, the European Soil Database has been distributed in vector format. More recently, interest was expressed for deriving a raster version of this database. In the specific case of MEUSIS, the advantages of the raster approach are listed below:

- Easy to identify the data per location. Each cell has an ID and its geographic location is determined by its position in the matrix cell.
- It is fairly easy to store data and to perform data analysis.

- It is easy to integrate data from different data sources or different data types. As a result soil data could be processed by other environmental indicators and can be imported in data models such as climate change ones.
- The pixel approach would make it easier for data to be updated.
- The structure is suitable to perform upscaling (bottom-up) from local to regional, national and European level.

The main disadvantage of the raster approach is that this technique is less precise in representing the real world, which means that it is not suitable for representing soil coverage complexity and it might not be always easy to persuade the general public about the potential usability of this technique. In Figure 1 portray an example on how pixel cells of $1km^2$ size may be represented in a higher resolution grid or raster of $10\ km^2$.

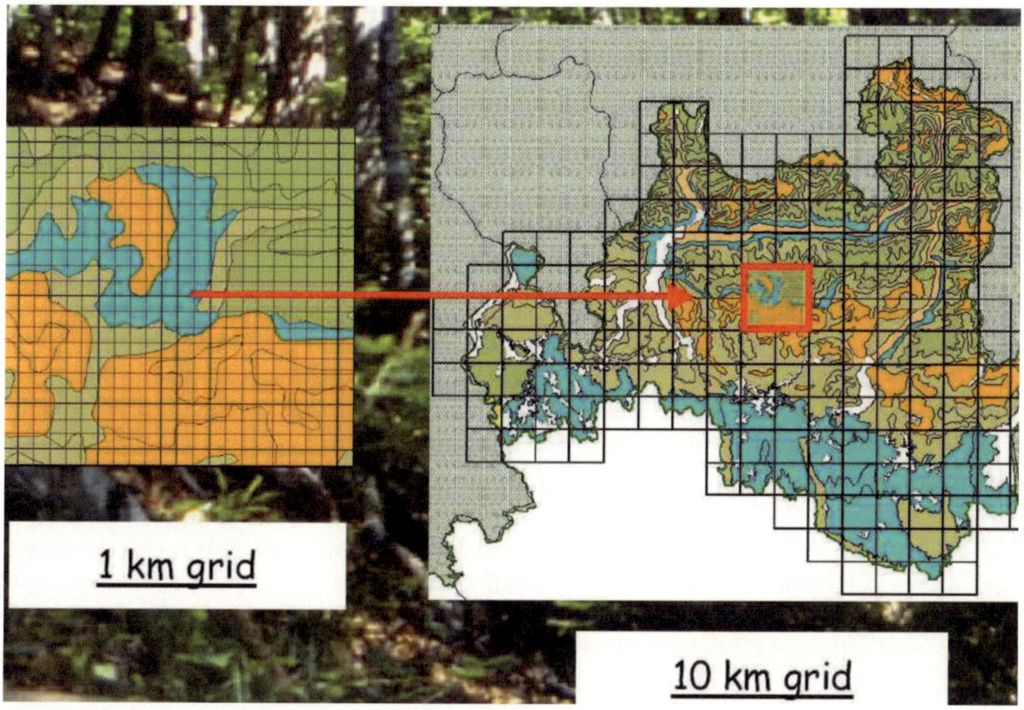

Fig. 1. Grid Example in 2 different resolutions

2. Upscaling

Upscaling of environmental indicators applied in regional analyses is sensitive to scale issues of the input Data (Bechini et al., 2011). Environmental assessments are frequently carried out with indicators (Viglizzo et al., 2006) and simulation models (Saffih- Hdadi and Mary, 2008). The environmental indicators have an increasing importance and are easily understandable by the general public. Those quantitative expressions measure the condition of a particular environmental attribute in relation to thresholds set by scientific community. However, decision makers use the environmental indicators to communicate with the general public.

When dealing with areas of different sizes and with information available at different scales, policy makers and decision makers need to either upscale their evaluations and simulations from small to large scale or downscale from large to small scale (Stein et al., 2001). Environmental indicators are dependent upon data availability and also upon the scale for which policy statements are required. As these may not match, changes in scales may be necessary. Moreover, change is scale may requested in research and modeling where the indicator is used as input parameter in a model. It has been recognised that the quality of indicators relies on the scale which they represent. The quality of the state of the environment at a local scale, for example, requires different information compared to the state of the environment at national scale.

From the one hand, ecologists criticize upscaling approaches insisting that it ecological knowledge is difficult to scale up (Ehleringer and Field, 1993). They support that environmental systems are organized hierarchically with multiple processes taking place across scales. When moving from a finer scale to a coarser one in this nested hierarchy, new processes may be encountered which is difficult to be translated in research results. The environmental systems are not non linear ones and no scaling rules can be imposed to express such a behaviour. Environmental systems are spatially heterogeneous due to spatial variations in climatic and soil conditions. As you can see from the references, this was mostly the trend in the 80's-90's while in the recent years there are many applications of upscaling in many environmental fields.

Scale for environmental indicators has barely been addressed in the literature. Scale issues are considered to be of importance (Bierkens et al., 2000) and advantages have been reported in hydrology (Feddes, 1995) and soil science (Hoosbeek and Bouma, 1998; McBratney, 1998). Upscaling is the process of aggregating information collected at a fine scale towards a coarser scale (Van Bodegom et al., 2002). Downscaling is the process of detailing information collected at a coarse scale towards a finer scale.

Scale is defined as the spatial resolution of the data. Scales, defined in terms of resolution and procedures, are presented to translate data from one scale to another: upscaling to change from high resolution data towards a low resolution, and downscaling for the inverse process. Environmental assessments at a small scale commonly rely on measured input, whereas assessments at a large scale are mainly based on estimated inputs that cannot be measured or outputs of modeling exercises.

Policy makers request to know also the uncertainty of environmental assessments in order to better interpret the results and proceed with the most suitable decision. The quantification of uncertainty implies the confidence level of indicators which can be measured with statistical measurement such as standard deviation.

Upscaling in complexity means that data quality degrades with decreasing complexity, because information is generalised and uncertainty increases. In literature, upscaling is defined as the process that replaces a heterogeneous domain with a homogeneous one in such a manner that both domains produce the same response under some upscaled boundary conditions (Rubin, 1993). The difficulty in upscaling stems from the inherent spatial variability of soil properties and their often nonlinear dependence on state variables. In 2004, Harter and Hopmans have distinguished four different scales: pore scale, local (macroscopic), field and regional (watershed). In this study the upscaled processes are performed between 3 scales: local, regional and national.

The scaling methods are applied before the geostatistical analysis in order to avoid dealing with multiple, spatially variable but correlated physical quantities. Environmental modelling requires the input spatial data to be in the same scale and upscaling/downscaling processes assist in transferring the input data in the requested scale. Geostatistics is used to make predictions of attributes at un-sampled locations from sparse auxiliary data. Upscaling is also used in disciplines or applications where there may be too much data which need to reduced to manageable proportions.

Based on King's approach for explicit upscaling in space (King, 1991), we will try to integrate the heterogeneity that accompanies the change in model extent by averaging across heterogeneity in the soil organic carbon data and calculating mean values for the model's arguments.

3. Material and methods

3.1 Indicators – Organic carbon

An environmental indicator is defined as a measure to evaluate or describe an environmental system. The indicator should be measurable and the threshold values attached to it would facilitate its presentation to the public. The indicators require to a scientific background and a sound method of evaluation (Gaunt et al., 1997). One of the main characteristics for the definition of an environmental indicator is the application in space and time. In this context, the indicator can be aggregated to a more coarse scale in order to serve decision making. Here, comes the contribution of statistics in comparing the indicators by using specific figures such as mean, median, mode, standard deviation, sample variance, quartile, ranges, etc.

Soil research and policy makers in the soil field needs statistics to support and confirm the impressions and interpretations of investigations in the field. The use of mathematics and statistics becomes more and more popular among soil scientists. The terms such as geostatistics become popular in the soil science community while new software tools facilitate such data processing with the help of more powerful computers.

However, Minasny and McBratney argued that better prediction of soil properties can be achieved more with gathering higher quality data than using sophisticated geostatistical methods and tools. However, it should be underlined the high cost and the time consuming for laboratory analysis of field data; that is why research in developing methods for the creation of soil maps from sparse soil data is becoming increasingly important. In the last 20 years, the development of prediction methods using cheap auxiliary data to spatially extend sparse and expensive soil information has become a focus of research in digital soil mapping (Minasny and McBratney, 2007). Examples of secondary information, named covariates, include remote sensing images, elevation data, land cover and crop yield data.

In order to describe the upscaling methodology, a data field such as the Organic Carbon (OC) content in the surface horizon 0-30 cm of the Slovakia Soil Database will be used. The Organic Carbon is a quantitative attribute measured as tones per hectare according to the following equation:

$$OC(t/ha) = Cox * BD * d$$

Where,
Cox (%) is the average content of organic carbon for topsoil/subsoil,
BD (g/cm^3) is the average soil bulk density for topsoil/subsoil,
d (cm) is the volume of topsoil/subsoil

Soil organic carbon is an important soil component as it influences soil structure and aggregation, soil moisture conditions, soil nutrient status and soil biota, and hence influences ecosystem functioning (Lal, 2004).

3.2 Changes in scale

Spatial scale refers to the representativeness of the singe measurements (or observations) for larger mapping units. The level of variation is different depending on the scale; few measurements at a coarse scale in a large area have a different variation from few measurements in a fine scale or many measurements in a large scale. Upscaling is the process of changing scale from fine to coarser one and it is performed with procedures such as averaging or block kriging. Use of confidence levels and ranges appears useful in upscaling. The use of GIS advanced systems is useful to visualise the affects of upscaled result and contribute better t communication with public and decision makers.

3.3 Aggregation technique and cell factor

Scale factors in general are defined as conversion factors that relate the characteristics of one system to the corresponding characteristics of another system (Tillotson and Nielsen, 1984). Aggregating functions in the upscaling methodology and spatial data process will be done using ArcGIS software. As a GIS technique, spatial join is proposed since spatial data from one layer can be aggregated and added to objects of the other layer, which is often referred to as the destination layer. Aggregation is accomplished via a cell fit criterion since many data cells from one source layer would fit in one cell in the destination layer. The modeller must decide how existing attributes will be summarized during aggregation (e.g., averages, sums, median, and mode). Aggregation of raster data always involves a cell size increase and a decrease in resolution. This is accomplished by multiplying the cell size of the input raster by a cell factor, which must be an integer greater than 1. For instance, a cell factor of 2 implies that the cell size of the output raster would be 2 times greater than cell size of input raster (e.g., an input resolution of 5km multiplied by 2 equals an output resolution of 10km). The cell factor also determines how many input cells are used to derive a value for each output cell. For example, a cell factor of 2 requires 2×2 or $4(2^2)$ input cells. The cell factor also determines how many input cells are used to derive a value for each output cell the following equation:

$$\textit{Output Cell Size} = \textit{Input Cell Size} \times \textit{Cell Factor}$$

In the proposed upscaling methodology, the value of each output cell is calculated as the mean or median of the input cells that fall within the output cell. In our study the scale factors will be 2, 5 and 10.

4. Methodology application of MEUSIS in Slovakia

The present chapter uses the results of a case study implemented in Slovakia in 2006 and the resulting Slovakia Soil Database. Due to financial resources, it is impossible to make such an assessment on a larger scale and one of the EU-27 member states has been selected in order to perform the testing phase. In 2005-2006 period, the SSCRI, using its expertise to identify the appropriate local data sources, compiled the Slovakian Soil Database on three scales following MEUSIS requirements and, eventually, provided structured metadata as a complement part of the data. The data are considered relatively new in the soil science domain if you think that the European Soil Database contains national data which have been collected in the '70s and imported in digital format in the '80s.

Due to their specificity in terms of soil geography (variability in soil organic carbon content) and their data availability, the selected pilot areas in Slovakia have contributed to the analysis of the feasibility of such an innovative approach. In MEUSIS, all geographical information (Attributes and Geometry components) are represented by the grid of regular spatial elements (pixels). The representation of various spatial resolution details follows the INSPIRE recommendations. In addition, three **spatial resolution levels** of geographical information have been defined for MEUSIS:

- 10 km^2 (10km x 10km) coarse resolution grid, corresponding to data collection in national level
- 5 km^2 (5km x 5km) medium resolution grid, corresponding to data collection in regional level
- 1 km^2 (1km x 1km), fine resolution grid corresponding to data collection in local level

Fig. 2. Demonstration of upscaling

4.1 Upscaling from 5km^2 grid towards the 10km^2 grid

According to the aggregation technique described above, 4 cells of 5km x 5km size are requested in order to upscale their value to one single cell of 10 km x 10 km. The aggregation of the 5km x 5km grid cells is performed using both the MEAN value of the 4 cells and the MEDIAN value of the 4 cells producing 2 output datasets of 129 cells sized at10 km^2 each. In the cases near the borders, less than 4 cells are aggregated in order "produce" a cell of a coarser resolution at 10km^2.

The aggregation of 4 data cells using the Median function has an interesting drawback since if there are 3 cells out of 4 (cases near the borders of the input data) with 0 value, then the Median value of the 4 data cells is taking 0 value while the Mean value is different than 0. In order not to take into account those "extreme" cases which may alter our analysis, we will exclude the 5 cells. That implies that the 2 upscaled dataset plus the original one enclose 124 cells.

The present analysis may be applied also in order to identify cases where the data provider has previously performed the "tricky" operation well-known as downscaling. The proposed methodology can serve also as a first data quality check in order to find out if the data providers have contributed with their original data or they have manipulated their data by downscaling their coarser resolution data to finer resolution ones.

In figure 3, the scatter diagram reports the original 10km^2 values on the Y axis and the Upscaled (MEAN, MEDIAN) data on the Y axis. It is obvious that there is a noticeable linear relationship between the 2 upscaled datasets and the original data as there is a major concentration of data values near a line.

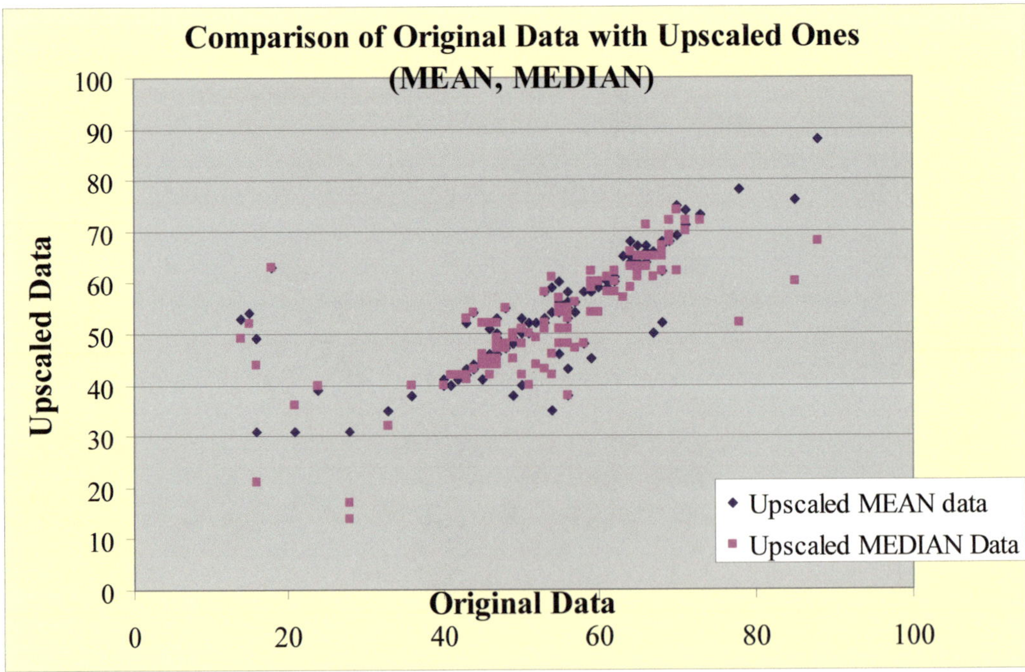

Fig. 3. Scatter Diagram of the Original data and Upscaled MEAN data

In the past, there were many theoretical references to an ideal MEUSIS as a nested system of hierarchical grids while in this analysis, we describe the results of the applied upscaling methodology in the Slovakian MEUSIS using both GIS operations and Statistical Analysis

(Descriptors, Scatter Diagram). Table 1 presents the core statistical indicators (Kavussanos, 2005) assessing the results of upscaling application.

Description of statistic	*Original Data 10km²*	*Upscaled data using MEAN*	*Upscaled data using MEDIAN*
Mean	52,96	53,76	52,29
Median	53	53	51,5
Mode	47	53	48
Standard Deviation	13,51	10,94	10,73
Sample Variance	182,61	119,58	115,18
Coefficient of Kurtosis	1,26	-0,03	1,30
Coefficient of Skewness	-0,65	0,25	-0,51
Range	74	57	60
Minimum	14	31	14
Maximum	88	88	74
P25 (First Quartile)	47	47	46
P75 (Third Quartile)	63	62	62
Count (Cells)	124	124	124
Confidence interval (95%)	2,40	1,94	1,91
Correlation Coefficient(r)		0,767	0,740

Table 1. Descriptive Statistics of the Upscaling Process from 5km² towards 10km²

The results of upscaling process which have used the MEAN value (named as Upscaled MEAN data) and the ones which have used the MEAN value (named as Upscaled MEDIAN data) will be compared against the Original data 10km² (supplied by the data provider) which is the criterion called to validate both processes. Find below the following remarks:

- The **Means** in both upscaled datasets are very close to the original data mean. Two are the possible explanations to this outcome:
  - Either the data sources for both the 10 km² Original and the 5 km² Original data are the same; this means that the original 5 km² numeric values, have previously been downscaled from the 10 km² Original ones. In practice, a newly introduced advantage of upscaling process is the detection of such data patterns. According to the data pattern, this is not the case in our datasets since the detailed data of 5 km² have a high variability inside the border of the 10km².
  - *Or* the use of the above mentioned upscaling method is producing satisfactory results.
- The **Median** values of both aggregated datasets are very close to the Median value of the original data. The **Mode** of upscaled MEDIAN data is very close to the mode of the original ones. Being almost the same, mean, median and mode of the upscaled MEAN data suggests symmetry in the distribution and once again confirm the theory that many naturally-occurring phenomena can be approximated by normal distributions (Dikmen, 2003).

Taking into account the three above mentioned measures of central tendency (Mean, Median, and Mode), we conclude that there are no extreme values that can affect the distributions of the three datasets. There is a small-medium variability regarding the Organic Carbon Content in the scale of 5km^2 and as a consequence the upscaling process gives positive results either using the MEAN or the MEDIAN.

- **Range** and **Quartile indicators** show that there is quite medium variability in the original data which becomes smoother in the upscaled datasets.
- The original data have a relative higher **Standard Deviation** than the two upscaled datasets and it is evident that the two aggregated datasets show a "smooth" variability as they have reduced the dispersion of the data.
- **Data Distribution**: Regarding the prediction of intervals, it is it has been observed that the distribution of both upscaled data tends to be a normal distribution and as a consequence we may use the Standard Normal Distribution. With a **probability of 95%,** the range of possible values for the parameter Organic Carbon content 0-30cm will vary according to the equation;

$$P(-1.96\sigma \leq X - \mu \leq 1.96\sigma) = 0.95$$

All the above mentioned measures of dispersion show that upscaling process has a tendency for more smother data comparing with the original values.

- The frequency distributions in all three datasets are platykurtic (**Coefficient of Kurtosis)** and have a negative **Skewness** (except the original data with a symmetric distribution)
- **Correlation Coefficient or Pearson Correlation Coefficient** (r) is a measure of the strength of the linear relationship between two variables. It is not our objective to prove that there is a dependency between the 2 datasets; instead a possible high value of Coefficient indicates how good predictions we can make if we try to upscale the detailed data. The original 10km^2 data are used to **validate** how good forecasts can be given by the aggregated values. The value 0,767 determines a quite strong relationship between the upscaled MEAN data and the original ones (It is also obvious from the Scatter Diagram in Figure 3).

4.2 Upscaling from 1km^{2}grid towards the 10km^2 grid

In order to update one cell of 10km x 10km, it is requested 100 cells of 1km x 1km. The data provider has collected data for 4.409 cells of 1km^2 which may be upscaled to 59 cells of 10km^2. In the cases near the borders, less than 100 cells are aggregated in order "produce" a cell of a coarser resolution at 10km. In Figure 4, the existing data covers only 14 1km^2 cells and the majority of the cells (11 out of 14) have 0 values. As a result the Mean is estimated with a value around 9 but the median will have a 0 value. In order not to take into account those "extreme" cases which may alter our analysis, we will exclude the 4 cells which have given results like the one shown above.

After implementing the upscaling process, the output datasets (Upscaled MEAN data, Upscaled MEDIAN data) have 55 common cells with the Original 10km^2 data. In the following paragraphs a more in depth statistical analysis will follow in order to assess the results of upscaling application.

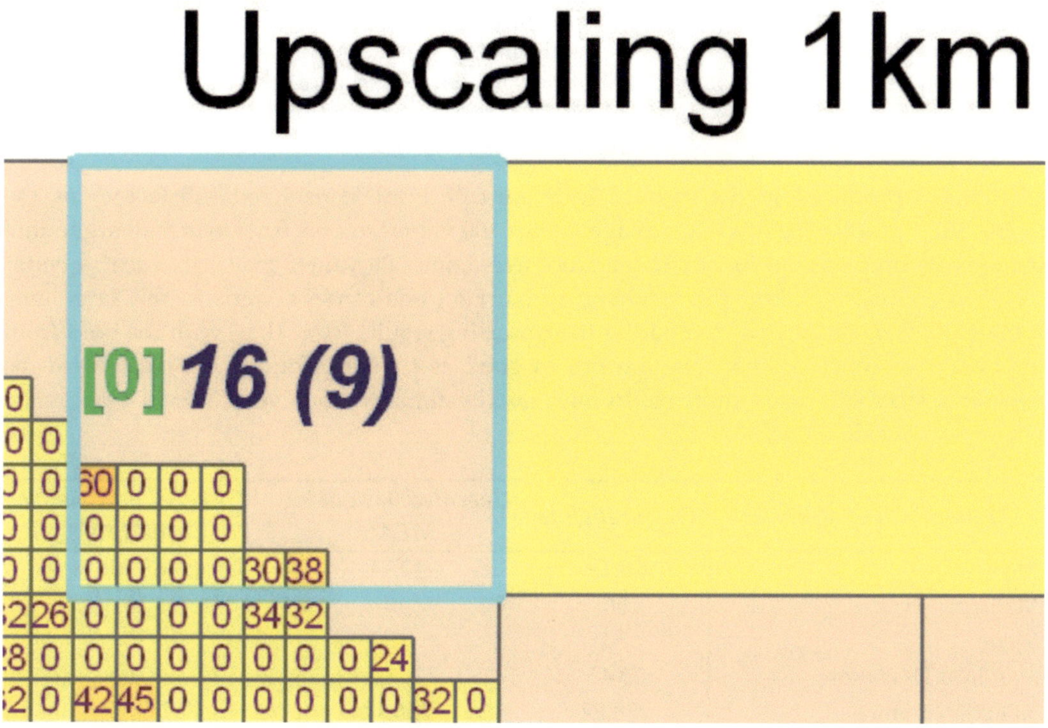

Fig. 4. The extreme case of MEDIAN upscale

Proceeding with the statistical analysis, some statistical descriptors are compared in the table 2 and the following remarks came out:

- Evaluating the **Mean** of the 3 datasets, we observe a slightly significant difference between the 2 Means of the upscaled data and the Mean of the original data. More than 10 tones per hectare difference may be explained as the upscaled data tend to have lower values than the original ones due to high dispersion of original data.
- Regarding the **Median** and the **Mode**, there is even a larger difference between the 2 upscaled datasets and the original data since the upscaling process has the trend to "produce" lower values.

Comparing the Upscaling results using the MEAN function with those using the MEDIAN function, we notice that the first ones tend to be better. The statistical indicators of the Upscaled MEAN data are closer to the Original data indicators. The upscaled MEDIAN data show a smoother dispersion and they show a big "concentration" around their mean.

- The **Range** of the Original data is higher than the one of the Upscaled MEAN data and much higher than the Upscaled MEDIAN data. The same comment is also referring to the P25 and P75 **Quartiles**.
- The **Standard Deviation** of the Upscaled MEAN data and the Original data are almost the same, while the standard deviation of the Upscaled MEDIAN data is much lower. The upscaled MEDIAN data show a very smooth variability while the other two datasets have almost the same variability.

- The **Correlation Coefficient** has a value of 0,49 between the Upscaled MEAN data and the Original data which express a medium-strong relationship (neither too strong, nor weak) between the 2 data distributions. Instead, this coefficient is smaller for the relationship between the Upscaled MEDIAN data and the Original ones which express a medium relationship between the 2 data distributions.

The results produced in the case of 1km^2 upscaling are considered satisfactory as the aggregation process that takes place aggregates 100 values to one. Scientists may argue that the upscale process may function well since averaging 100 values may "produce" a better result in an area of 10km^2 than picking up (survey) one random value in this large area (Original Data). At the end, comparing the upscaling results from 1km^2 with the ones from the 5km^2, we conclude that they are not as good as the latter ones. This remark can be explained since it is more probable to have good estimates when you upscale 4 cells than when you upscale 100 cells.

Description of statistic	*Original Data*	*Upscaled data using MEAN*	*Upscaled data using MEDIAN*
Mean	54,13	42,71	43,13
Median	56	40	44
Mode	50	29	30
Standard Deviation	15,43	16,00	10,56
Sample Variance	238,22	256,14	111,52
Coefficient of Kurtosis	1,29	1,11	0,20
Coefficient of Skewness	-0,77	0,98	0,06
Range	76	73	56
Minimum	12	16	16
Maximum	88	89	72
P25 (First Quartile)	47	33	35
P75 (Third Quartile)	65	52	50
Count (Cells)	55	55	55
Confidence Interval (95%)	4,17	4,33	2,85
Correlation Coefficient(r)		0,490	0,401

Table 2. Descriptive Statistics of the Upscaling Process from 1km^2 towards 10km^2

4.3 Upscaling from 1km^{2}grid towards the 5km^2 grid

In this case, the hierarchical grid system requests 25 cells of 1km^2 in order to update 1 cell of 5km^2. In the Slovakia Soil Database there are available 4.409 cells of 1km^2 and the upscaling process had as an output 207 cells of 5km^2. In this case, it was more evident the problem of the 0-value MEDIAN cells described above (with the Figure 4). In order not to alter the comparison results, the 20 cells with 0-value have been excluded and the outputs of 187 upscaled cells of 5km^2 will be compared in table 3.

Proceeding with the statistical analysis, some statistical descriptors are compared in the table 3 and the following remarks came out:

- The **Mean** values of the upscaled datasets are very close but still quite "distant" from the Mean value of the Original data. Around 8-9 tones per hectare difference may be explained as the upscaled data tend to have lower values than the original ones due to high dispersion of original data. Of course, the variability is less than the previous upscaling exercise since 25 cells is aggregated comparing with the 100 cells in the previous chapter.
- The **Standard Deviation** of the Upscaled MEAN data and the Original data are almost the same, while the Standard Deviation of the Upscaled MEDIAN data is much lower. The same "pattern" has been noticed in the previous upscaling exercise.
- The **Correlation Coefficient** has a value of 0,62 between the Upscaled MEAN data and the Original data which express a quite-strong relationship between the 2 data distributions. This indicator is used only to forecast how good can be possible predictions of the original data based on the upscaling processes.

Comparing the Upscaling results using the MEAN function with those using the MEDIAN function, we study that the first ones tend to follow the data pattern of the original data. Instead, the upscaled MEDIAN data show a smoother variability since they are more concentrated around their mean value. The statistical indicators, in the case of $1km^2$ upscaling towards $5km^2$, can be considered somehow in between the other 2 exercises with closer trend towards the results of the $1km^2$ to $10km^2$ upscaling. This remark can be explained since statistically it is more probable to have worst estimates when you upscale 25 cells than when you upscale 4 cells and better estimates than upscaling 100 cells.

Description of statistic	*Original Data*	*Upscaled data using MEAN*	*Upscaled data using MEDIAN*
Mean	54,98	46,21	45,75
Median	57	40	45
Mode	55	38	36
Standard Deviation	21,42	22,69	12,65
Sample Variance	458,82	514,97	160,12
Coefficient of Kurtosis	5,11	10,24	1,07
Coefficient of Skewness	-0,01	2,75	0,52
Range	161	154	84
Minimum	0	15	15
Maximum	161	169	99
P25 (First Quartile)	49	34	36
P75 (Third Quartile)	65	51	53
Count (Cells)	207	187	187
Confidence Interval (95%)	2,94	3,27	1,83
Correlation Coefficient(r)		0,62	0,54

Table 3. Descriptive Statistics of the Upscaling Process from $1km^2$ towards $5km^2$

5. Cross-comparison and conclusions on the 3 upscaling exercises

Major objective of this chapter is to analyse further the statistical indicators that have been described above, find out some more "interesting" relationships between various factors and compare the 3 upscaling exercises.

5.1 The "non-perfect squares" coverage effect

It has been observed in all three upscaling exercises that some squares have aggregated less input detailed data than required according to the Cell factor definition in the Technical Implementation. This observation is noticed in the borders of the data area. The concept of "**non-perfect squares**" is defined for those upscaled data cells where less than required data cells are aggregated.

In table 4, the Ration of Real to Expected squares can be defined as the percentage (%) of more cells that have been "produced" in the upscaling process due to the "non-Perfect Square" fact. In the first case there are 8,6% more cells than the expected ones, in the $1km^2$ towards $5km^2$ there are 17,4% more cells and in the $1km^2$ towards $10km^2$ upscaling there are 33,8% more cells. It is obvious that the Ratio of real to expected squares has a very strong positive relationship to the Cell Factor since it is increasing as the Cell Factor increases. Performing a regression analysis, the following outputs are found:

Ration = 1,02 + 0,031 * Cell Factor With coefficient of Determination: **R^2 = 0,9990**

Upscaling Exercise	*Cell Factor*	*Nr. of Input Cells*	*Expected squares (in case of perfect matching)*	*Real upscaled squares*	*Ratio of Real to expected*
5km towards 10km	2	475	118,75	129	1,086
1km towards 5km	5	4409	176,36	207	1,174
1km towards 10km	10	4409	44,09	59	1,338

Table 4. Analysis of "Non-Perfect Square"

The results are interesting allowing the modelers to identify how many more cells will have if they use an alternative Cell Factor. Even if this analysis may take different values in another country, the relationship between Cell Factor and additional cells will be always positive according to the "Non-Perfect Square" concept.

5.2 The role Correlation Coefficient (r) in predictions

Another interesting analysis can be considered the relationship between the Correlation Coefficient (r) in each of the 3 upscaling exercises with the Cell factor. In practice, this coefficient indicates how good can be the predictions given by the upscaling process validating them with the Original data.

In table 5, it is obvious that there is a negative relationship between the Correlation Coefficient (how good the predictions of upscaling can be) with the Cell Factor. As Cell Factor increases then the upscaling process will predict less precisely the real values.

Upscaling Exercise	*Cell Factor*	*Correlation Coefficient*
5km towards 10km	2	0,767
1km towards 5km	5	0,62
1km towards 10km	10	0,49

Table 5. Relation of Correlation Coefficient to Cell Factor

5.3 Lost of variation and dispersion variance

Commonly variation is lost when data are upscaled. This is modelled by the mean of the dispersion variance (Dungan et al, 2002) which quantifies the amount of lost variance between the 2 scales. Upscaling has a clear effect on spatial variability and this could be an advantage and disadvantage. In general for environmental data, if the interest focuses on observing extreme values in space, then upscaling is disadvantageous as the coarser scale variation tends to be smoother. But in case policy making involves recognition of general pattern then smoothing may be considered advantageous. We conclude that the latter is the case where soil organic carbon belongs to. The data variability or variance is smoothening since the upscaled values become smaller compared to the real finer scale data and this fact has been observed in all three upscaling exercises.

For comparison of the variability between the different sources, the coefficient of variation (Post el al, 2008) or the variances may be used. Alternatively, in the table 3, there is a comparison of the Variances, Ranges, Cell Factor, and Number of output cells between the 3 upscaling exercises. It is well known and it is proven in present case that variability is affected by the sample size and the extreme scores. The sample size is the number of output cells. It is supposed that variance should decrease as the number of output cells increases. This is not the case in the upscaled results because **the most important factor is the Range which determines the variance**. The high variability is due to the extreme values and as a consequence of the high ranges. This is proven in the orange part of the Table 3 and the trend of the variability in any of the 3 datasets (and upscaled exercises) is strongly affected by the trend of the Range in any direction of the table.

Upscaling Exercise	*Origina l data*	*Upscaled MEAN data*	*Upscaled MEDIAN data*	*Cell Factor*	*No of Output cells*
	Variance (Range)				
5 km^2 towards 10 km^2	182,61 (74)	119,58 (57)	115,18 (60)	2	124
1 km^2 towards 10 km^2	238,22 (76)	256,14 (73)	111,52 (56)	5	55
1 km^2 towards 5 km^2	458,82 (161)	514,97 (154)	160,12 (84)	10	187

Table 6. Cross Comparison of Variance, Range, Cell Factor and No of Cells in Upscaling.

The dispersion of variance quantifies the amount of lost variance lost between scales. It is obvious from the table 3 that the median decreases the variance in upscaling.

5.4 Smoothing effect

Variation is lost when upscaling is performed. In case policy makers are interested in extremes values then upscaling has a disadvantage as either low or high values are smoothened. The smoothing effect is visible in figure 5 where the upscaled values have a smooth appearance. Instead the original 1km^2 values allow the policy maker to identify the extreme cases.

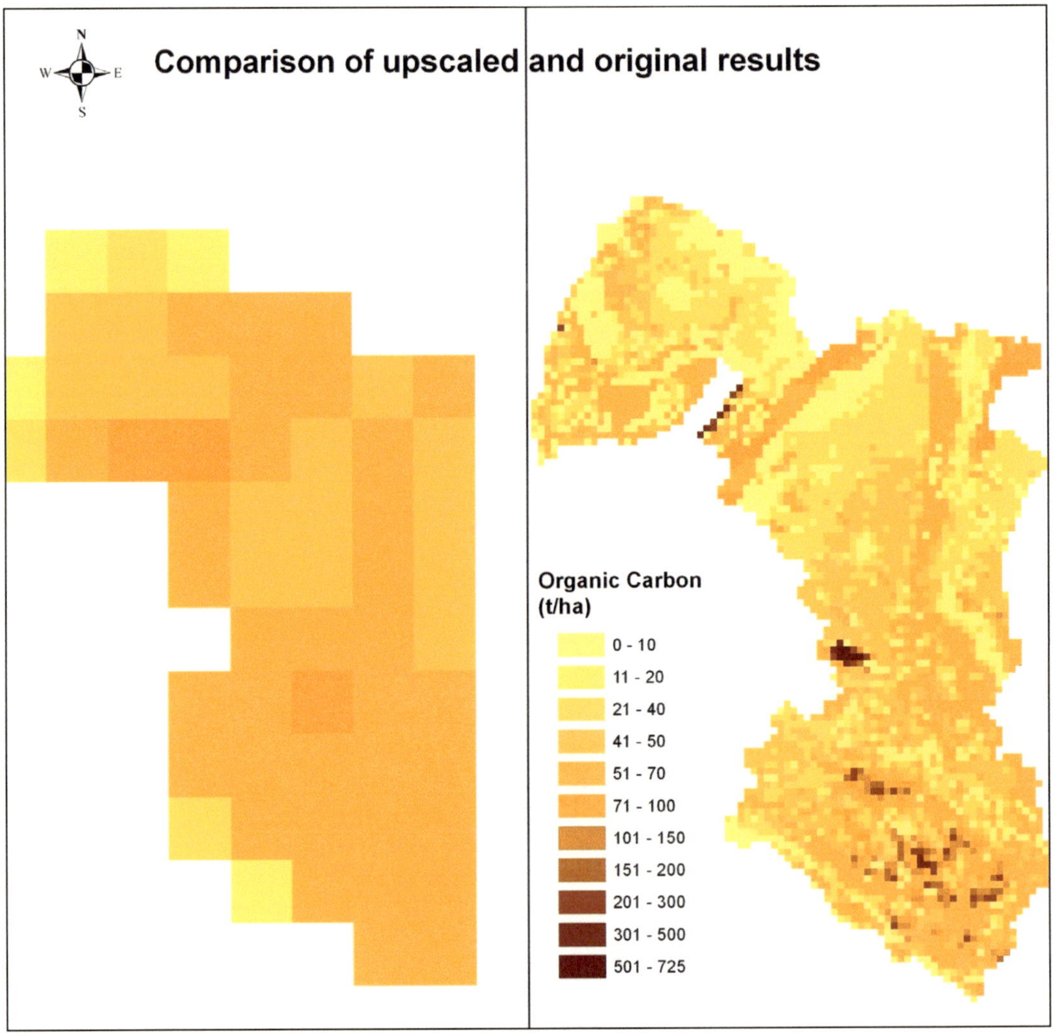

Fig. 5. The smooth effect in upscaling for the region Trnava in Slovakia

In case the policy maker is interested in the general pattern of the environmental indicator, then the upscaling proved to be advantageous. The advantage/disadvantage of upscaling depends also on the study area. In case the policy maker is interested in a small local region/province then the upscaled results may not be sufficient for his decision; instead in a larger scale (national), the identification of a pattern is much better succeeded with upscaled results than the raw data. Most of upscaled data are in the range between 51-70 t/ha C in the left part of the figure 5. In the majority of the cases, policy making is not based on the single observations but on general pattern. Instead a spatial study focusing in a specific area is disadvantageous using upscaled data. Comparison in time is better performed for the upscaled results since it allows the user to identify changes in block of cells.

Another reason for upscaling data is to ensure confidentiality during dissemination of data. This may be achieved by aggregated to various coarser scales than the size of data collection. European laws are quite strict in personal data treatment and land information data are quite sensitive and may affect the price of parcels. Suppose that you own an agricultural land parcel inside the1km^2 grid cell sample size and that information related to the sensitive environmental data (Organic carbon content, pH - Acidity, Heavy metal content, salinity...etc) about this cell are published. The parcel price is immediately affected by such publication and then the personal data protection authorities intervene and don't permit this kind of sensitive information dissemination. Instead, the process of data aggregation and the upscale of various environmental parameters in coarser scale make feasible the publication of low resolution land thematic maps without taking the risk of personal data violation. This implies that such a map must guarantee that individual entities (soil data) cannot be identified by users of the data. Aggregation is the traditional means for ensuring such confidentiality.

6. Spatial prediction and digital soil mapping

Digital Soil mapping (DSM) is the geostatistical procedure based on a number of predictive approaches involving environmental covariates, prior soil information in point and map form, (McBratney et al., 2003) and field and laboratory observational methods coupled with spatial and non-spatial soil inference systems (Carre et al., 2007). It allows for the prediction of soil properties or classes using soil information and environmental covariates of soil.

High-resolution and continuous maps are an essential prerequisite for precision agriculture and many environmental studies. Traditional, sample-based mapping is costly and time consuming, and the data collected are available only for discrete points in any landscape. Thus, sample-based soil mapping is not reasonably applicable for large areas like countries. Due to these limitations, Digital Soil Mapping (DSM) techniques can be used to map soil properties (Yigini et al., 2011).

As an example of the application of geostatistical techniques to produce continuous map of soil properties can be seen in the study conducted in Slovakia (Yigini et al., 2011). The authors studied to interpolation of point data to produce continuous map of soil organic carbon content in Slovakia. The regression kriging technique was applied and Corine Land

Cover 2006 data, SRTM 90m, European Soil Database (ESDB), climate, land management data were used as covariates. As a result, the soil organic carbon map was produced in raster format at a spatial resolution of 100 meters (Figure 6).

Digital Soil Mapping (DSM) can be defined as the creation and population of spatial soil information systems by numerical models inferring the spatial and temporal variations of soil types and soil properties from soil observation and knowledge and from related environmental variables (A.E. Hartemink et al., 2008). For soil mapping purposes, geostatistical techniques can be used to predict the value of the soil property at an unvisited or unsampled location by using auxiliary data (Figure 6). Most used interpolation methods are listed below;

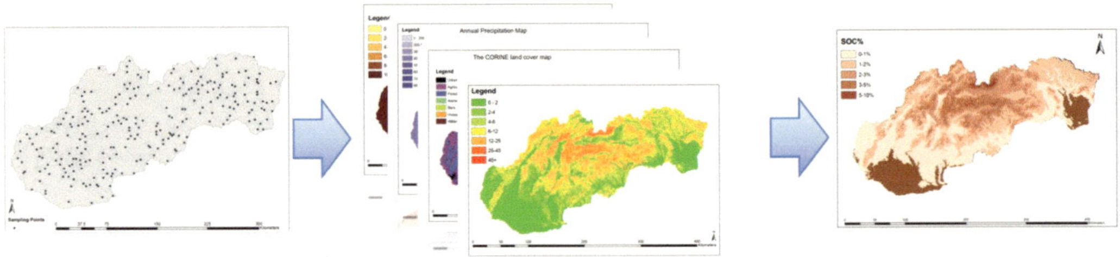

Point Data **Auxiliary Data** **Final Continuous Map**

Fig. 6. Soil Properties can be mapped using geostatistical techniques

1. *Inverse distance weighting (IDW)*

Inverse Distance Weighted (IDW) is a technique of interpolation to estimate cell values by averaging the values of sample data points in the neighbourhood of each processing cell.

2. *Regularized spline with tension (RST)*

Regularized Spline with Tension (RST) is an accurate, flexible and efficient method for multivariate interpolation of scattered data (Hofierka et al., 2002)

3. *Ordinary kriging (OK)*

Ordinary Kriging is a geostatistical method used for regionalization of point data in space. Because it is similar to multiple linear regressions and interpolates values based on point estimates, it is the most general, widely used of the Kriging methods (Ahmed and Ibrahim, 2011)

4. *Ordinary co-kriging (OCK)*

Co-kriging allows samples of an auxiliary variable (also called the covariable), besides the target value of interest, to be used when predicting the target value at unsampled locations. The co-variable may be measured at the same points as the target (co-located samples), at other points, or both. The most common application of co-kriging is when the co-variable is cheaper to measure, and so has been more densely sampled, than the target variable (Rossiter, 2007)

5. *Regression Kriging (RK)*

Regression kriging is a spatial prediction technique which adds the regression value of exhaustive variables and the kriging value of residuals together (Sun et al., 2010).

7. Conclusions

On the basis of this study, the following conclusions can be drawn:

- The multi-scale nested grids approach can be proposed as a solution in many cases where the data owner does not allow the distribution/publication of detailed data but is willing to distribute degraded data (in coarser resolution). The aggregation methodology can be considered a valuable one which contributes to the degradation (without losing the real values) of very detailed data and may allow the scientific community to access valuable information without having any copyright problems.
- For a number of reasons upscaling can be useful in soil science domain: respect of privacy and data ownership, easy adaptation to model requirements, update of spatial databases in various scales and simplification of thematic maps.
- Upscaling methodology has proven to be good enough for identification of "data patterns". The upscaling process can easily identify if soil data have been downscaled before a possible aggregation for reporting reasons.
- Upscaling has a serious drawback in case the source dataset in the finer scale has high spatial variability. This has been shown in the upscaling process from 1km^2 towards the 10km^2. The descriptive statistics show the smooth effect that upscaling may cause in high variability cases. Upscaling involves recognition of general pattern in data distribution and this can be considered an advantage for environmental indicators. In any case the upscaled output doesn't represent the real world but it is a smooth approximation. The upscaling from local scale to upper scales involves trade-offs and compromises.
- Despite the limitations, the scale transfer method presented here was well-suited to the data and satisfied the overall objective of mapping soil indicators in coarser scale giving appropriate responses to policy makers. Moreover, a series of newly introduced concepts/indicators such as "Non-Perfect Square" Coverage, Correlation Coefficient for predictions and Lost of Variation can be introduced for further research and evaluation.
- Digital Soil Mapping (DSM) offers new opportunities for the prediction of environmental indicators in various scales.

8. References

Ahmed A., Ibrahim M., Production of Digital Climatic Maps Using Geostatistical Techniques (Ordinary Kriging) Case Study from Libya. International Journal of Water Resources and Arid Environments 1(4): 239-250, 2011 ISSN 2079-7079

Bechini L., Castoldi N., Stein A. Sensitivity to information upscaling of agro-ecological assessments: Application to soil organic carbon management (2011) Agricultural Systems, 104 (6), pp. 480-490.

Bierkens, M.F.P., Finke, P.A., De Willigen, P., 2000. Upscaling and Downscaling Methods for Environmental Research. Kluwer Academic Publishers, Dordrecht.

Cantelaube P., Jayet P.A., Carre F., Bamps C., Zakharov P. Geographical downscaling of outputs provided by an economic farm model calibrated at the regional level (2012) Land Use Policy, 29 (1), pp. 35-44.

Carre F., McBratney A.B., Mayr T., Montanarella L. Digital soil assessments: Beyond DSM (2007) Geoderma, 142 (1-2), pp. 69-79.

Dikmen, O., Akin, L., Alpaydin E., 2003. Estimating Distributions in Genetic Algorithms. Computer and Information sciences, Volume 2869/2003, pp. 521-528

Dungan, J. L., Perry, J. N., Dale, M. R. T., Legendre, P., Citron-Pousty, S., Fortin, M.-J., Jakomulska, A., Miriti M., and Rosenberg, M. S. 2002. A balanced view of scale in spatial statistical analysis. Ecography 25, pp. 626-640

EC, 2006. European Commission, 2006. Proposal for a Directive of the European Parliament and of the Council establishing a framework for the protection of soil and amending Directive 2004/35/EC. Brussels, 22-9-2006. COM (2006)232 final.

Ehleringer, JR and Field C.B 1993, Scaling physiological process: Leaf to globe, Academic Press, San Diego a.o, 388

Feddes, R.A., 1995. Space and Time Variability and Interdependencies in Hydrological Processes. Cambridge University Press, Cambridge.

Gaunt, J.L., Riley, J., Stein, A., Penning de Vries, F.W.T., 1997. Requirements for effective modelling strategies. Agric. Syst. 54, 153–168.

Hartemink, A.E., A.B. McBratney & L. Mendonca (eds) 2008 Digital soil mapping with limited data. Springer, Dordrecht. 445 pp. ISBN 978-1-4020-8591-8.

Harter, T. and J. W. Hopmans, 2004. Role of Vadose Zone Flow Processes in Regional Scale

Hydrology: Review, Opportunities and Challenges. In: Feddes,R.A., G.H. de Rooij and J.C. van Dam, Unsaturated Zone Modeling: Progress, Applications, and Challenges, (Kluwer, 2004), p. 179-208.

Hofierka J., Parajka J., Mitasova H.,Mitas L., Multivariate Interpolation of Precipitation Using Regularized Spline with Tension, Transactions in GIS (2002) Volume: 6, Issue: 2, Publisher: Wiley Online Library, Pages: 135-150 ISSN: 14679671

Hoosbeek, M.R., Bouma, J., 1998. Obtaining soil and land quality indicators using research chains and geostatistical methods. Nutr. Cycling Agroecosyst. 50, 35–50.

INSPIRE, 2007. INSPIRE EU Directive, Directive 2007/2/EC of the European Parliament and of the Council of 14 March 2007 establishing an Infrastructure for Spatial Information in the European Community (INSPIRE), Official Journal of the European Union, L 108/1 50 (25 April 2007).

Jones, R.J.A., Hiederer, B., Rusco, F., Montanarella, L., 2005. Estimating organic carbon in the soils of Europe for policy support. European Journal of Soil Science 56, 655–671.

Kavussanos, M.G. and D. Giamouridis, Advanced Quantitative Methods for Managers Vol. 2 - Economic and Business Modelling. Hellenic Open University, Patras, 2005

King, A.W. 1991. Translating models across scales in the landscape, in Turner, M.G and Gardner, R.H(Eds), Quantitative methods in landscape ecology, Ecological studies, Springer, New York, Vol. 82, pp 479-517

Lal, R., 2004. Soil Carbon Sequestration Impacts on Global Climate Change and Food Security. Science 304 (2004), pp. 1623–1627.

McBratney, A.B., 1998. Some considerations on methods for spatially aggergatinbg and disaggregating soil information. Nutr. Cycling Agroecosyst. 50, 51–62.

McBratney, A., Mendonça Santos, M.L., Minasny, B., 2003. On digital soil mapping. Geoderma 117, 3–52.

Minasny B., McBratney A.B. Spatial prediction of soil properties using EBLUP with the Matérn covariance function (2007) Geoderma, 140 (4), pp. 324-336.

Panagos P., Van Liedekerke M., Jones A., Montanarella L. European Soil Data Centre: Response to European policy support and public data requirements (2012) Land Use Policy, 29 (2), pp. 329-338, doi:10.1016/j.landusepol.2011.07.003, ISSN: 02648377

Post, J., Hattermann, F., Krysanova, V., Suckow, F., 2008. Parameter and input data uncertainty estimation for the assessment of long-term soil organic carbon dynamics. Environmental Modelling & Software. Volume 23, Issue 2, February 2008, Pages 125-138

Rossiter D. G., 2007Technical Note: Co-kriging with the gstat package of the R environment for statistical computing.

Rubin, Y., and D. Or. 1993. Stochastic modeling of unsaturated flow in heterogeneous media with water uptake by plant roots: The parallel columns model. Water Resour. Res. 29:619–631.

Saffih-Hdadi, K., Mary, B., 2008. Modeling consequences of straw residues export on soil organic carbon. Soil Biol. Biochem. 40, 594–607.

Stein, A., Riley, J., Halberg, N., 2001. Issues of scale for environmental indicators. Agric. Ecosyst. Environ. 87, 215–232.

Sun W., Minasny B., McBratney A., Local regression kriging approach for analysing high density data. 19th World Congress of Soil Science, Soil Solutions for a Changing World 1 - 6 August 2010, Brisbane, Australia. Published on DVD

Tillotson, P.M., and D.R. Nielsen. 1984. Scale factors in soil science. Soil Sci. Soc. Am. J. 48:953–959

Viglizzo, E.F., Frank, F., Bernardos, J., Buschiazzo, D.E., Cabo, S., 2006. A rapid method for assessing the environmental performance of commercial farms in the Pampas of Argentina. Environ. Monit. Assess. 117, 109–134.

Van Bodegom, P.M., Verburg, P.H., Stein, A., Adiningsih, S., Denier van der Gon, H.A.C.: Effects of interpolation and data resolution on methane emission estimates from rice paddies. Environ. Ecol. Stat. 9(1), 5–26 (2002)

Yigini Y., Panagos P., Montanarella L., Spatial Prediction of Soil Organic Carbon Using Digital Soil Mapping Techniques in Slovakia - Volume 75, Number 3, June 2011, Mineralogical Magazine, Goldschmidt Abstracts 2011 - ISSN 0026-461X, Online ISSN: 1471-8022

2

Ontology Approach in Lens Design

Irina Livshits, Dmitry Mouromtsev and Vladimir Vasiliev
National Research University of Information Technologies, Mechanics and Optics, Russia

1. Introduction

Contemporary lens-CAD systems are powerful instruments for optical design ("CODE V", "OSLO", "SYNOPSYS",…). Some of them provide user with suggestions considering suitable starting point using a database of stock lenses from various vendors, what limits them to the number of existing solutions. Proposed algorithm synthesizes lens schemes for any combination of technical requirements starting from only one basic element.

To explain why this idea came to us, we have to remind that we are from the university, and teaching students stimulates to explain how to design OS (not a very big difference to whom: computer or student). Our university has started optical design practice since 1930th, so, we had accumulated big experience in optical system design. Unique combination of Information technologies and Optics in ITMO and active team which consists of both experienced and young generations of specialists.

2. Optical design and ontology

What is an Ontology? Short answer: An ontology is a specification of a conceptualization. This definition is given in the article (Gruber, 1993).

What is lens design? Short answer: Optical lens design refers to the calculation of lens construction parameters (variables) that will meet a set of performance requirements and constraints, including cost and schedule limitation (Wikipedia).

For us the application of ontology to lens design gave a new inspiration to the process of starting point selection of optical system (OS). Close cooperation between optical engineers and specialists of information technologies made it possible to apply artificial intelligence to optical design and create a software for "composing" optical schemes.

It is well known that there are a lot of different kinds of optical design software for analysis and optimization, but the selection of starting point (or so called structural scheme of optical system) still remains mostly the function of human optical designer. This procedure is one of the most important steps in the optical design and it in more than 80% determines the success of the whole project. This is the most creative step of design process, which was called by Professor Russinov as "optical systems composing" similarly to composing music, where instead of sounds, optical designer uses the optical elements. We present lens classification and its link with the process of optical design composing. In Figure 1 we present our explanation on important design steps.

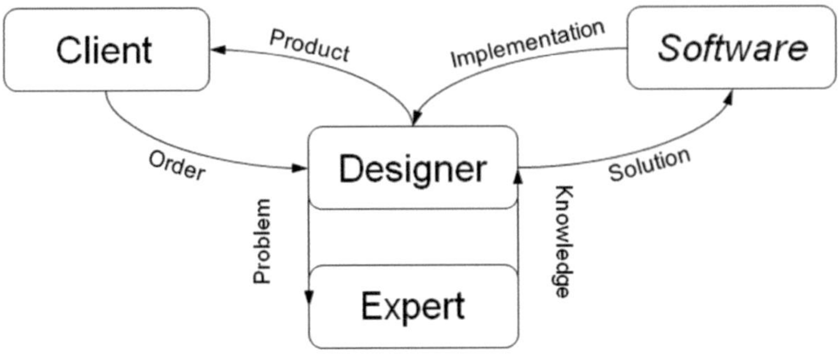

Order	– *general technical requirements*
Problem	– *functional requirements*
Knowledge	– *starting point*
Solution	– *structural scheme, parametrical requirements*
Implementation	– *parametrical synthesis, image quality optimization*
Product	– *technical documentation (or manufactured OS)*

Fig. 1. Design steps

In figure 2 it is shown the proposed approach taking into consideration the relations between designer and expert, and in figure 3 - stages of the optical design procedure.

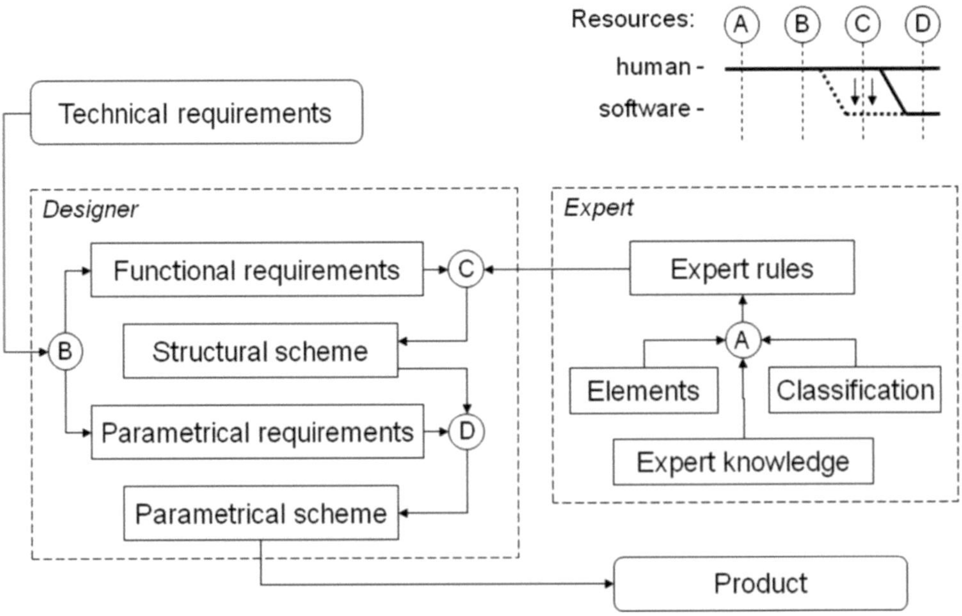

Fig. 2. The proposed approach in terms of relations between human and software resources as well as designer and expert

Looking at Fig.3, it seems obvious that if starting point is good, all the rest stages will be implemented very fast. But in case starting point has not enough parameters, we have to repeat the step of starting point selection (changing the starting point) until it satisfies the customer requirements.

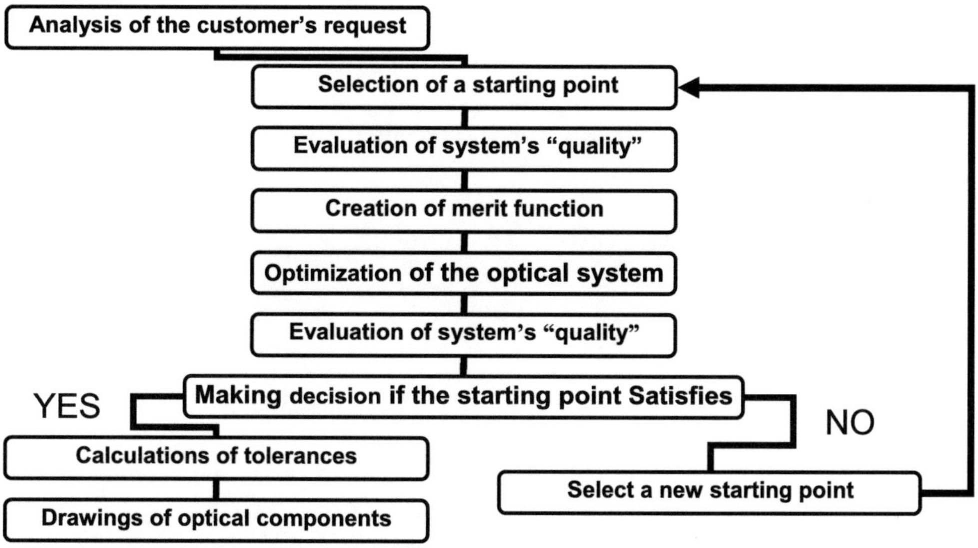

Fig. 3. Stages of the optical design procedure

3. Optical classifications and starting points

We give below some basic determinations of frequently used definitions useful for better understanding:

- Optical element (OE) is understood here as one reflective or combination of two refractive surfaces. Examples of OE are a mirror or a single lens.
- Optical module (OM) is a combination of several optical elements. Examples of OM are doublets, eyepieces, objectives – as parts of microscope optical system.
- Optical system (OS) is a combination of several optical modules. Examples of OS are telescope (includes several OM: objective lens, relay lens, eyepiece), microscope, etc.

Due to their functions in optical systems all optical elements are classified into four big groups:

- Basic Elements - are used to form the optical power in an OS, they are always positive.
- Correction Elements - are used to correct residual aberrations of basic elements. Correction elements can be both positive and negative and also afocal, which will depend on the aberration type.
- "Fast" Elements - are used for developing the aperture of an optical system, they have only positive optical power, but in distinction to basic elements, they work only from the finite distance.
- "Wide-angular" Elements - are used for developing the field angle in an OS, they are negative or afocal.

There are two basic types of data used to describe optical systems. The first are the general data that are used to describe the system as a whole, and the other is the surface data that describes the individual surfaces and their locations. Usually, an optical system is described as an ordered set of surfaces, beginning with an object surface and ending with an image surface (where there may or may not be an actual image). It is assumed that the designer knows the order in which rays strike the various surfaces. Systems for which this is not the case are said to contain non-sequential surfaces.

Entire lens space is subdivided into 3 zones: (1st zone is in front of the aperture stop, 2nd zone is inside the aperture stop region, 3d zone is behind the aperture stop) (see Fig. 4).

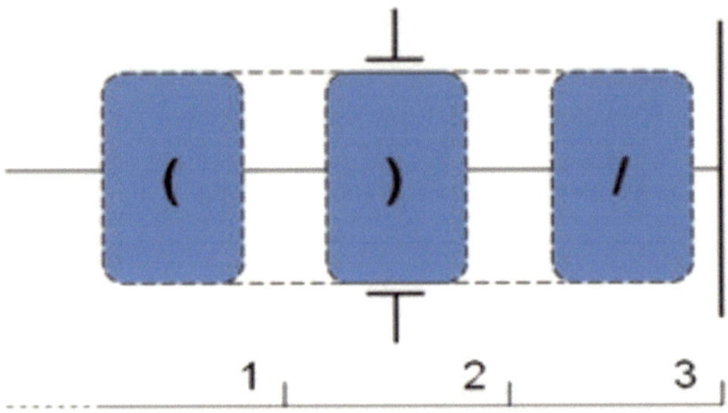

Fig. 4. Surface Location

The general data used to describe a system includes the aperture and field of view, the wavelengths at which the system is to be evaluated, and perhaps other data that specify evaluation modes, vignetting conditions, etc. If we describe these data in symbolical values we've got general classifications, see bellow.

Before one starts the optical design, it is very important to classify optical system using different classifications depending on the customer's request. Different types of characteristics are used for optical systems' classifications and there exist big amount of the classifications. There are many different approaches how to design a lens.

General classifications describe optical systems properties in conventional values. For example, if we designate the object (image) infinite position as "0" and finite position as "1", we would have the most general classification which divides all optical systems into four big classes due to object-image position, Table 1:

Conventional notation of Systems' class	Name of the systems' class
"00"	binocular type
"01"	photographic lens type
"10"	microscope objective type
"11"	relay lens type

Table 1. General classification depending on object-image position

Technical classification operates with physical values. If we input physical values Real physical values for seven optical characteristics (J, W, F, L, Q, S, D), then we get the technical classification, which is of the most influence to the starting point selection for the objectives ("01" type). Technical classification is presented in Table 2, and the link between general and technical classifications is shown in Table 3.

Notation	Name	Units
J	Aperture speed	nondimentional
W	Angular field	Angular units
F	Focal length	mm
L	Spectral range	Nm
Q	Image quality	Wave units
S	Back focal distance	mm
D	Entrance pupil position	mm from the first surface

Table 2. Technical characteristics for photographic objective

Notation for characteristic	Conventional notation depending on technical data
J	"0"; OS is not fast; D/F'<1:2.8
	"1"; OS is fast; 1:2.8<D/F'<1:1.5
	"2"; OS is super fast; 1:1.5<D/F'
W	"0"; OS with small angular field;
	"1"; OS with average angular field;
	"2"; wide angular OS;
F	"0"; short focal length OS; F'<50 mm
	"1"; average focal length OS; 50mm<F'<100 mm
	"2"; long focal length OS; F'>100 mm
L	"0"; monochromatic OS;
	"1"; ordinary polychromatic; 10nm<
	"2"; super polychromatic correction;
Q	"0"; "geometrical " image quality;
	"1"; "intermediate" image quality;
	"2"; "diffraction" image quality;
S	"0"; OS with short back focal length; S'<F';
	"1"; OS with average back focal length; 0.5F'<S'<F';
	"2"; OS with long back focal length; S'>F';
D	"0"; with entrance pupil located inside OS
	"1"; with entrance pupil located behind OS; (removed back entrance pupil);
	"2"; with entrance pupil in front of OS (removed forward entrance pupil).

Table 3. Links between general and technical classifications

Example of estimation of system's class in terms of general classification is given for a Cook triplet with following value of characteristics:

OS in not fast, so J=0,
OS with average angular field, so W=1,
OS with short focal length F=0,
ordinary polychromatic OS, so L=1,
OS with "geometrical " image quality, so Q=0,
OS with back focal length S'=43 mm, so S=2,
Entrance pupil is inside the OS, so D=0.

The sum of all seven general characteristics is called index of complexity (IC) of the objective, for our triplet it is equal:

IC=0+1+0+1+0+2+0=4;
Index of complexity (IC) varies from 0 to 14.

Selection of starting point for optical systems depends very much on the systems' complexity. From experience we can say that system with IC>7 is a complex system and, as a rule, to design such a lens, it is necessary to invent (optical scheme will have "know-how" solution). Please, notice: in spite of that characteristic "D" (aperture stop position) cannot be called "technical or, even, general characteristic", it belongs to scheme construction, we included this symbol into our classification, because it gives significant input into the starting point selection.

Numbers "0,1,2" are symbols, which belong to general classification and indirectly connected with the selection of starting point for OS.

"0" is symbol for the technical characteristic of OS, which can be realized in the easiestOS.
"1" is symbol for technical characteristic which would indefinitely require more elements to build OS than in case "0", and
"2" is for advanced technical characteristic which would require the most complex OS for achievement the required data.

Using the classification described above we can describe 3^7 = 2187 classes of OS, which are located between class "0000000" and "2222222", for example, "2222222" describes fast wide angle long FOCL OS, polychromatic with expanded spectral range, diffraction limited, with increased BFL, and APS coincident with exit pupil. It is very hard to design OS, which belongs to this class.

A complete list of optical systems for today's applications would require hundreds of entries, but a few of the design tasks that have been handled by traditional optical design software are listed in the following table. Design tasks classification is presented in Table 4.

Imaging Systems	Non-imaging systems	Laser systems	Visual systems (working with human eye)
System Layout	Illumination Systems	Fiber couplers	Microscopes
Lens Design	Solar Collectors	Laser focusing	Telescopes
Laboratory Instruments	Faceted reflectors	Scanners	Low vision aids
Optical Testing	Condensers	Cavity design	Virtual reality
Astronomical Telescopes	Light Concentrators	Beam delivery	Night vision

Table 4. Design tasks classification

So, as the result of the analysis of the customer's request we must have clear understanding what kind of optical system we are going to design, its general and technical characteristics, and its possible construction. Evaluation of the system's complexity is also important to know before selecting starting point.

4. The problem of a starting point selection

Many programs approach the starting point by supplying a number of standard or sample designs that users can apply as starting points (relying on the user's knowledge to select or generate a suitable starting design form). Smarter approaches are being explored, including expert systems (Donald Dilworth's ILDC paper, "Expert Systems in Lens Design"), and the intriguing possibility of training neural network to recognize a good starting point (research presented by Scott W.Weller, "Design Selection Using Neural Networks"). Some designers use database programs (for example, LensView,...) which recently appeared in the market. Creation of starting point is the main stage of the whole design process. If starting point was successfully matched we can get the result very fast. Bad starting point leads to failure of the design process after loosing some time for understanding the wrong choice. Besides matching the starting point the merit function has to be created.

The procedures of selecting the surfaces' types for the optical elements (OE) construction and the selecting the OE themselves for structural schemes construction are done using the finite set of selection rules and is called structural synthesis of optical scheme. Formula for structural synthesis scheme contains the type, the quantity and the arrangement of the OE.

The procedure of determining optical elements parameters in the selected optical scheme is called parametrical synthesis.

Our approach leads to receiving the optimal number of the elements in optical systems and puts all of them in certain strict sequence, which makes them more efficient both from technical and economical point of view. Anyway, this part of the general approach to optical design process, as well as other parts is programmed as "open access (entry)", and, moreover, it offers additional opportunities to its development and correction.

Structural syntesis is based on using for lens design the surfaces with well-known properties only, such as working at its aplanatic conjugates, concentric about the aperture or the chief ray, flat or near image surfaces. In Russia this approach was developed by Mickael Russinov (Russinov,1979) and his successors (Livshts at al, 2009), (Livshits&Vasiliev, 2010) and in the USA by Robert Shannon (Shannon, 1997). The main feature of this method is the complete understanding of the functional purpose of each optical surface.

Due to the predicting properties of this approach it is possible to formalize the process of structural scheme synthesis, what allowed, in its turn to create the simple algorithm and elaborate the synthesis program.

The main concept of the method is:

- Every optical system (OS) consists of the finite set of optical modules (OM);
- Each OM has its own function in the OS and consists of a finite set of optical elements (OE);
- Each OE can be formed using only the finite set of optical surfaces' types.

The procedures of selecting the surfaces' types for the OE construction and the selecting the OE themselves for structural schemes construction are done using the finite set of selection rules and is called structural synthesis of optical scheme.

The structural scheme construction based on the two levels hierarchy of the components is presented. The objects of the lower level are optical surfaces and the objects for the upper level are optical elements. This approach made it possible to resolve the components of any structural scheme according to the hierarchy levels.

Rule examples:

- If only air spaces differ among the several configurations, the problem becomes that of the zoom lens (true zoom lens - special case of multi--configuration OS).
- If any other parameters of the lens are to zoom, such as wavelengths or element definitions (for inserting and removing sections of the lens), the true multi-configuration form of zoom must be used.

5. Selection rules for objects, optical surfaces and elements for structural scheme synthesis, attributes and ties

Optics - expert determines the applicability of each OE, used in the structural scheme. He fixes the applicability index value for every OE.

Multiplicativity (maximum quantity of the same type optical elements in the certain position of structural scheme) is also determined by optic-expert in conformity with the heuristic rules. As it was shown in (Livshts at al, 2009), optical system can include only one basic element and the quantity for each of wide-angular, correction and light powerful elements can vary from 0 to 3, moreover, it is possible to have from 0 to 3 correction elements on each of three positions allowed for these elements. In conformity with the heuristic rules the following optical elements' sequence is accepted (the structure of optical scheme is presented in Figure 5).

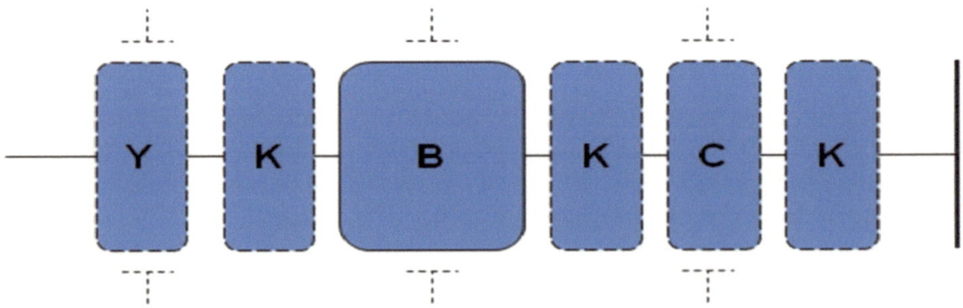

Fig. 5. Composition of Elements

So, in the high-performance optical system we have wide-angular, basic and fast elements. It is possible to put correction elements between them and after the light powerful element. This structure will be more simple if it is not necessary to have high aperture speed or wide field angle, then the corresponding optical elements (light powerful or wide-angular) are absent, but basic and correction OE are always present.

The permissibility of the optical elements neighbouring is analyzed. It is determined by the position of OE in the scheme and its thickness, for example, OE with "III" thickness cannot stand together with another thick element in one optical scheme, but OE with thickness "II0" and "00I" are fine to be neighbours.

Formal rules of cementing optical elements were elaborated. It is possible to cement two neighbouring OE if their surfaces which have to be cemented are of the same type.

The selection of the objects for putting them into the upper level is done on the basis of the set of the heuristic rules. The structural schemes' variants are formed using these rules. The best variant becomes the first in the structural schemes' list. The other variants are disposed in certain order in accordance to the diminishing of the total index of applicability for all OE of the structural scheme.

The input data for the selection rules are seven optical characteristics, which are given in the technical specification (J, W, F, L, Q, S, D) (Livshts at al, 2006) and the optical features of surfaces and elements.

The overall conventional scheme for starting optical design is present in figure 6.

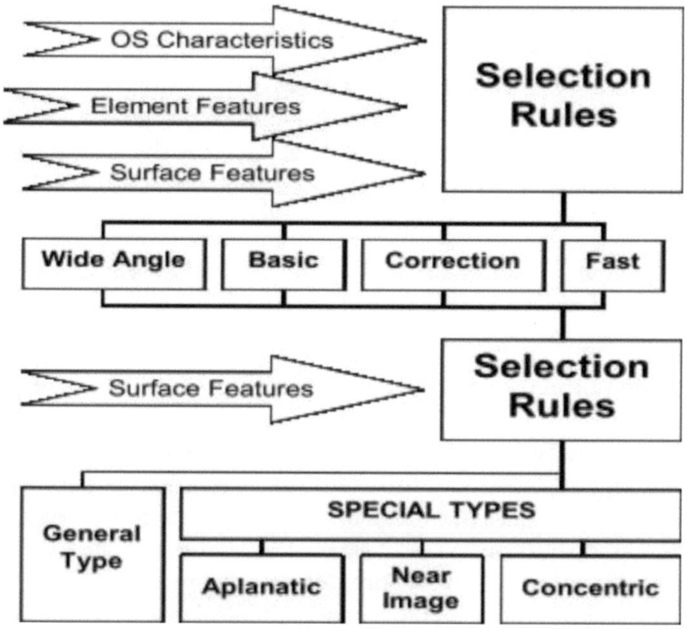

Fig. 6. Conventional scheme for starting optical design

6. Knowledge based methods

There is already a long story of using expert systems to solve different design problems. Expert Systems (ES) - are the most widely used class of AI applications, focused on disseminating the experience of highly qualified specialists in the areas where the quality of decision-making has traditionally depended on the level of expertise, for example, CAD, medicine, law, geology, economics, etc.

ES are effective only in specific "expert" areas, where an empirical experience is important. R1 system was one of the first successful attempts to use expert systems in the industry in the early 1980s (McDermott, 1980). This system is designed to assist developers in determining the configuration of a computer system constructed from different units of the family VAX.

All ES have similar architecture. The basis of this architecture is the separation of knowledge embedded in the system, and algorithms for their processing. For example, the program solves the quadratic equation, and, uses the knowledge of how to solve this kind of equations. But this knowledge is "hardcoded" in the text of the program and it cannot been either read or changed by user, if the original source code is not available. If the user wants to solve a different type of equation he/she should ask a programmer to create a new program.

Now, suppose the task is set slightly differently: the program being run must read the type of the equation and the method of its solution from a text file and the user is allowed to enter new ways of solving equations, for example, to compare their efficiency, accuracy, etc. The format of this file should be "friendly" both to a computer and a user. This way of organising the program will allow to modify its functionality without the help of a programmer. Even if the user chooses only one type of equations, the new approach is preferable to the former , because to understand the principle of solving equations, it is only necessary to examine the input text file. This example, despite its simplicity and non-typical domain of ES applications (for solving mathematical equations specialised software packages are used, rather than expert systems), illustrates the architecture of ES - the presence in its structure the knowledge base, available for the user's view directly or by means of a special editor. Knowledge base is editable that allows someone to change the behaviour of ES without reprogramming it.

Real ES may have a complex, branched structure of modules, but any ES always have the following main blocks (Figure D1. Structure of the ES):

- **Knowledge Base** (KB) is the most valuable component of an ES core. It is a set of domain knowledge and methods of problem solving, written in a readable form to non-programmers: expert, user, etc. Typically, knowledge of KB written in a form close to natural language. The written form of knowledge is called a knowledge representation language. Different systems may use different languages. In parallel to this "human" representation, KB can be saved in an internal "computer" representation. Conversion between different forms of representation should be done automatically since editing of KB does not suppose the work of the programmer-developer.
- **Reasoner** or Inference engine (R) is module simulating the reasoning on the basis of expert knowledge stored in the knowledge base. The reasoner is a constant part of any ES. However, most real-ES have built-in functionality to control of inference using the so-called "meta-rules" also saved in KB. An examples of meta-rules is given below:
  IF aperture is high (J=2);
  THEN check the elements with high index of appcicability first.
  This rule allows to adjust the reasoning process taking into consideration expert's knowledge (heuristics in optical design)
- **Editor** of the knowledge base (E) is intended for developers of ES. This editor is used for adding new rules to knowledge base or edit existing ones.

- **User Interface** (UI) is a module designed to interface with the user, allowing the system requests necessary data for its operation, and outputs the result. The system mat has fixed interface that focuses on a certain mode of input and output, or may include a **tool of designing custom interfaces** for better user interaction.

The authors have included a new module to ES architecture - Ont - the ontology of optical elements.into this work It allows ones to use a generic and extensible domain vocabulary of the rules for the KB. Ontology will be discussed below in detail.

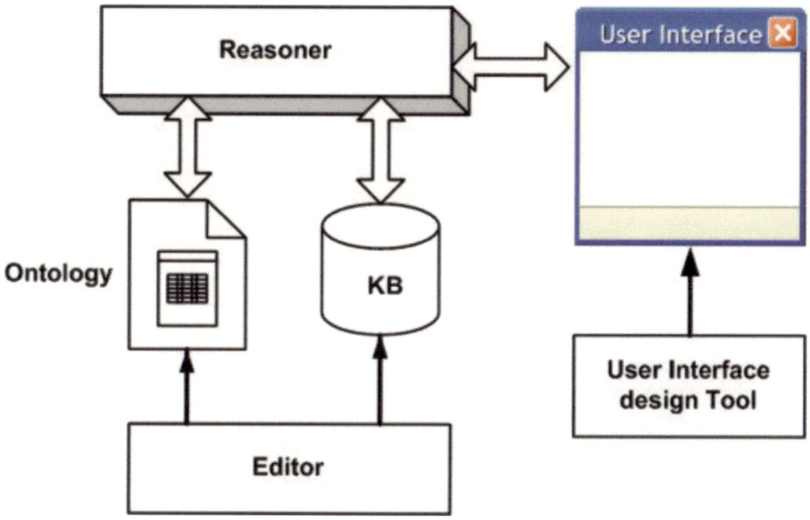

Fig. 7. Structure of the ES

Knowledge representation in the form of production rules is most common in expert systems, because the records of KB are actually knowledge written on a subset of natural language. The consequence is that the rules are easy to read, they are simple for understanding and modification, the experts have no problem to formulate a new rule, or to point out the fallacy of an existing one.

Production systems are a model based on production rules, allowing to describe knowledge about solving problems in the form of rules of "IF condition, THEN action».

The concept of "production systems" is a special case of knowledge based systems. The idea of representing knowledge in the form of products appeared in the work of Emil Leon Post (Post, 1943).

The main components of a production system architecture are (Figure 8.):

- KB production rules;
- Working memory;
- Controlling recognition-action cycle.

Reasoning modelling is based on the process of pattern matching, in which the current state of the solutions are compared with existing rules to determine further action.

The knowledge base contains a set of production rules or simply productions, which are condition-action pairs that define the basic steps of problem solving. The condition part (IF-part) rule is a pattern, where we can determine at what point you want to use (activate) the rule for the next stage of solving the problem. Part of the action (THEN-part) describes the corresponding step of solutions. The conditional part of the rule is also called the antecedent, and part of the action - consequent.

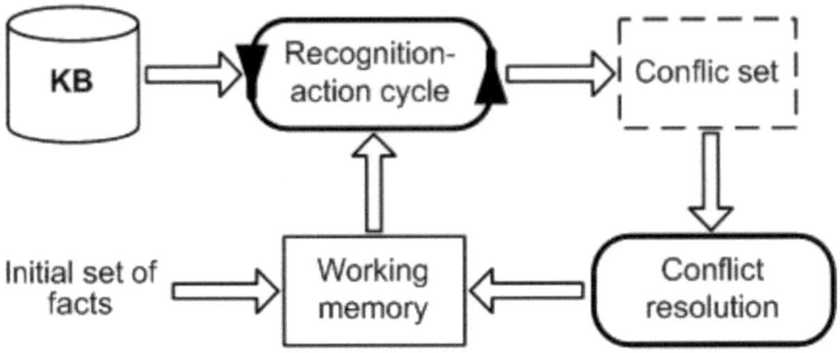

Fig. 8. Production system architecture

Working memory contains the current set of facts constituting a world model in the process of reasoning. Initially this model contains a set of samples, representing the starting description of the problem.

During the recognise - act cycle facts from the working memory are matched with the conditional parts of rules in the knowledge base. If the condition of a rule matches a pattern, it is usually placed in a conflicting set. Products contained in the conflict set are called admissible, since they are consistent with the current state of working memory. When the cycle-detection operation is finished, the process of conflict resolution, in which one of the acceptable products is selected and activated takes place. Finally, the working memory is modified in accordance with THEN-part of the activated rules. This whole process is repeated until the samples in the working memory will not fit any of the rules of KB.

Conflict resolution strategies differ in different implementations productional models and can be relatively simple. For example, select the first of admissible rules. However, many systems allow the use of sophisticated heuristics for choosing rules from a set of conflict. For example, the system OPS5 supports the following conflict resolution strategies (Brownston at al, 1985):

- Refraction is to prevent infinite loops: after activation of a rule it can not be used again until they change the contents of working memory.
- Recency is to focus the search on the same line of reasoning: preference rules are that there are facts that have been added in the working memory of the latter.
- Specificity prefers a more specific rules before more general, one rule is more specific than another if it contains more facts in the conditional part.

As the conditions and actions in the rules may be, for example, the assumption of the presence of some property that evaluates as true or false. The term action should be interpreted broadly: it may be a directive to carry out any operation, recommendation, or modification of the knowledge base - the assumption that there is any derivative properties. An example of a production is the following expression:

IF Aperture speed is low,
THEN base element with "III" thickness.

Both IF and THEN parts of a rule allow the multiple expressions, combined by logical connectives AND, OR, NOT:

IF Entrance pupil position located inside
AND NOT Angular field is small,
THEN correction element with "II0" thickness.

In addition to production rules knowledge base should include the simple facts which are coming in through the user interface or inferred during reasoning process. The facts are simple statements such as "Aperture speed is low." The facts, as true assertions are copied into the working memory for use in a recognise - act cycle.

Sequential activation of the rules creates a chain of inference (reasoning). In the present work we use the data-driven search, in which the process of solving the problem starts with the initial facts. Then, applying the admissible rules, there is a transition to the new facts. And it goes on until the goal is reached. This process is also called "forward chaining".

Forward chaining of reasoning applies to problems where on the basis of available facts it is necessary to determine the type (class) of an object or phenomenon, to give advice, to diagnose, etc. These tasks include, for example, design, data interpretation, planning, classification, etc. The conclusion, based on data applied to problems in the following cases is that:

- All or most of the data set in the space of the problem, for example, the task of interpretation is to select the data and presenting them for use in the interpretation of a higher level.
- There is a number of potential goals, but only a few ways to use initial facts.
- It is very difficult to formulate a goal or hypothesis because of redundancy or the source data of a large number of competing hypotheses.

Thus, a search, based on the initial facts in the problem, is used to generate the possible ways of solving it. Forward chaining algorithm is usually based on the search strategy the initial facts are added to the working memory and then its content is compared sequentially with the antecedent of each rule in BR. If the contents of working memory leads to the activation of a rule, after modifying the working memory the next rule is analysed. When the first pass over KB is completed, the process repeats, beginning with the first rule.

Separation of the knowledge base and inference machine is an advantage of expert systems. During the inference process all the rules of the system are equal and self-sufficient, that is all that is necessary for activation of the rules contained in its IF-part, and some regulations may not directly cause the other. The reasoner work is independent of the domain, which makes it universal. But sometimes, to get the solutions, some intervention to standard output process is required. For this purpose, some production systems allow one to enter specific rules into the knowledge base to manage the process of withdrawal - metarules. Metarules are not involved directly into the process of reasoning, but determine the priority of execution the regular rules. Thus, some structuring and ordering of rules is introduced in the knowledge base.

In this work the knowledge base of the general optical system consists of two modules:

- The rules for structural synthesis of optical systems.
- The ontology of optical elements.

The first important part of the knowledge base contains the optical systems structural synthesis rules. This approach based on the rules has proved its effectiveness for solving optical design problems during many years of expert system development and using. Rules based systems provide a formal way of representation of recommendations, guidance and strategies. They fit ideally in the situations when knowledge of field of application appears from the empirical associations, accumulated during the years of solving problems in the domain. Rules based presentations of knowledge are clearly understandable and easy readable. It is possible to modify the rules or add new one, or find a mistake in the existing rules.

So, as a result of CAD process of structural synthesis of optical system due to the technical specifications it is possible to get several technical solutions (scheme variants). Because of that, the ranking technology has to be used, so, the less profitable solutions will be excluded and will not appear in the final list of optical elements.

The formal presentation of the selection rules of optical system structure (as a starting point) is based on logic expressions using boolean operation conjunction (logical AND) and implication (logical consequence). This is the most convenient type of formalisation, as such equations could be easily interpreted into understandable rules "IF - THEN", which significantly simplifies the work of the expert. Besides, using formal mathematical approach, logical equations could be transferred to a more compact equivalent minimal notation, then the knowledgebase becomes "lighter". Every logic equation determines a condition of the application of the certain optical element in the designed optical system.

There is an analysis of the existing optical constructions created by generations of Russian optical designers in accordance with the theory of the synthesis and optical systems composing created by Professor Russinov. This theory together with its further development gave an opportunity to extract and generalize database consisting of more than 400 rules.

7. Ontology approach

The leading paradigm of structuring the information or content is an ontology or hierarchy of conceptual frameworks (Guarino, 1998). From the methodological point of view - this is one of the most "systematic" and intuitive ways.

By definition of Tom Gruber (Gruber, 1993), who was the first to use this concept in the field of information technology: an ontology is specification of a conceptualization – it is not only a philosophical term for the doctrine of being. This term has shifted to the sciences, where nonformalized conceptual models are always accompanied by a strong mathematical definitions. In accordance of the definition of an ontology, many conceptual structures: a hierarchy of classes in object-oriented programming, conceptual maps, semantic networks, etc. could be easily determined.

Ontology is an exact specification of a domain, or a formal and declarative representation including the vocabulary (or names) of pointers to the domain terms and logical expressions, describing what these terms mean, as they relate to each other, and how they can or may not be related to each other. Thus, ontologies provide a vocabulary for representing and sharing knowledge about a certain subject area and a lot of relations established between terms in the dictionary.

In the publication (Gavrilova, 2005) there proposed the following classification of modern ideas and research works in the field of ontology. The proposed systematisation of ontology illustrates the views of several research groups.

Ontology or a conceptual domain model consists of a hierarchy of domain concepts, relationships between them and the logical axioms that operate within the framework of this model we describe:

- by the type of relationship:
  - taxonomy - the leading relationship is «kind-of» («is-a»);
  - partonomy - the leading relationship is "is part" ("is», «has part»);
  - genealogy - the leading relationship if "father-son" ("a descendant of the predecessor");
  - attribute structure;
  - cause and effect - the leading relationship if «if-then»;
  - mixed ontology - the ontology with other types of relationships.
- by owner or user:
  - individual (personal);
  - shared (group):
    - belong to the country,
    - belong to the community (eg scientific)
    - owned company or enterprise;
  - common (opened).
- by language:
  - informal;
  - formalized;
  - formal - in languages RDFS, OWL, DAML + OIL, etc.
- by domain:
  - science;
  - industry;
  - education, etc.
- by the design goals:
  1. for design;
  2. for learning;
  3. for research;
  4. for management;
  5. for knowledge sharing;
  6. e-business.

The ontology is necessary tool for optical systems structural analysis. The purpose of this analysis is to determine the function of the every element of optical system with the consequent formalising of the design procedures. The ontology makes it possible to formalise most of the steps of optical design process and determine the cutoff values for indices of applicability of the certain elements in certain optical schemes.

This approach has a set of essential advantages because it allows to combine the creation of structured dictionary of notions in the optical domain with the technical classification used in lens design. As a result, the combination of just two procedures makes it possible to use existing optical design experience for design of new optical systems.

The ontology development is based on knowledge engineering, where the main problem is the correct search of objects (individuals), classes (sets of concepts) and the relationships between these structures.

Algorithm used for ontology engineering was as same as proposed (Gavrilova, 2003):

1. Forming glossary of a problem area, i.e. acquisition and extracting of concepts - the basic glossary in the subject field.
2. Extracting of notions (bottom to top). For example, we can start from forming the class of general concepts "a lens" and "an optical system" Then we can specify the general class "a lens" by extracting sub-classes "positive" and "negative". Further from the class of "positive lens" we can inherit, for example, such elements as "basic" and "fast".
3. Abstracting concepts (bottom-up). For example, first define the classes for the elements of "correction lens for "coma" and "corrective" lens for "astigmatism". Then it creates a common superclass for these two classes - "corrective lens", which in turn is a subclass of the most abstract concept of "lenses".
4. Distribution of the concepts on the levels of abstraction. Cyclic execution of steps 2 and 3.
5. Setting of some other relationships between concepts (properties, parts, etc.), a glossary, and their combination.
6. Refactoring of the ontology (specification, the resolution of contradictions, synonymy, redundancy, inaccuracy, restructuring and addition).

Ontology to be created belongs to the taxonomy scheme, i.e. hierarchal structure of goals and results from easy to complex organised by generalisation-specialisation relationships, or less formally, parent-child relationships. Mathematical taxonomy is a tree of classification of certain number of the objects. In the top of this structure is uniting uniform classification, or the root taxon, which belongs to all of the objects of this taxonomy. Taxons located below the root taxon are more specific elements of the classification. "Optical system", "lens", "surface", "material" were chosen as the upper level concepts. After that the taxonomy was structured in correspondence with the purpose, main characteristics and specific construction of optical system. It is of great importance that the proposed ontology allows to classify and create the semantic search of solution in the database of the optical patents.

For the formal description of the ontology the Web Ontology Language (OWL) is used. OWL is one of the family of knowledge representation languages for authoring ontologies. The languages are characterised by formal semantics and RDF/XML-based serializations for the Semantic Web. OWL is endorsed by the World Wide Web Consortium (W3C) and has attracted academic, medical and commercial interest.

OWL is designed primarily for identifying and representing of Web ontologies, which may include descriptions of classes, instances of classes and properties. Description logics being the underlying formal semantics of OWL, allows to obtain the facts which are not represented in the Web Ontology explicitly, but is followed (inferred) from its definition. Moreover, these effects may be based on a single document or multiple distributed documents that are combined with the use of special algorithms.

The main differences between OWL-XML and XML Schema are as follows:

- Ontology, in contrast to XML Schema, allows to represent knowledge, and not the data format. Most XML-based specifications consist of a combination of data formats and protocol specifications, which are attributed to a specific semantics.
- One more advantage of OWL ontologies is the possibility of performing reasoning (inference of knowledge). Moreover, these systems can be largely universal, ie do not depend on a specific subject area.

OWL exists in three dialects: OWL Lite, OWL DL and OWL Full. Each of these dialects is an extension of a simpler predecessor, both in the expressive possibilities of information and that is connected with the inference of knowledge.

The main concepts of OWL are class and individual, or instance. The differences between them require some clarification. Class - it's just a name and a set of properties that describe a set of individuals. Individual is a member of this set. Thus, the classes must correspond to a set of concepts in some domain, and individuals should correspond to real objects, which can be grouped into these classes.

When creating ontologies the distinction is often blurred in two ways:

- Levels of representation. In certain contexts, something that clearly is a class that can independently be an instance of something else.
- Subclass or instance. It is very easy to confuse the relationship type instance of the class with the class-subclass.

An example of the ontology for optical design is present on Fig. 9.

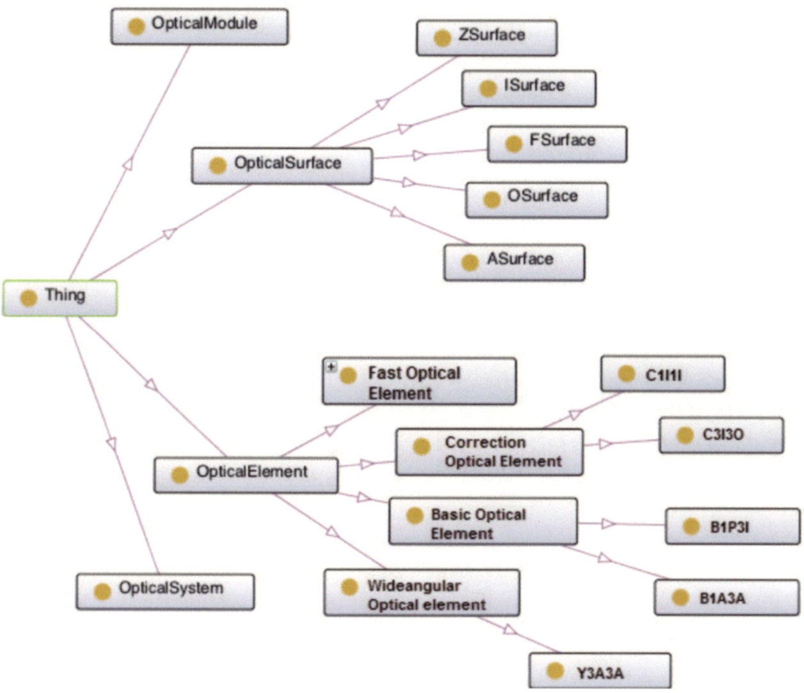

Fig. 9. A part of Optics design ontology

8. Conclusion

Presented research confirms the statement that application of information technologies to optical design brings new quality even to very traditional area of physics. Artificial intelligence, in particular experts systems, not only opened new horizons for optical designers, but attracted young researchers and software engineers, who are very important for saving and development of optical knowledge inheritance.

9. References

Brownston L., Farrel R., Kant E., Martin N. 1985 *Programming Expert Systems in OPS5. An Introduction to Rule-Based Programming.* Reading, Addison-Wesley: MA.

Gavrilova T., Laird D. 2005. *Practical Design Of Business Enterprise Ontologies In Industrial Applications of Semantic Web* (Eds. Bramer M. and Terzyan V) Springer. 61–81.

Gavrilova T.A. 2003. Ontological approach to knowledge management in the development of corporate information systems. *News of Artificial Intelligence* (2): 24-30. (in russian)

Gruber T. R. 1993. A Translation Approach To Portable Ontologies. *Knowledge Acquisition* 5 (2): 199–220.

http://wikipedia, the free encyclopedia. Wikipedia.org

Irina Anitropova, Simple method for computer-aided lens design with the elements of artificial intelligence, Proc. SPIE 1780, 1992.

Irina L. Livshits, Vladimir N. Vasiliev, Optical systems classification as an instrument for getting knowledge from optical expert, 7th Int'l Conf. on Optics-Photonics Design & Fabrication, pp. 13-14, 2010.

Irina Livshits, State-of-the-art in Russian and Former Soviet Union optical design, 2nd Int'l Conf. on Optics-Photonics Design & Fabrication, pp. 285-287, 2000.

L. Livshits, I. G. Bronchtein, V. N. Vasiliev, Information technologies in CAD system for lens design, Proc. SPIE 7506, 2009. doi:10.1117/12.837544

Livshits, A. Salnikov, I. Bronchtein, U. Cho, Database of optical elements for lens CAD, 5th Int'l Conf. on Optics-Photonics Design & Fabrication, pp. 31-32, 2006.

McDermot D., Doyle J. 1980. Non-monotonic logic I. Artificial Intelligence 13: 14–72.

N. Guarino (ed.), *Formal Ontology in Information Systems. Proceedings of FOIS'98, Trento, Italy, 6-8 June 1998.* Amsterdam, IOS Press, pp. 3-15.

Post E. 1943. Formal reduction of the general combination problem. *American journal of Mathematics* 65: 197–268.

Robert R. Shannon, "The Art and Science of Optical Design", Cambridge University Press 1997, ISBN 0-521-58868-5

Russinov M. Technical Optics. Mashinostroenie. Leningrad, 1979, 488 p. (in russian)

3

Quality Management of the Passenger Terminal Services on the Base of Information System

Vaira Gromule and Irina Yatskiv
JSC „Riga International Coach Terminal",
Transport and Telecommunication Institute,
Latvia

1. Introduction

Integration of Latvia in the Common European Market and its joining the EU has highlighted new demands to passengers' transportation - high mobility, inter-modality, comfort observing of passengers' rights as well as new requirements to the interaction of transport and environment. It is impossible to exercise complete account of all these requirements without a systematic approach and applying the modern instruments to the formation and management of the passengers' services market.

Bus and coach transport today is in hard and constant competition with the other modes of public transport. It is necessary to enlarge the network of transportations by increasing the accessibility of services in order to manage passengers' transportation by coaches more attractive for passengers than it is done today as well as to increase the number of passengers. In this situation the role of terminal is vital. Following the best examples of passengers' transportation by air, it would be useful for the terminals to unite in cooperation with transportation companies, and to build a common network of ticketing and information to the passengers of several European states. At the end it will bring to the so-called "virtual" terminal on the basis of using the up-to-date information technologies and general technical standard, thus making a unified Information System for passengers.

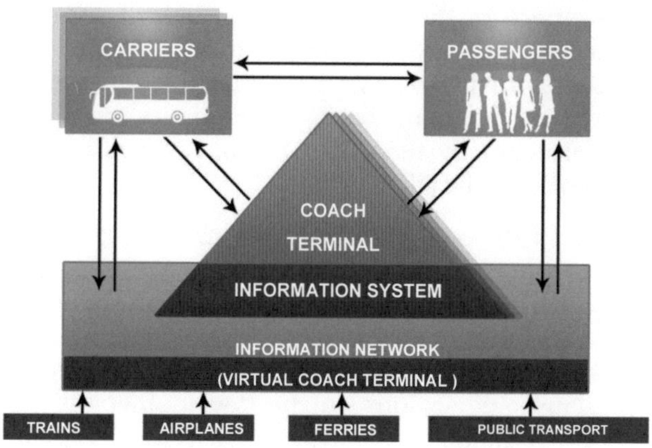

Fig. 1. General scheme of a "virtual" terminal

Raising the efficiency of the terminal control in conformity to the system approach requirements is greatly liaised with the formation of the coordinated management system including strategic, tactic and operative decisions as well as with the provision of the information-analytical base of managerial decision-making of the above types and working out the corresponding instrumentation based on the monitoring and estimation of the indicators of the inner-organisation development.

Nowadays, the good information system becomes the key moment of the development strategy of transport industry. The development of the information system is also an essential factor for coach terminals, as passengers' transport infrastructure objects, in their transformation into *passenger logistics centres* (PLC). By definition a coach terminal is a linear construction consisting of specific buildings, platforms and a territory for the rendering of services to passengers and coaches during the routes. To ensure an effective operation of such a linear construction, to be able to render high quality services both to passengers and to haulers in conformity with their needs, the functions and operational activities of a coach terminal have to be evaluated at a larger scale. We would like to suggest considering a coach terminal as *passenger logistics hub,* taking the operational and development model of the JSC „Riga International Coach Terminal" (RICT) as a basis.

The objective of the development concept of the JSC "Riga International Coach Terminal" is as follows: „To develop the JSC "Riga International Coach Terminal" as a new passenger modular transfer and service point meeting the future requirements for high culture and diversity of passenger servicing and interlinking with other types of public transport - the railway, urban public transport, sea port and airport".

To develop an effectively operating hub of logistics, there has to be an assessment of the main critical factors for the successful operation of such hub (Gromule & Yatskiv, 2007a): location, support by government, infrastructure, qualified labour forces, information technologies, etc. The development of information technologies that includes the IT and telecommunication infrastructure, the WEB based easy interface and e-commerce platform allow to ensure the access to both the passengers and hauler companies, thus widening the range of the coach terminal operation and services.

The role of information system in transport is important from the point of view of the quality of service for travellers. Taking into account the fact that the services of a passenger terminal are integrated into the whole chain of passenger transportations and are accepted by the user as a single service of the chain, development of a complex approach to the analysis of the passenger terminal service quality is quite topical. For passengers, there are several important aspects of travel - route, timetable (frequency of trips), time of travel, service reliability, security, etc. Some of these characteristics are objectively estimated and stored in the terminal Information System (IS) (Gromule, 2007); some of them are subjective and need constant questioning of the clients.

The chapter gives overview of the concrete passenger terminal IS and the possibilities of its employment as the decision support system (DSS) and as the basis for realizing of the PLC conception. There is also defined the place of the IS in the quality system. The example given in the chapter is the IS *Baltic Lines* worked out at the beginning for RICT specially and used now all around Latvia and issued for many Bus and Coach Terminals of the European Union. There are formulated suggestions on the development of the given system and formation on its basis of a virtual logistics hub as the basis and essential part of realizing the PLC conception in the chapter.

The chapter gives consideration of the quality system existing at the terminal and development of the systematic approach to the analysis of the service quality based on both the objective data stored in the terminal information system and on the subjective data. The methodic of estimating and analysing the index of punctuality as a reliability measure is presented. There is formulated the algorithm suggested for employment in the DSS of the IS *Baltic Lines*.

For analysing the factors influencing the choice of a coach as a transport mean there is employed the econometric modelling on the basis of the discrete choice models' theory. In building the models there are considered both the social-economic characteristics of passengers and the characteristics of the given service: time-table, network, etc. The detected key characteristics of the service are analysed from the point of view of their influence on the overall estimation of the quality.

The main accent in the complex approach is made on the formation of an integral (composite) quality indicator (IQI) and the detection, on this basis, of those particular attributes of quality which considerably impact the overall estimation of quality. This approach allows control and management of the service quality, coordination of special practical steps aimed at the correction of particular attributes of quality with the account of their possible influence on the overall estimation of the service quality - on IQI.

2. Review of Information systems for coach and bus transport

Analysing the experience of using information systems for this mode of transport it can be stressed upon that basically the systems provide the sale and refund of tickets, information for passengers and reports. It does not give complete information about all possibilities of travel (routes). Also, in the era of intermodality and co-modality the node of connections (terminal) has become the important part in the process of service quality provision. That's why the Information system for terminal or system, which covers like the tasks for carriers and for terminal, is needed.

There are the different realizations of such kind of the system but most of them implemented only for realization the tasks of carriers. One of the examples - the system PLUSBUS (Ten facts, 2011) in England that has developed in cooperation of carriers but the functions of terminal are not realized. But in general the chain of passenger services provides the largest passenger flow in terminal. In the terminal a comfortable, fast and convenient service for passengers must be provided while waiting for a transfer and opportunities from one coach to another or other modes of transport. By this it is expedient to introduce additional features in the IS for collecting and processing these services, for instance, dispatch information, information on return tickets, denial of travel, booking sites, and so on.

The German experience can be mentioned as an example of using such systems, DELFI system having started its development in 1996 and its test exploitation happened in 2000. The vision of DELFI – to create an integrated travel information service for the customer out of an apparently integrated information base – has led to the approach of connecting the existing systems by means of communication (DELFI, 2006). Advanced techniques for optimising the "inter-system" search continuous itineraries have been developed. Itinerary information will be created by composing the information of all the participating systems through the open interfaces and harmonised meta information.

Another example of bus information system is NextBus that functions in San Francisco and other American cities. The core of the NextBus system is a GPS satellite (How NextBus works, 2008). The system tracks public transportation buses in the real time and dynamically calculates the estimated arrival times of the bus at each stop. This estimated time is displayed on the Internet and on the screen at each bus stop. Users can access the information from their mobile phones or PC. The NextBus system is also used in Finland (in rural areas) and other countries.

The further development of the systems of the kind is to implement the Decision Support System modulus. The task of development of the analytical part of this system is being set. From our point of view, the advanced approach to the development of such kind of the system took place in Bangkok (Borvornvongpitak & Tanaboriboon, 2005). There is the bus transit system with the developed analytical part. The analytical part of bus transit system can be used for evaluating bus performance through the developed bus indicators. Also the index of punctuality, see: (Kho et al., 2005), can be the basis for analysis of the quality of passengers' service.

The Baltic Lines system (Gromule, 2007), which described below in this chapter, is created to manage information and economic relationship in the sphere of coach transportation for the whole totality of participants of passenger transportation: coach terminals and their branches, coach operators, agencies that sell tickets, passengers, etc. Availability of the flexible tuning of the inner functions of the system both within one company in the industry and for the co-operation of the different coach operators within the same region, as well as ability of fast localization with taking into account specific features of the country is a distinctive feature of the Baltic Lines system.

Parallel to the use of IS „Baltic Lines" in the Terminal for Customer services cashiers working in the other ticketing systems such as Toks (Lithuania); LuxExpress (Estonia); Hansabuss (Estonia) and Norma-A "Ecolines" (Latvia). Some of them are connected to the database level. Tickets and information are available through IS „Baltic Lines". Connection of the carriers occurs through web interface. All of the systems ensure the sale and refund of tickets, information for passengers and reports. Each of the mentioned system covers only a segment of the market carriage of which serves only a part of the carriers. It does not give complete information to passengers about all the possibilities of travel (routes). IS „Baltic Lines" unites all the information about the possibilities of service from the Riga Coach Terminal.

3. Information system as the basis quality system of terminal services

The main conditions for realizing the conception of a logistics centre lie in the development of a system of the logistics centre management and its integration into a global network that is possible only on the basis of the all-round application of information technologies.

The implementation of the Riga International Coach Terminal (RICT) IS „Baltic Lines" in 2003 made it possible to form an integrated ticket sales/reservation accounting system that ensured a new level of passengers' and carrier service quality (Gromule, 2007; Gromule & Yatskiv, 2007b). Bringing of the IS *Baltic Lines* of the terminal into operative allowed creating an integrated system of selling/reserving tickets (Fig.2) that provided servicing passengers and transportation companies at a new quality level.

The IS „Baltic Lines" used by the coach terminal collects, processes, stores, analyses and disseminates the information providing the following principal functions:

- coach timetable and operative information about the changes;
- information about the coach movement: arrival, departure, location at the platforms, delay;
- ticket reservation and sales system, including: planning of routes, using services of several hauler companies and vehicles; different ways of payment and communication;
- observation of passengers' rights in accordance with normative documents;
- management and control system of the coach terminal service processes;
- processing of operational information in economic activity accounts and control.

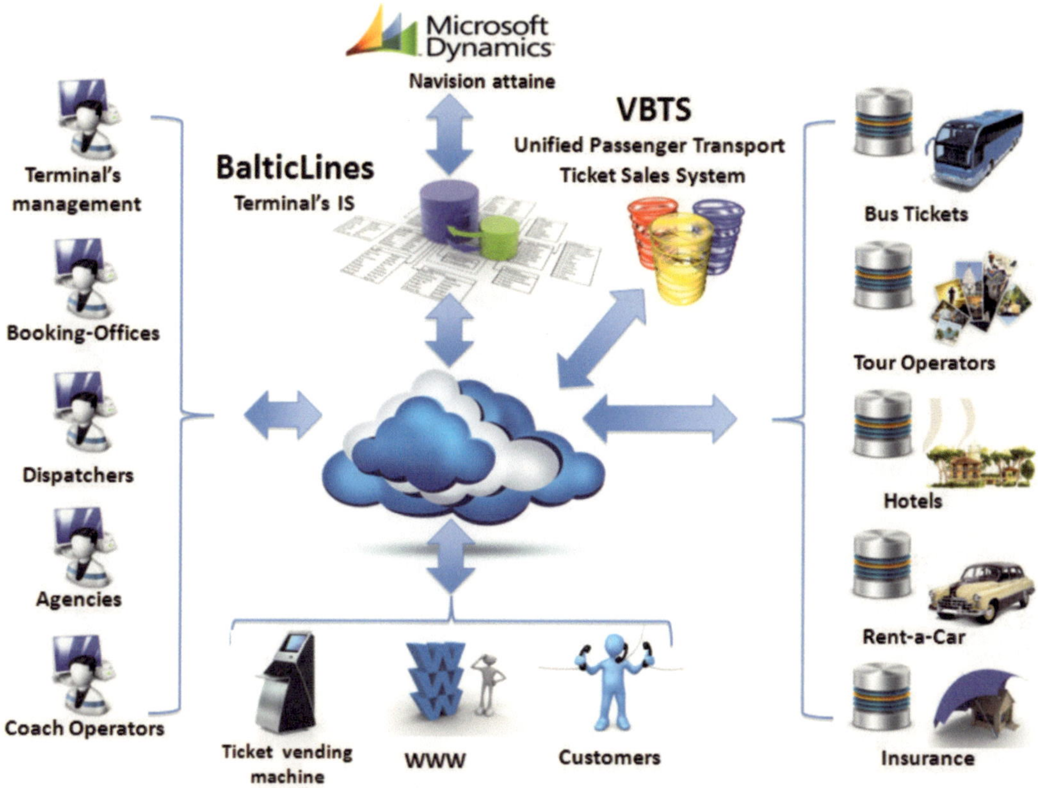

Fig. 2. Scheme of functioning of IS Baltic Lines

In order to ensure these functions, the coach terminal must process a large amount of operatively changing data coming from multiple sources of information, both internal and external. The data processed in the system is exported both for the internal use at the enterprise and to external users. The information flow is depicted on Figure 3.

The structure of the IS *Baltic Lines* is formed by ten modules with the continuous inter-exchange of information flows as it is shown on Figure 4. Organisation of the outward and inward information flows of the IS Baltic Lines provides necessary connection between the users of the system and other IS, such as book-keeping accounting in the IS *Navision Attaine*, selling tickets at www.bezrindas.lv and others.

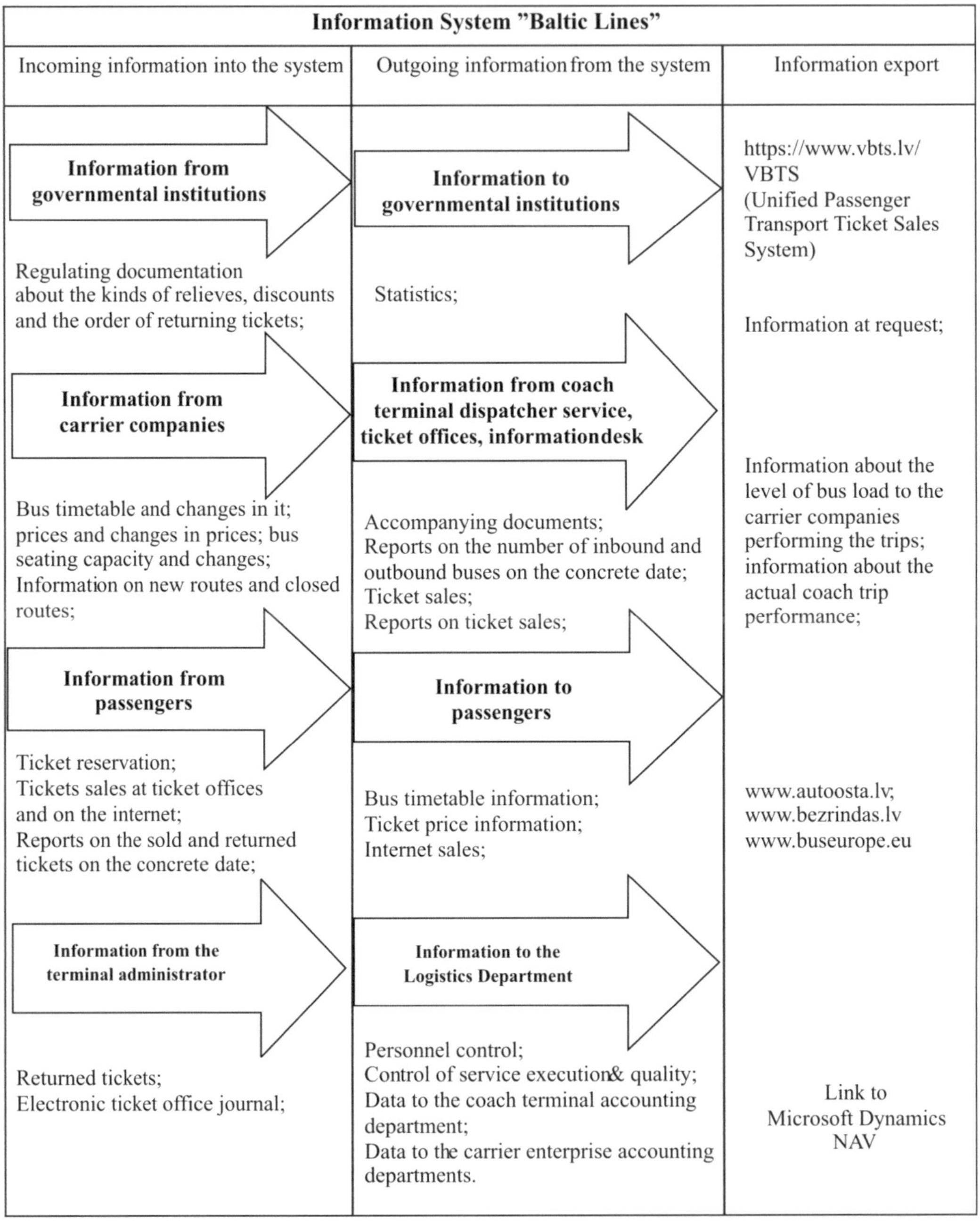

Fig. 3. Information flows of the coach terminal information system

The functional structure of the system envisages different users of the system:

At the terminal: system administrator; logistics specialists; administration; dispatchers, cashiers; information service;

Other users of the system: travelling agencies selling tickets; transportation companies; employees of the State, Ltd. "Direction of Auto-transport" and clients.

The users' rights are spelt out in conformity with the users' functions, performed operations and levels of responsibility.

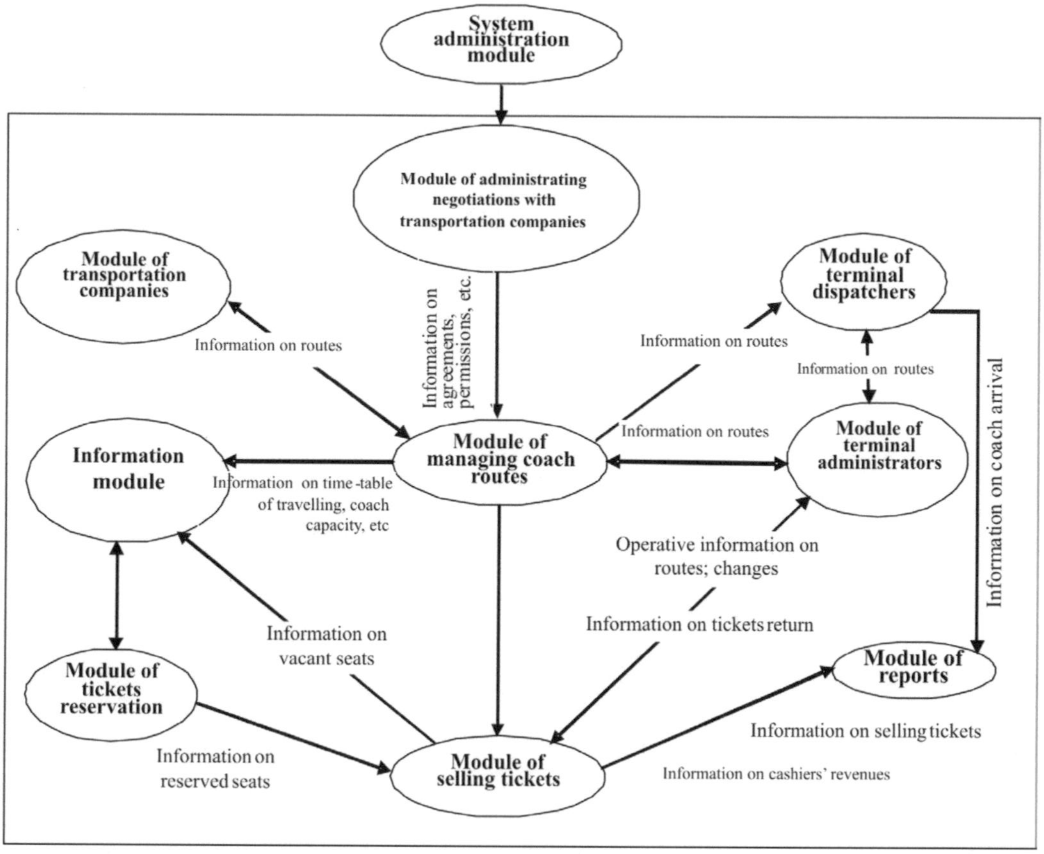

Fig. 4. Interaction of information flows in the IS Baltic Lines

The IS of *Baltic Lines* provides for:

- passengers:
  - A new level of service - possibility of reserving or selling public transport tickets for all trips in Latvia (no matter what the location of the passenger is);
  - Possibility of buying tickets through the Internet (print, send by *e-mail* or mobile phone);
- transportation companies and terminals:
  - New possibilities of attracting passengers and raising the number of clients;
  - Reduction of the tickets selling costs;
  - Improving the efficiency of the work by means of an accelerated and unified process of tickets selling;
  - Quality management;

- Increasing the quality of financial accounts;
- Possibility of the operative statistics analysis;

- the State Ltd. "Direction of Auto-transport":
  - Accessibility to operative statistics;
  - Possibility of controlling quality and transportations' volume;
  - Getting finance information.

4. A complex approach to estimating the quality of terminal services

The theoretical basis of the quality system in public transport might be presented in a form of a „quality loop" (Fig.5), which components might be divided into two parts: customers - passengers and service providers - carriers. Expected Quality is the level of quality that is required by the customer.

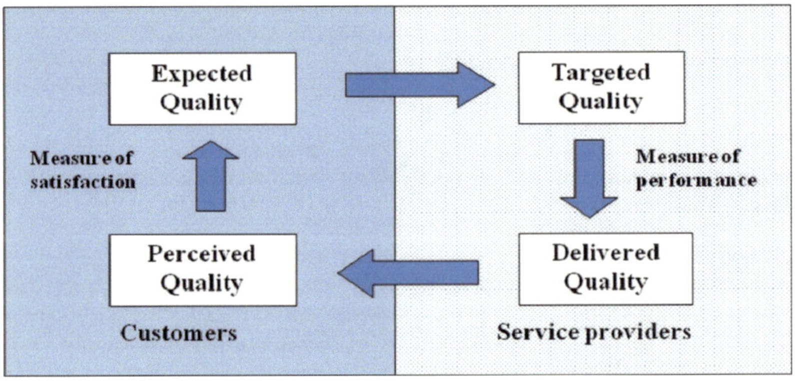

Fig. 5. The parts of "Quality Loop" (Portal, Written material, 2003)

Targeted Quality is the level of quality, which service provider or manager of mobile system is aiming to provide to the customers as a consequence of his understanding of the customer expectation. Delivered Quality is the level of quality effectively achieved in the provision of mobility services by the different components of system. Perceived Quality - the level of quality perceived by the user-customer (Portal, Written material, 2003).

The difference between the Expected Quality and Perceived Quality reflects a measure of the customer satisfaction. The difference between the Targeted Quality and Delivered Quality reflects problems with the service design or anything else connected with the provision of service. In our case the Perceived Quality on top level consists of two parts: the Perceived Quality, which is provided by the direct service provider (carrier companies) and the Perceived Quality, which is provided by a terminal. The complexity of this particular case research is connected with the fact that customer often doesn't divide the Perceived Quality in two parts and estimates the Perceived Quality as a single whole (placing own part and carrier's part on coach terminal).

In 2004 RICT received the Quality Standard ISO 9001:2000 certificate within the operational sphere of passenger traffic servicing and provision, ticket sales and trip record keeping management. In 2010 the RICT received the ISO 9001:2008 certificate, which acknowledges its high quality management systems compliance with international standards and criteria. A major part of our attempts to enforce the quality of terminal services is the use of modern IT systems. The quality management system for the RICT consists of three hierarchical levels (Fig.6):

1. Documents of policy, which include the formulation of quality assurance guidelines, aims and objectives, organisational structure, the sphere of certification, etc.
2. All processes that concerns the company.
3. A database, which ensures the functions of the company.

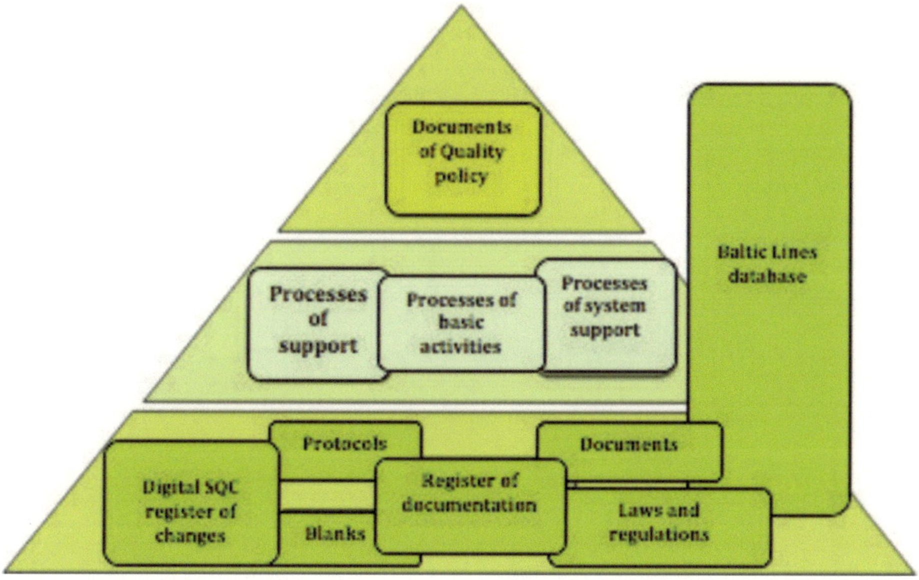

Fig. 6. The structure of the quality management system

The IS *Baltic Lines* constantly storing and processing in real time big volumes of updating information is used for making decisions at both the level of strategic planning, management control and tactic planning and the level of operative planning. To support decision-making in the system of public transport and at all stages of providing services, a certain volume of information is used at every level of decision-making. While defining the volume of this information, it is necessary to take into account what actions and processes are controlled and what level of influence on the whole system is.

Considering the IS *Baltic Lines* as an example, we can define two stages of its development:

- realisation of collecting primary statistic data on technological processes,
- providing necessary instrumentation to support management decision-making, (the analytical part, which included analysis of the statistic data and prognosis of the indicators of the quality and efficiency).

Figure 7 presents the system of complex analysis of the terminal services' quality that includes a number of tasks of the quality analysis on the basis of information from the objective and subjective factors.

One of the main tasks is calculation of *the quantitative criteria of the service quality.* In addition to the existing criteria under calculation today that characterize the coach terminals services, for example, the work of dispatchers, the number of the tickets sold, the number of the errors made, the authors suggest calculation of some additional criteria on the basis of the objective information of the terminal IS that characterizes the following: the reliability (index of punctuality); the coefficient of network covering; the congestion of coaches, etc.

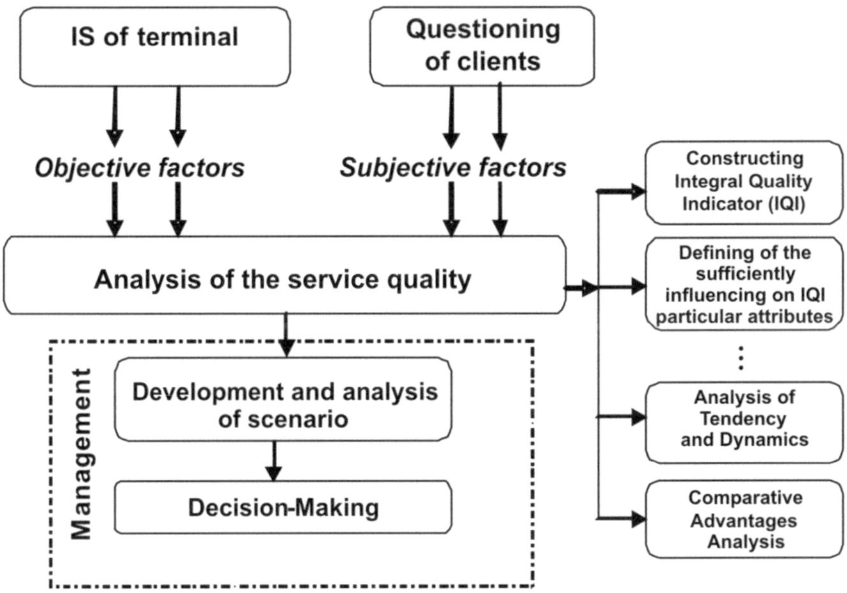

Fig. 7. System of complex analysis of the terminal services' quality

These criteria characterize the quality of the service provided, first of all, by a transportation company, and the terminal hardly influences these services. But this is not evident for the client, consequently client estimates the quality in general; therefore constant monitoring of these indicators is important for managing the terminal. For calculating the above-mentioned criteria we need information that is not always available in today's terminal IS.

An integral part of the quality system is clients' questionnaire. A system of questionnaire has been developed that is designed for solving the following tasks (see Table 1):

- analysis of comparative advantages (clients' choice of the transport mode);
- analysis of mobility;
- analysis of the constituents of the general estimation of service quality and defining of the sufficiently influencing particular attributes.

№	Required Interval	Title	Target Group	Task	Expected Results	Management Level
1	Once a year	Passenger survey on the quality of services	Passengers	Passenger satisfaction analysis	Use of the results for the quality management system. Development and improvement of services	Operational
2	Once a year	Carrier survey on the quality of services	Carriers, coach drivers	Carrier satisfaction analysis	Use of the results for the quality mana-gement system. Development and improvement of services	Operational
3	Regular	Consideration of the customers' applications and complaints	Customers	Customer satisfaction analysis	Service quality improvement	Operational
4	Regular	Consideration of the applications and complaints from the personnel	Personnel	Personnel satisfaction analysis	Human resources system improvement	Operational
5	At least once a year, preferably automatically	Register and analysis of delays, passenger survey	IS database, passengers	Punctuality index calculation, analysis of influencing factors	Analysis and increasing of reliability	Strategic, operational
6	2-3 years	Transport mode choice and preference survey	Passengers	Identification of the factors that influence passenger choice of transport mode	Determination of the most important factors in attracting passengers to a certain mode of transport	Strategic
7	3-5 years	Survey on the level of services and infrastructure of the coach terminal	Experts	Identification of important particular attributes of quality	Determination of the integral indicator of service quality and the major quality influencing factors	Strategic

Table 1. Surveying system for monitoring of the quality of services provided by the terminal

5. Analysis of the transportations reliability on the basis of the punctuality index

One of the considered in (Kittelson et al, 2003) reliability indices is punctuality index. Punctuality of coach operation is quantitative measure of reliability from the viewpoint of users. This index indicates the magnitude of time gap between actual and scheduled arrival times. Research of this index in combination with different factors, influencing on this index; and in an ideal development of the model for evaluation of punctuality is a difficult task, possible only at presence of plenitude of information and its pithiness. By the developed information system of the Riga Coach Terminal the decision of the mentioned task in the designed module of decision-making is not possible.

Punctuality reflects reliability of the transport enterprise activity and is accounted by passengers in choosing a transportation company and a mode of transport. If we consider railways and coach transportations we'll see that railways are much more reliable means of transportation since its reliability is not dependent on jams and weather conditions. On the other hand, this mode of transport is less available as compared to coaches because not all regions have access to the railway network. In such competitive market, combination of comfort and service may play a deciding role in choosing a transport mode. And if transporting time does not differ greatly, to fall within the timetable may become a problem for the coach transport, especially if we consider realisation of inter-modality of transportations.

The work suggests the method of calculating and analysing the index of punctuality as a measure of reliability of coach transportations. The index for the *i-th* trip with the κ points of arrival is calculated as the value of the time interval between the actual time of arrival of the transport means at the j point for the *i-th* trip t_{ij}^f and the planned time of arrival t_{ij}^r :

$$h_i = \sum_{j=1}^{k} \left(t_{ij}^f - t_{ij}^r \right) * w_j \, ,$$

where

w_j – a weighting coefficient for the j point equals

$$w_j = \begin{cases} 0, \textbf{ if } t_{ij}^f < t_{ij}^r \\ 1, \textbf{ if } t_{ij}^f > t_{ij}^r \end{cases} .$$

The task of exposure of different factors, stronger than all influencing on this index, is important for top management best of all.

The authors offered the following ways of investigation:

- calculation of the punctuality index for the examined period of time for a sample of the analysed trips on the basis of the data of the terminal IS;
- calculation of the descriptive characteristics of a random value – punctuality index;
- investigation, on the basis of the analysis of variance, of the degree of influence on the punctuality index of the following factors: (1) weather conditions; (2) day of the week; (3) time of the day; (4) direction of entering the city, etc.

Approbation of the above-mentioned methods on the data of RICT has been performed by the authors only in reference to the final stop since information about the time of arrival and departure of the coaches in the intermediate points of the route is lacking in the current version of IS. The results of the approach application are published in the authors' papers (Gromule et al., 2008a; Gromule, 2008).

For instance, it is concluded, the significant influence of the direction of entering the city on reliability - the hardest delays have been checked with the trips entering the city in the Latgale direction (see Fig.8). For the data of 2007 the value of the *F* criterion equals 38.45 and the critical level - $F(3,1125)=2.61$. As a result, some alternative routes of entering the city in case of jams in the regular directions have been suggested.

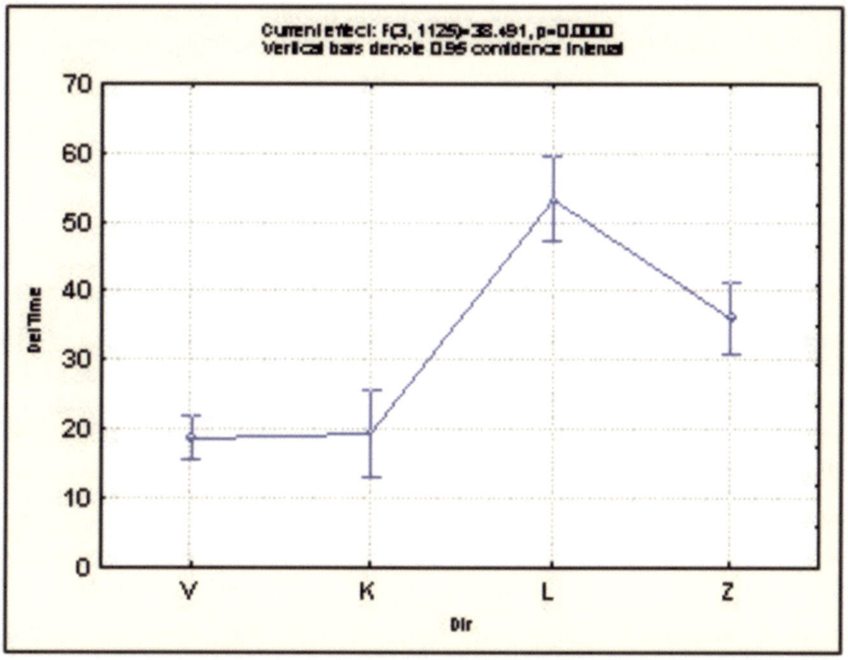

Fig. 8. 95% significant intervals for the delay time depending on 4 directions: L-Latgale, Z - Zemgale, K- Kurzeme, V- Vidzeme (July, 2007)

Application of the mentioned methods to the data of the terminal IS gives possibility of solving the task of influencing on the reliability of both controlled and non-controlled factors, such as:

- Strategies of managing the process, which can be and are used for reacting to the problems of reliability with the purpose of their minimization.
- State of transport means and quality of their maintenance.
- Sufficiency of transport means and personnel (drivers, dispatchers, etc.) available and required for the trips according the timetable in the given day.
- Introduction of priority for coach transportations, for example, a special traffic line for coach transportations, special traffic lights.
- Difference in driving skills, knowledge of the route, keeping to the timetable.

- Length of the route and number of stops, which increase the probability of the coach delay in the route.
- Transport conditions (in the streets), including traffic congestions, delays of traffic lights, manoeuvres at parking, different accidents, highways' building or current repair, etc.

6. Model of an integral indicator of the terminal services quality

Quality has a complex character and depends on many categories and dependence is not constant, therefore, we need a mechanism that tracks the influence of particular categories of quality on the integral indicator of quality.

It is of great importance for running a coach terminal to have internal logistics of its operation, the level of infrastructure, the variety and quality of services rendered. The most significant preconditions are characterised by the following (access possibilities, content and layout of information, comfort and customer service, security and environment).

It is no unique approach to measuring service quality. But, it is accepted that the quality of service is usually a function of several particular quality factors (attributes) and determining of each factor weight is the key moment of measuring quality. The theory of linear composite indicator constructing (Nardo, 2005) and statistical methods are used for definition of weights of aggregation function. In our research we have taken at the basis the approach, which is developed in D.Peña works (Peña, 1997a; Peña & Yohai, 1997b).

Authors suggest an algorithm of building a function for an integral (composite) indicator of quality which benchmarks the quality of different terminals services and revealing important quality categories influencing the total quantity indicator (Gromule et al., 2008b; Gromule et al., 2009; Gromule et al., 2010a). The linear indicator of quality assumes that function may be presented in the form

$$Q_i = \sum_{j=1}^{k} \beta_{ij} X_{ij} ,$$

where weight β_{ij} measures a relative importance of the attribute X_j in relation to the quality of service for the i-th client. Selection of a model of type and estimation of the mean weight of each attribute are the main problems in this task. The given work suggests an algorithm of calculating weights based on a regression analysis with restrictions on coefficients signs and values.

So, we have a task of estimating the unknown parameters with these restrictions. Suppose that the estimates of overall quality of service – Y_i, (i = 1,..., n) and estimates of attributes (particular quality indexes), which define quality of service – X_{ij}, for k-th concrete attributes (i=1, ... , n; j=1, ..., k) are made on the basis (0-5) scale. Let the quality of service is unknown variable, which is measured by user's estimation Y_i and determined as follows

$$Y_i = \mathbf{\beta}^{\mathrm{T}} \mathbf{x}_i + Z_i ,$$

where $\mathrm{x}_i = (X_{i1}, \ldots, X_{ik})$ – estimations of attributes, made by i-th user,

$\mathbf{\beta} = (\beta_1, \ldots, \beta_k)^{\mathrm{T}}$ – vector of unknown weights,

Z_i – error of measuring (residual), which assumption is normally distributed $Z_i \sim N(0, \sigma_z^2)$.

Models assumptions are assumptions of the classical regression analysis, with the exception of the assumption about model coefficients. It is logical to assume that the increase in an estimation of partial attribute should lead to increase in an estimation of the overall quality. In this case dependence between the overall quality and partial attributes should be with a positive sign. The second restriction – usual for weight – on value. Taking these conditions into account let's enter the restrictions on parameters (weights for partial attributes of quality) into model and restriction of the weights vector is the following:

$$\beta_j \geq 0 \text{ for } j=1,\ldots,\text{k and } \sum_{j=1}^{k} \beta_j = 1 .$$

Therefore, we have a task of estimating the unknown parameters with these restrictions. The research suggests an algorithm, which is drawn on Figure 9 and presented in publications (Gromule et al., 2009; Gromule et al., 2010a; Gromule et al., 2010b).

At *the first step of algorithm* an estimation of a vector-column with unknown parameters β is finding at which value of function *f*(β) is minimum and the condition "the sum of these parameters (weights) are equal 1" is satisfied. If the received vector has negative elements, transition to the step 2, if not, then transition to the step 3.

At the second step (in case of *s* negative elements presence in a vector of parameters β ($\beta_i < 0$)) the following updating (modification) of initial matrix X is made: the lines concerning negative estimations are excluded from consideration. Transformed matrix X dimension $(k\text{-}s)\times n$ goes on a repeated estimation of parameters, i.e. transition to the step 1 is made.

In case of the component positivity in a vector of parameters β (*the third step*) calculation of standard purpose function *f*(β) in a method of the least squares, which is necessary to minimize, is made.

At *the fourth step* search of optimum value of the purpose function is made. Assume that altogether number of the remained positive parameters equals *l*. By serial zeroing (all possible combinations on one, on two, on three etc. on *l* remained positive parameters) and searching of all received values of the purpose function at given combinations of parameters such set is defined at which the purpose function *f*(β) is minimum. Answering to the minimum value of the purpose function *f*(β) the vector β, which is not containing negative elements, is the task's decision.

The result of algorithm work is vector-column β (dimension $k\times l$) containing estimations of unknown regression model parameters only with nonnegative signs and the sum of these parameters (weights) is equal 1.

Approbation of the suggested approach was made on the basis of the results of questioning of 44 experts in transport, which was performed in spring 2009. The questionnaire included 22 particular attributes of quality distributed on 7 groups: accessibility (availability); information; time characteristics of service; customer service; comfort; safety; infrastructure

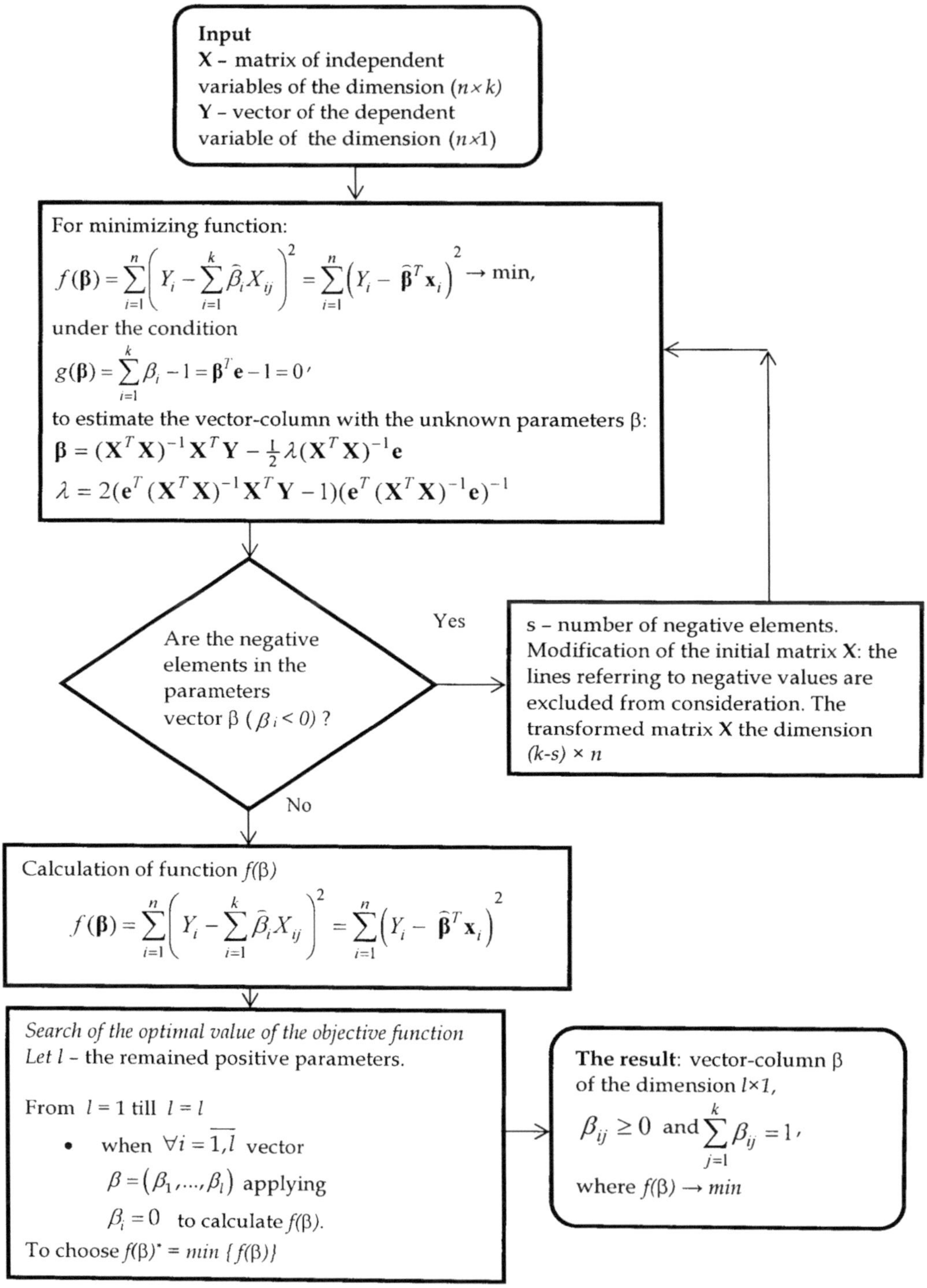

Fig. 9. The algorithm of building a function for an integral (composite) indicator of quality

and environment (Table 2). The overall quality of service was evaluated too. The overall quality service was estimated on a scale 0-5 as well as particular attributes of quality.

Title of chapter in questionnaire	Coding	Description of variable	Coding
1. Accessibility	W1	Accessibility for external participants of traffic	X1
		Accessibility for terminal passengers	X2
		Ticket booking	X3
2. Information	W2	General information in terminal	X4
		Information about trips in positive aspect	X5
		Information about trips in negative aspect	X6
3. Time	W3	Duration of trip	X7
		Punctuality	X8
		Reliability/trust	X9
		Coach time schedule	X10
4. Customer service	W4	Customer trust to terminal employees	X11
		Communication with customer	X12
		Requirements to employees	X13
		Physical services providing	X14
		Process of ticket booking	X15
		Services provided by coach crews during boarding/debarkation	X16
5. Comfort	W5	Cleanness and comfort in terminal premises and on terminal square	X17
		Additional opportunities/services providing in coach terminal	X18
6. Reliability/safety	W6	Protection from crimes	X19
		Protection from accidents	X20
7. Environment	W7	Dirtying, its prevention	X21
		Infrastructure	X22
	W8	Overall estimation	X23

Table 2. Particular Attributes of Quality

The analysis of coordination (consistency) of questionnaire questions was made by means of Cronbach alpha coefficient

$$\alpha = \frac{k}{k-1}\left(1 - \sum_{i=1}^{k} \frac{s_i^2}{s_{sum}^2}\right),$$

where k - amount of questions (in our case - particular quality attributes), s_i^2 - variance of i question and s_{sum}^2 - variance of sum of questions.

The results of questionnaire (estimates of particular attributes of quality) have demonstrated high indices of the internal coordination. A value of Cronbach alpha coefficient is equal to 0.933 and the standardized value is 0.93. It has allowed making an assumption about reliability of results. The lowest value of correlation is between resultant estimate and variables x7 («trip duration») and x8 («punctuality»).

The results of questionnaire (estimates of particular attributes of quality) have demonstrated high indices of the internal coordination. A value of Cronbach alpha coefficient is equal to 0.933. It has allowed making an assumption about reliability of results. The lowest value of correlation is between overall quality estimate and variables: x_7 («trip duration») and x_8 («punctuality»).

It is important to analyse the descriptive characteristics of particular attributes of quality, too. The attributes connected with infrastructure ($\overline{x}_{22}$ =3.035) and environment ($\overline{x}_{21}$ =3.182) have the lowest estimates. It corresponds to a true situation: today the Coach Terminal is experiencing difficulties and looking for new squares for moving and further repair of the existing territory. The following low estimated attributes are «Cleanness and Comfort in Terminal Premises and on Terminal Square» ($\overline{x}_{17}$ =3.419), «Protection from Crimes» ($\overline{x}_{19}$ =3.500) and «Physical Services Providing» ($\overline{x}_{14}$ =3.550). These attributes also depend directly on the infrastructure state of the Coach Terminal.

Experts have given the highest estimates to the particular quality attributes of «Coach Time Schedule» ($\overline{x}_{10}$ =4.409) and «Accessibility/Ticket Booking» ($\overline{x}_3$ =4.5) that is also explainable. The issues of accessibility (opportunity of ticket booking in the terminal ticket offices and in the Internet and via the mobile telephone) are considered by the management of the Riga Coach Terminal as priority and therefore high estimations of these attributes are obvious.

The above mentioned fact, that respondents are the high-qualified transport specialists, allowed as to assume that the sample is homogeny and the assumption about equal variance of residual is fulfilled.

The final formula of the developed model according the algorithm showed on Figure 9 is the following:

$$y_i^* = 0.144x_{1i} + 0.082x_{4i} + 0.171x_{7i} + 0.050x_{8i} + 0.133x_{11i} + 0.141x_{12i} + \\ +0.058x_{13i} + 0.128x_{19i} + 0.093x_{22i}$$

where x_{1i} – accessibility for external participants of traffic
x_{4i} – general information in terminal
x_{7i} – duration of trip
x_{8i} – punctuality
x_{11i} – customer trust to terminal employees
x_{12i} – communication with customer
x_{13i} – requirements to employees
x_{19i} – protection from crimes
x_{22i} – infrastructure.

The quality of the obtained model is tested obligatory: the Standard Error of Estimate (SEE) makes about 9% in relation to the mean value of the overall estimate.

Knowledge of the weights allows regulating of the attributes according to their relative importance for the user and shows the key attributes from the point of view of improving quality. For example, revealing the fact of the importance of the x_{11i} and x_{12i} corresponding to the group of quality attributes "Customer service", underlines the importance of measures of managing the coach terminal personnel. And, the second place according to significance X_1 - "Accessibility for external participants of traffic" - confirms a correctness of a strategic goal of the terminal's management - to make it as a modern passenger logistics centre with the high level of intermodality.

The practical result of building the given models is revealing the importance of particular attributes of quality in their influence on the evaluation of the quality provided by a passenger terminal - coach terminal. It will allow the administration to take more grounded measures of improving the quality of service. Figure 10 shows the scheme of possible usage of the quality indicator for decision-making.

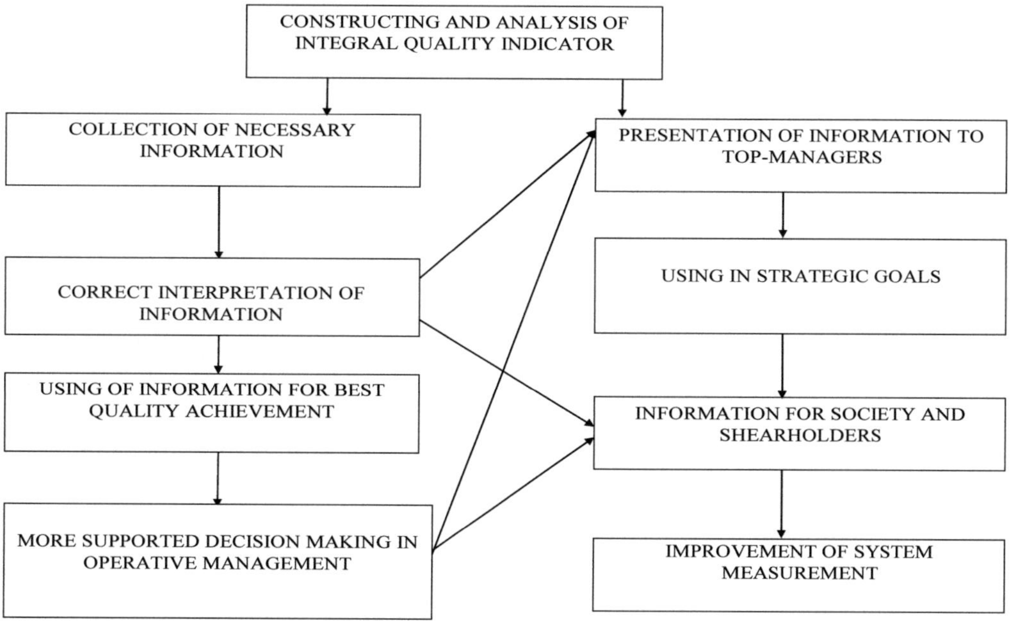

Fig. 10. Scheme of using an integral quality indicator

7. Models of examining the reasons of the transport mode choice by passengers

To make passenger transportations by public transport more attractive for passengers and to increase the number of passengers, it is necessary to enlarge the network of transportations by increasing the accessibility of services. For this, the theory of discrete choice, which is being developed by scientists Ben-Akiva, Lerman (Ben-Akiva & Lerman, 1985) and others (McFadden, 1974), has been used. In the disaggregated models of a discrete choice there are accounted the factors, which influence generation of trips: social status, way of life and other characteristics of an individual. Besides, the behaviour of an individual is influenced by the characteristics of a transport mode, such as: cost and time of transfer, punctuality, comfort, suitability and quality of the transport infrastructure. A discrete choice model predicts a decision made by an individual (such as mode or route choice.) as a function of any number of variables. In the research we have investigated the influence of a wide range of factors to passenger's choice, estimated their marginal effects. Discovered key factors and their influence directions can be used for improving the services of coach and railway carriers and terminals.

To develop models, which allow taking into account influence of numerous factors on the volume of the passenger turnover and transport needs of every individual traveller, it is necessary to have a well developed system of transport research and surveillance.

In this research a *discrete choice model* (Ben-Akiva & Lerman, 1985) is used for predicting a preferred transportation mode. The mathematical formalization of the model can be presented as:

$$P(y=1|x=X)=F(X^T\beta),$$

where y - a discrete variable, which equals to 1 if a passenger accepts an alternative and 0 if he declines it (a binary choice);

X - a set of explanatory variables;

β - a vector of unknown coefficients to be estimated;

F - a function, transforming a set of real numbers into [0, 1].

An econometrical base is different from a simple regression in this case - we need to estimate the conditional probability of a particular choice alternative as a function of the set of explanatory variables. There are no exact practical rules for this selection of the F function form (some recommendations can be found at (Hausman&McFadden, 1984: McFadden., 1984)). Usually F is a standardised normal cumulative distribution function (the model is called *probit* in this case) or a cumulative logistic distribution function (the model is called *logit* respectively). Both logit and probit models give similar results for intermediate values of $X^T\beta$ (the function form makes a difference for larger deviations - the logistic function has fatter tails). There is no systematic difference in the results of logit and probit models estimation in our case, so the logit models only are used in this research.

There is a complication with an analysis of estimated coefficients $\hat{\beta}$. We can calculate the influence of each explanatory variable x_i as:

$$\frac{\partial P(y=1|X^T\beta)}{\partial x_i}=\frac{\partial F(X^T\beta)}{\partial x_i}=f(X^T\beta)\cdot\beta_i,$$

where f is a probability density function.

The majority of explanatory variables are discrete (qualitative) ones in our case, so we can't use the derivatives for marginal effects calculations and use the discrete change formula instead:

$$P(y=1|X^T\beta,x_i=1)-P(y=1|X^T\beta,x_i=0).$$

To measuring goodness of fit we use an analogue to the R^2 - McFadden's likelihood ratio index (McFadden, 1974):

$$LRI=1-\frac{Ln(L)}{Ln(L_0)},$$

where $Ln(L)$ - a value of the likelihood function for the full model,

$Ln(L_0)$ - a value of the likelihood function for the model with a constant only.

The authors demonstrate the approach to build a model of choosing a transport mode on the route Riga-Daugavpils on the basis performed passengers' questionnaire at the RICT. There were built two models of the discrete choice of the transport mode for trips to Riga-Daugavpils (Gromule et al., 2010; Pavlyuk et al., 2011). The first stage choice ("use a car" vs. "don't use a car") represented by an usual discrete choice model (the Model I) estimated on the base of the full sample, and the second stage ("use a train" vs. "use a coach") represented by a conditional discrete choice model (the Model II) estimated on the base of the restricted sample. There were built two discrete choice models (Fig. 11).

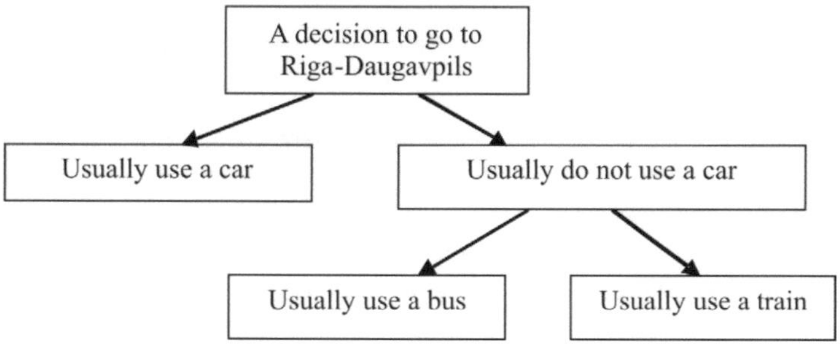

Fig. 11. Two-level scheme of decision (Passenger's decisions hierarchy)

We suppose that a passenger doesn't choose a usual transport from all three possible alternatives directly, but his decision includes two steps. At the first step the person decides to use or don't use his own car (the choice can be restricted with an absence of the own car). At the second stage, if he decided to use a public transport, he chooses either a coach or a train.

As alternatives of modes of transport the following vehicles were used: a car, a train, a coach. There was considered a consistent model of the discrete choice. The first stage choice ("use a car" vs. "don't use a car") represented by an usual discrete choice model (the Model I) estimated on the base of the full sample, and the second stage ("use a train" vs. "use a coach") represented by a conditional discrete choice model (the Model II) estimated on the base of the restricted sample. There was examined the influence of a wide range of factors on the passenger's choice, evaluated their particular effects. To test this supposition we have used a procedure developed by Hausman and McFadden (Gromule, 2008), usually called a test of independence from irrelevant alternatives.

All meaningful coefficients in the models had the explained signs (and therefore, correct directions of influence). Both models had a high percentage of correctly classified cases.

The final formula for Model II, which includes the significant variables and estimates the probability for choice "use a train" vs. "use a coach", is the following:

$$P(vid\_train) = Logistic(x) = \frac{e^x}{e^x + 1}$$

with

$$\begin{aligned} x = {} & -2.919 - 1.785 time\_12\_18 + 1.976 riga - 2.079 why\_habit + 2.657 why\_price - \\ & -1.988 age40\_60 - 1.867 direct + 1.014 freq\_year + 1.178 destn\_final + 1.167 alt\_cheap + \varepsilon' \end{aligned}$$

where *time_12_18* – a variable «departure time from 12:00 till 18:00»;
riga – a variable «a person travels from Riga»;
why_habit – a variable «a person states a habit as a reason for coach selection»;
why_price – a variable «a person states a price as a reason for coach selection»;
age40_60 – a variable «a person is from 40 till 60 years old»;
direct – a variable «a trip is a direct one (vs. a return one)»;
freg_year – a variable «a person travels this way once a year or rarer»;
destn_final – a variable «person's destination is the terminal point»;
alt_cheap – a variable «a person thinks that a train is cheaper than a coach».

There are 86.27% of cases are classified correctly. Also we note a high level of coincidence for the rare alternative (13 of 18 passengers who usually use a train are classified correctly).

On the basis of the built models there were made the conclusions about most attractive features of coach transportation, particular features of passengers, etc. For instance, it was found out that the majority of passengers, preferring city transport, arrived at the Coach Terminal 15-30 minutes before the departure. This time interval may be used to analyse the coach terminal possibilities of offering additional services.

On the basis of the performed econometric modelling with the help of the discrete choice theory, we can make the conclusions:

- considering further possibility of using this kind of analysis on a constant basis in the system of quality of a passenger terminal, we may divide the explaining variables into two parts - observed and non-observed ones. The values of the observed variables (for example, point of destination) can be received without direct contact with person, and the values of the non-observed variables (for example, opinion about service) can be received only by questionnaire. Therefore, practical application of such models for decision-making requires thoroughly planned and wide transport surveillance;
- the detected key factors and their directions of influence are vitally useful for quality monitoring and may be used for improving the quality of services of coach and railway transportation companies and terminals.

8. Conclusions

By the development of IS the passenger terminals can offer integration of the functions of the service provider (terminal, transportation company) including planning, managing and controlling of the whole complex of transportations so as to achieve long-term strategic aims and to promote business development. This aim can be achieved by means of introducing into practice of the direct interaction between the information systems used by the passenger terminal and the information systems used by transportation companies, institutions regulating the industry.

The above-developed analytical instruments make up a system of monitoring of the quality of the terminal services, which aim is improving the manageability of the terminal. Solving the tasks of management in complex systems today lies in the sphere of designing of corporate information systems, the integral part of which is the decision support system (DSS).

The authors have developed the analytical instruments of decision-making, which may become the basis of the DSS for any passenger terminal IS:

- the methods of the reliability analysis with calculating the punctuality index of the coach traffic and revealing the factors, which influence reliability,
- the discrete-choice models for revealing the factors, which influence the coach transportations from other modes of transport,
- the algorithm for constructing an integral quality indicator, which helps to estimate influence of every particular indicator on the overall estimate of quality.

Use of the analytical instruments developed by the authors on the base of objective and subjective data will allow, by improving the adaptability of the terminal, increasing the competitiveness not only of the terminal but of the passenger transportations under service, too.

Availability of such complex system with the integrated analytical instruments allows making efficient decisions on terminal resources management.

9. References

Ben-Akiva, M., Lerman, S. (1985). *Discrete Choice Analysis: Theory and Application to Travel Demand (Transportation Studies)*. Massachusetts: MIT Press, 1985. 384 p.

Borvornvongpitak, N., Tanaboriboon, Y. (2005). Development of computerized Bangkok bus transit analytical system, *Journal of the Eastern Asia Society for Transportation Studies*, Vol.6, 2005, pp.505-518.

DELFI documentation: Report on the current status of the DELFI – system implementation / Edited by S.Schnittger, 2006.

Gromule, V. (2007). Development of Information System for Coach Terminal. In: *Proceedings of the 7th International Conference "Reliability and Statistics in Transportation and Communication" (RelStat'07)*. Riga: Transport and Telecommunication Institute, 2007, pp. 44-52.

Gromule, V. (2008). Analysis of the quality of service of the Riga coach terminal from the viewpoint of travellers. In *Proceeding of the 8th International Conference Reliability and statistics in transportation and communication (RelStat'08)*. Riga: Transport and Telecommunication institute, 2008, pp. 87–95.

Gromule, V., Pavlyuk, D. (2010). Discrete Choice Model for a Preferred Transportation Mode. In: *Proceedings of the 10th International Conference "Reliability and Statistics in Transportation and Communication"* (RelStat'10). Riga: TTI, 2010. pp. 143-151. CD.

Gromule, V., Yatskiv, I. (2007a). Coach Terminal as an important element of transport infrastructure. In: *Proceedings of the International Scientific Conference "Transbaltica 2007", Vilnius 11-12 April 2007.* Vilnius, 2007.

Gromule, V., Yatskiv, I. (2007b). Information System Development for Riga Coach Terminal. In: *Proceedings of the 6th WSEAS Int. Conference on System Science and Simulation in Engineering (ICOSSSE'07)*. Venice, Italy, 2007, pp. 173-178.

Gromule, V., Yatskiv, I., Kolmakova, N. (2010a). Estimation of Weights for the Indicators of Quality of Service. In: *International Symposium on Stochastic Models in Reliability Engineering, Life Science and Operations Management*. Ber-Sheeva, Israel, 2010, pp. 1180-1187.

Gromule, V., Yatskiv, I., Kolmakova, N. (2010b). Public Transport Service Quality Estimation on the Basis of Statistical Analysis. In: *The Third International Conference "Problems of Cybernetics and Informatics"*. Baku, Azerbaijan, 2010, pp. 232-235.

Gromule, V., Yatskiv, I., Kolmakova, N., Pticina, I. (2009). Development of the Indicator of Quality of Service for Riga Coach Terminal. In: *Proceedings of the International Conference "Reliability and Statistics in Transportation and Communication"* (RelStat`09). Riga: TTI, 2009. pp. 124-133. CD.

Gromule, V., Yatskiv, I., Medvedevs, A. (2008a). Development of quality indicators system as analytical part of information system for Riga coach terminal. In: *International Conference Modelling of business, industrial and transport systems.* Riga, Latvia: Transport and Telecommunication Institute, 2008, pp. 278–283.

Gromule, V., Yatskiv, I., Medvedevs, A. (2008b). Investigation of bus and coach service quality on the basis of information system for Riga coach terminal, *Transport and Telecommunication*, Vol. 9, No 2, 2008, pp. 39-45. ISSN 1407-6160

Hausman, J., McFadden, D. (1984). A Specification Test for the Multinomial Logit Model, *Econometrica,* Vol. 52, 1984, pp. 1219-1240.

How NextBus works, 2008 - http://www.nextbus.com/corporate/works/index.htm

Kho, S.-Y., Park, J.-S., Kim, Y.-H., Kim, E.-H. (2005). A development of punctuality index for bus operation, *Journal of the Eastern Asia Society for Transportation Studies,* Vol.6, 2005, pp.492-504.

Kittelson, P., Quade, B. Hunter-Zaworski, K. (2003) *Transit Capacity and Quality of Service Manual, 2nd edition.* Washington, DC: Transportation Research Board, National Academy Press, 2003.

McFadden, D. (1974). The Measurement of Urban Travel Demand, *Journal of Public Economics,* Vol.3, 1974, pp. 303-328.

McFadden, D. (1984). *Econometric Analysis of Qualitative Response Models: Handbook of Econometrics, Vol. 2.* Amsterdam: North Holland, 1984 pp. 1395-145.

Nardo, M., a.o. (2005). *Handbook on Constructing Composite Indicators: Methodology and User Guide.* OECD Statistics Working Paper, 2005. Vol. 3. 108 p.

Pavlyuk, D., Gromule, V. (2011). Application of a Discrete Choice Model to Analysis of Preferred Transportation Mode for Riga-Daugavpils Route. *Transport and Telecommunication*, Vol. 11, No 1, 2011, pp. 40-49. ISSN 1407-6160

Peña, D. (1997a). Measuring service quality by linear indicators. *Managing Service Quality, Vol. II / Edited by Kunst and Lemmink.* London: Chapman Publishing, Ltd., pp 35-51.

Peña, D. and V. Yohai (1997b). A Dirichlet random coefficient regression model for quality indicators, *Journal of Statistical Planning and Inference,* Vol. 136, Issue 3, March 2006, pp. 942-961.

PORTAL - Transport Teaching Material, 2003. Transport and land use. Written material. EU - funded Urban Transport Research Project Results.

Ten facts about PLUSBUS, 2011. http://www.plusbus.info/sites/default/files/pdfs/Facts%20about%20PLUSBUS.pdf

4

Document Image Processing for Hospital Information Systems

Hiroharu Kawanaka[1], Koji Yamamoto[2], Haruhiko Takase[1] and Shinji Tsuruoka[3]
[1]*Graduate School of Engineering, Mie University*
[2]*Suzuka University of Medical Science*
[3]*Graduate School of Regional Innovation Studies, Mie University*
Japan

1. Introduction

In this chapter, we introduce document image processing methods and their applications in the field of Medical (and Clinical) Science. Though the use of electronic health record systems are gradually spreading especially among big hospitals in Japan, and e-health environment will be thoroughly available in near future [1–3], a large amount of paper based medical records are still stocked in medical record libraries in hospitals. They are the long histories of medical examinations of each patient and, indeed, good sources for clinical research and better patient care. Because of the importance of these paper documents, some hospitals have started to computerize them as image files or as PDF files in which the patient ID is the only reliable key to retrieve them, however most hospitals have kept them as they are. This is due to the large cost of computerization and also the relatively low benefit of documents that can only be retrieved by patient ID. Indeed, the true objective of computerization of paper records is to give them functionality so that they can be used in clinical research such as to extract similar cases among them. If we cannot find out any practical solutions to this problem, large amounts of these paper based medical records will soon be buried in book vaults and might be discarded in near future. Thus we are confronted with a challenge to devise a good system which is easy to run and can smoothly incorporate the paper based large histories of medical records into the e-health environment.

In an e-health environment, health records are usually treated using an XML format with appropriate tags representing the document type. Here the document type means the scope or rough meaning of contents. Therefore, a good system might have such functions as to create XML files from paper documents that also have appropriate tags and keys representing the rough meaning of contents. Fortunately, most paper based medical records have been written on fixed forms depending on the clinic or discipline, such as diagnoses placed in a fixed frame of a sheet, and progress notes in another frame, etc., and these frames usually correspond to the document types. It would seem rather easy to assign an appropriate XML tag to each frame if we could determine the form or the style of the paper. And if such a frame can be determined and the scope of the contents in it is fixed, then translation into text from the document in that frame might be accurately performed by using dictionaries properly assigned to the scope. Also, as collaborative medicine spreads, many recent medical records have been typed so that they can easily be read among the team members; which also improves the accuracy of translation. Therefore, if we can determine accurately the style of the document, many stylized documents which will have XML tags corresponding to the frames in it may be fixed and the contents will be rendered into a text file with good accuracy. With this premise we started to investigate a new indexing system for paper documents [4–7]. The key elements of our investigation are document image recognition, keyword extraction, and automatic XML generation. This chapter will be devoted to the introduction of our work and some recent topics about the document image processing method used in the healthcare sector.

After describing experimental materials used for this study in section 2, the proposed method will be presented in section 3. The results and discussions about the proposed method will come in section 4, other related topics in medical sector in section 5, and lastly, concluding remarks and future scope will come in section 6.

2. Materials

As it is very important to know the power and limitations of the idea we first used typed and stylized documents with frames or tables archived at the medical record library at Mie University Hospital. These documents were scanned by an optical image scanner with gray scale of a resolution of 300 dpi. The images thus obtained are the target of this research. The resolution of 300 dpi is the minimum requisite to satisfy the law for digital archiving of medical documents in Japan. To know the extensibility and power of our system, handwritten medical records were also tested, which we only discuss in the discussion. Extension of our method to atypical medical documents though stylized but without frames is also discussed in that section.

3. Document image recognition method for resemble case search

3.1 Employment of a master information

As is stated in the introduction, almost all paper-based medical records are written in stylized sheets. When the use of computers was not so common as today, each clinical department designed the sheets carefully so as to fulfill their clinical examination requirements. Indeed, the styles used in each clinic were the result of a long history of contemplation. Titles and frame lines to the frames were in many cases printed out on blank sheets, and bundles of blank sheets were stocked at the medical record library and the medical affairs office, which were used for in many years. To save running cost, these blank sheets have gradually been output from computers where frame lines and/or ruled lines were sometimes omitted, but, the majority of medical records archived at the library were written on these stylized sheets with frame lines. In our research, these blank sheets were used to obtain master information to determine the type of the sheets of the images examined. The blank sheets were scanned and thus obtained images we call "master images", and the master information is generated from the "master images". The master database consists of information about the positions and types of the corners of each frame in a sheet and XML tags representing the contents of each frame. The method of determining the positions and the types of the corners of each frame of master information is the same as is used in analyzing images examined, but adding XML tags to each frame was done using knowledge about the sheets used. Using the master information clarifies the XML structure and makes the extraction of strings inscribed by users easy. As the XML tag in the master database is given from outside, it is quite robust in creating XML files. We employed the master database to the proposed system aggressively so as to cover all kinds of blank sheets used in Mie University Hospital. Generally speaking, employment of such a master database will improve the reliability of our system when the processed objects are regarded as stylized documents with frame lines.

Here, to make the statement more clearly, we use the word "sheet type" as the type of sheet included in the master information and "document type" as the type of document of each frame which directly relates to the XML tag. The word "table" is also used to mean a frame with frame lines, while the term "cell" means the contents in one cell of the table, and "cells", the plural of "cell", also means the contents in the table.

3.2 Outline of our system

Figure 1 illustrates the outline of the proposed method. The images obtained from paper-based medical documents have some factors, such as noise, tilts and so on, that deteriorate the accuracy of the following processes. These factors are reduced (or removed) by pre-processing described in 3.3, and some features to determine the sheet type are extracted from them. After this, each cell in the documents is extracted using cell positions and master information. The extracted cell often has images, e.g. schema images, sketches, as well as character strings. Thus such images are also extracted from the cell images. The extracted character strings are converted into text data by OCR engine, and the obtained text data are stored into a database. The extracted schema images are also recognized by a schema recognition engine, and the recognition results, i.e. schema name, annotation and its position etc., are also registered into the database. After this, an XML file is generated using the master information.

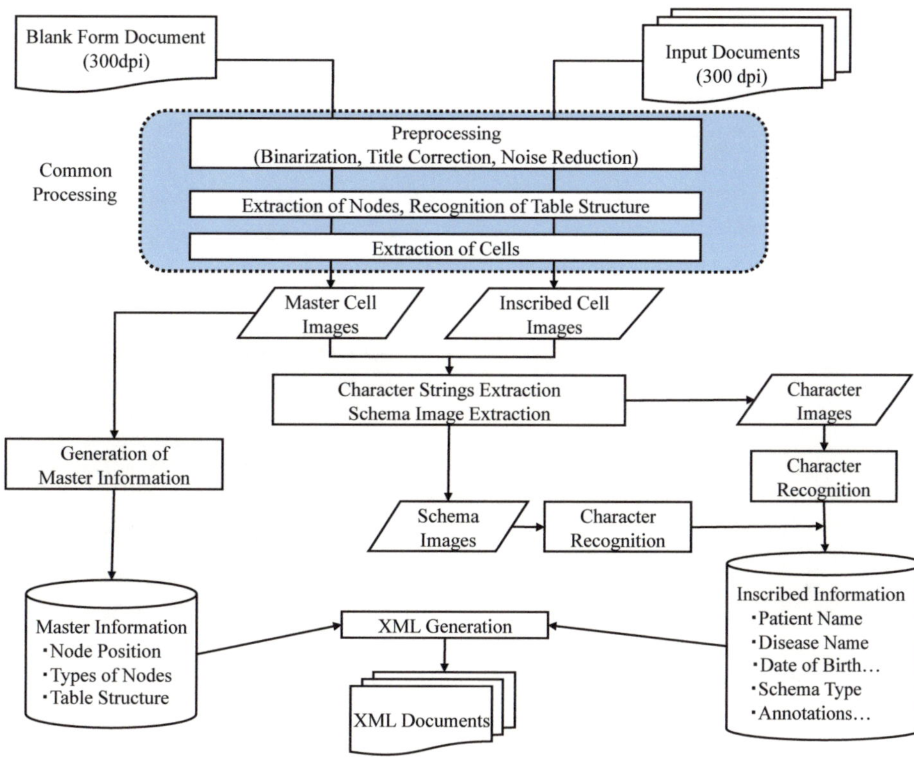

Fig. 1. Flow of the Tabular Document Recognition

3.3 Pre-processing

In this study, binarization, tilt correction and noise reduction techniques are applied to the input images as pre-processing. In the binarization process, Otsu's method was used [8, 9]. In his method, the threshold for binarization is determined by discriminant analysis using a density histogram of the input image. Therefore, no fixed threshold for each image is required. In the tilt correction process, the LPP method is used to correct the tilt of the images [10]. Figure 2 illustrates the rough image of LPP. In the LPP, the target image, i.e. the input image, is divided into n_s sub-regions and marginal distributions of each region are obtained. In this case, horizontal projection histograms are used as the marginal distributions. Next, correlations between each region (α_k) are calculated by

$$\alpha_k = \max_{-\beta \le y \le \beta} \left[\sum_j P_k(j) P_{k+1}(j-y) \right] = \sum_j P_k(j) P_{k+1}(j-\alpha_k). \tag{1}$$

$$(k = 1, 2, 3, \cdots, n_s - 1)$$

Here, $P_k(j)$ means the j-th value of the horizontal projection histogram of the k-th sub-region, and β does the range of calculation. These value indicate misaligns of the phases in each region, which are equivalent to the ratio of the tilt. As the result, the tilt angle of the paper θ is given by

$$\theta = tan^{-1} \frac{\alpha_m}{S_w}. \tag{2}$$

Here, α_m is the average of α_k, and S_w is the width of each sub region. the LPP method can detect the tilt of images with high accuracy with low calculation effort. For an image size of 1024×1024 pixels, the theoretical detection accuracy is about 0.06 degree and the detection

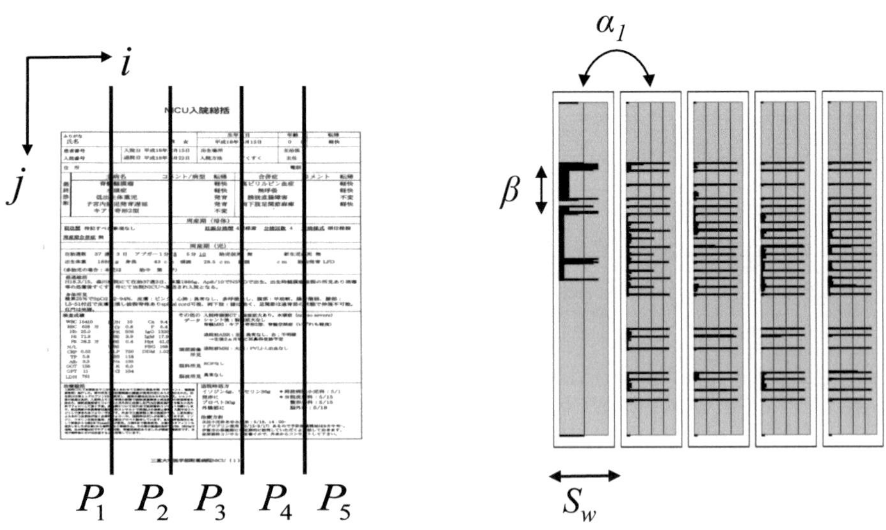

(a) Input Image (b) Obtained Marginal Distribution

Fig. 2. Tilt Correction using the LPP Method

range is from –10 to 10 degrees. We use the LPP method only, because images tilted by more than 10 degrees do not occur in practical cases. As a final step of pre-processing, a median filter is applied to the images to reduce speckle noise and salt and pepper noise.

3.4 Sheet type recognition using node information

Generally speaking, a tabular form document has at least one table, and its form and location heavily depend on sheet type. In other words, features of the table in the document would be the key information for sheet type recognition. Thus we extract crossover points of ruled lines, which we call "Nodes", from the document, then positions and types of these nodes are used for the sheet type recognition.

3.4.1 Feature extraction

Figure 3 shows the outline of feature extraction for sheet type recognition. As a first step, ruled lines in the input images are extracted using black pixels forming a straight line. When there is a horizontal connected component that consists of n_h black pixels, it is regarded as a horizontal solid line. The same process is also applied to extract vertical ruled lines. In this study, the value of n_h is decided experimentally as 50. The length of 50 pixels is equivalent to about 4.2mm when the resolution of the input images is 300 dpi. Of course, the value of n_h affects the extraction accuracy of ruled lines. And in some cases, partial lines of characters or underlines in the image are also obtained as shown the circular parts in the figure 3(b). These parts may influence the processes follows. But in the proposed method, the detection of crossover points can remove these surplus lines, and the determination of value of n_h is not so significant. As a matter of fact, these surplus lines are removed by adjusting the value of n_h. Now the next step is to decide the types and positions of nodes. Since ruled lines usually have some width, the node where these ruled lines crossover usually form a rectangle. We set the node position as the center of gravity of such a rectangle. Then, from the node position, ruled lines are traced toward outside until they reach other lines. All ruled lines which failed to meet other lines are discarded. By doing so, the pattern of the node is decided.

Figure 3(c) shows the outline of the classification method. Generally speaking, a table consists of nine types of crossover points, which are called "Node" in this paper, and non-crossover points [11–13]. We express the table in the document using these features. In our method, ruled lines around the target nodes are searched first. In the case shown in Figure 3(c), when a ruled line exists above the target node, then, node No.1, 2 and 3 are excluded as candidates. In the next step, ruled lines are also searched for on the left, right and bottom of the target node. As a result, the target node is identified as node type 4. The same process is applied to all nodes in the image. The extracted nodes' numbers and their positions are stored into the database for sheet type recognition and cell image extraction. These features can express the structure of the table, and elements in the table can be extracted by using the nodes' types and their positions.

3.4.2 Determination of sheet type

Figure 4 illustrates the outline of our sheet type recognition technique. We first set a ROI of size $n_{roi} \times n_{roi}$ pixel to each node thus obtained in the above section. Then, we search whether the same type of node exists in the same ROI of a sheet in the master database, and count up the successful cases and calculate the degree of coincidence to the sheet in the master database as the ratio of the number of successes to the total number of nodes of that sheet registered in the master database. Lastly we determine the sheet type of the image as that which has the

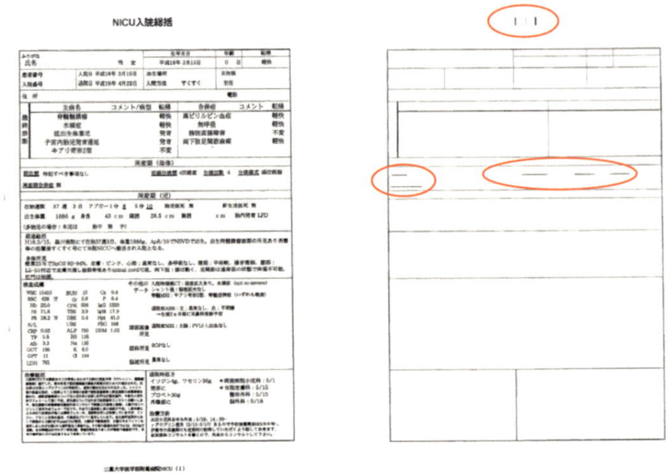

(a) Input Image (b) Detected Ruled Lines

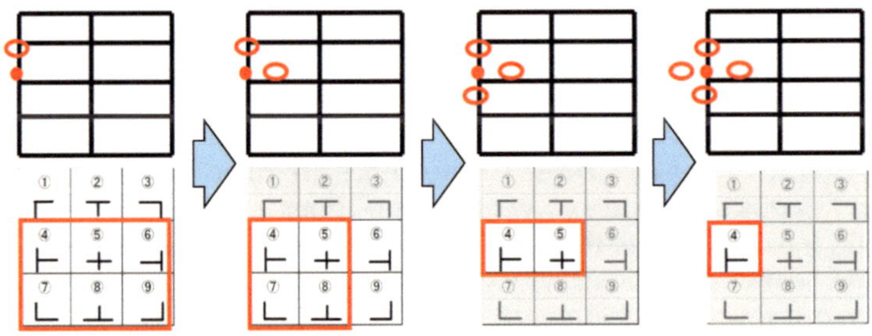

(c) Node Type Detection

Fig. 3. Extraction of Node Type and Position from Input Images

highest degree of coincidence among the master database. As the master database contains all types of sheets used at Mie University Hospital, and the occurrence of an irregular type of sheet will be very rare if at all, the proposed method can determine the sheet type with quite good accuracy.

3.5 Detection and extraction of character strings in each cell

3.5.1 Cutout of cell images using node matrix

The elements of the table which we call "cells", are extracted using node information. In this study, we use a matrix using the node's number called "Node Matrix". Figure 5 illustrates the generation process of the node matrix. The node matrix expresses the structure of table, thus we can extract cells from the table by using the matrix and the positions of these nodes. Figure 6 shows the outline of the cell extraction method. The node located on the top-left in the document is set as the starting point of the extraction. Then the matrix is scanned from the start point left to right until the nodes with a downward element, i.e. node 1 – 6 in Figure 5, appear. In this case, node 2 appears first as the node with a downward element. The node is the top-right point of the cell and the matrix is scanned from this point to the bottom again.

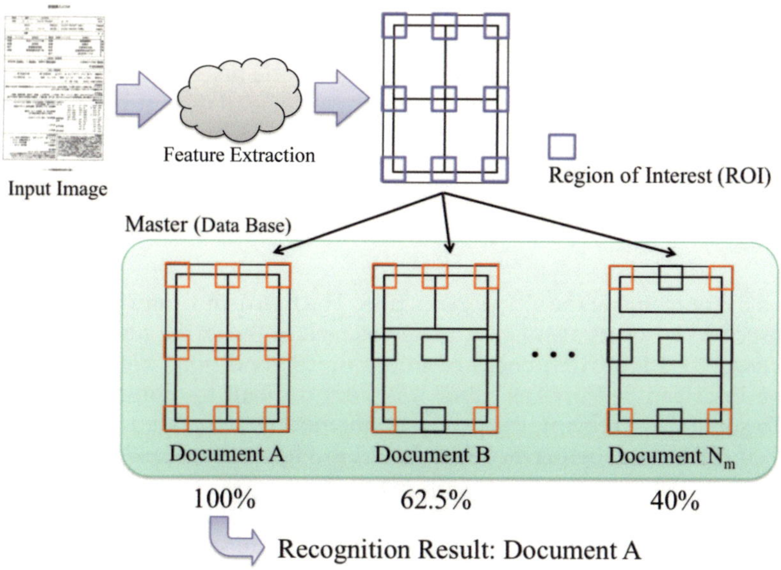

Fig. 4. Outline of Sheet Type Recognition

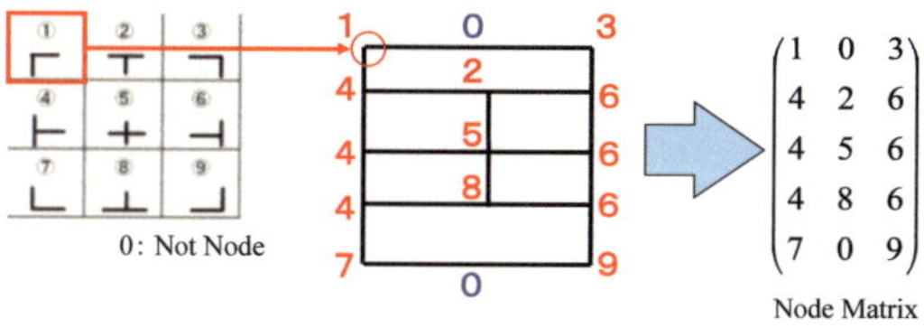

Fig. 5. Generation of Node Matrix

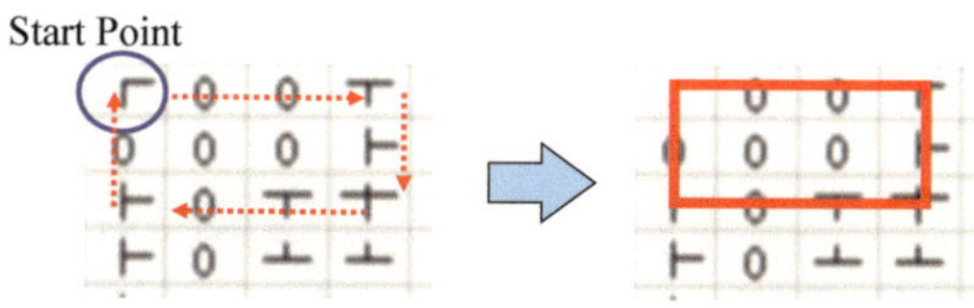

Fig. 6. Extraction of Cells from Table

When the node with a left element such as nodes 2, 3, 5, 6, 8 and 9 appears, the node is regarded as the bottom-right of the cell. The same process is repeated until the start point appears again. In this paper, the same process is applied to all nodes in the matrix to extract all cells in the table. Of course, the position of each node is stored into the database, thus we can finally cutout each cell from the table by using the information.

3.5.2 Detection of strings and character recognition

String regions in all the cells have to be extracted to recognize characters and generate an XML document. The proposed method extracts the regions using the master information. In this chapter, the cell image extracted from a blank table is called the "Master Cell Image", and the one from a table inscribed by users is called "Inscribed Cell Image", respectively. Since the master cell image sometimes has images coming from the title printed in the blank sheet, the string regions inscribed by users in each cell are extracted by a subtraction between the master cell image and the inscribed cell image. However, when the position of the master cell image does not match that of the inscribed cell image, these regions cannot be extracted correctly. Therefore, our method calculates the ratio of difference between these images first, and then the position for the subtraction process is determined to solve the above problem. In this process, the ratio of difference is obtained by the sum of the number of pixels with different values in each pixel, and the string regions in the cell image are extracted by the subtraction process.

Figure 7 shows the outcome of the string extraction. The figure indicates that the inappropriate regions not inscribed by users are also extracted as well as the string regions inscribed. These results are caused by slight differences of tilt or input conditions between the master cell image and the inscribed cell images. But, it is very difficult to eliminate these differences completely. To solve this problem, the proposed method was changed to improve extraction accuracy. Specifically, the labeling process shown in Figure 8(a) was added. As a first step of the procedure, the labeling process is applied to the master cell image, and next the black pixels belonging to the large connected components are changed to white. After this, the same subtraction process is done again. Figure 8(b) shows a result of the improved method. It is obvious that characters in the master cell image are erased completely and strings inscribed by users are appropriately extracted compared with the result in Figure 7. Actually the extraction accuracy of the improved proposed method depends on that of the labeling process. In the case of the printed documents, variations of character size and distance between characters are not significant, thus the accuracy of the improved proposed method is high enough for practical use. In preliminary experiments, false extraction of string regions such in Figure 7 was not detected.

3.6 Schema image recognition method

3.6.1 Features for schema detection

Generally speaking, extracted cell images consist of some elements such as character strings, dotted (or broken) lines and schema images. In our method, as a first step, four features are extracted from the cell images to discriminate these elements. In this section, we focus on

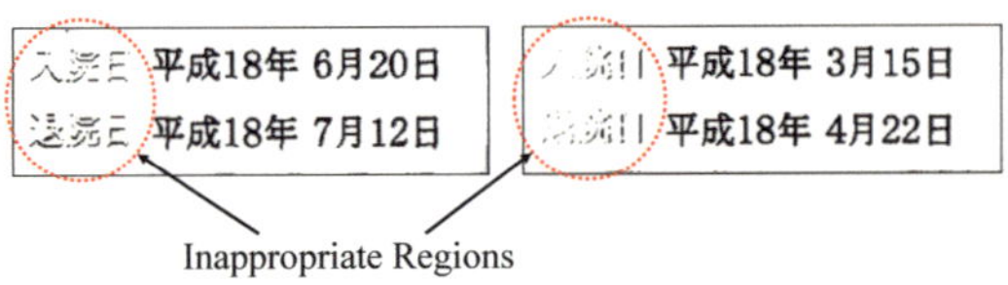

Fig. 7. Result Example of String Extraction

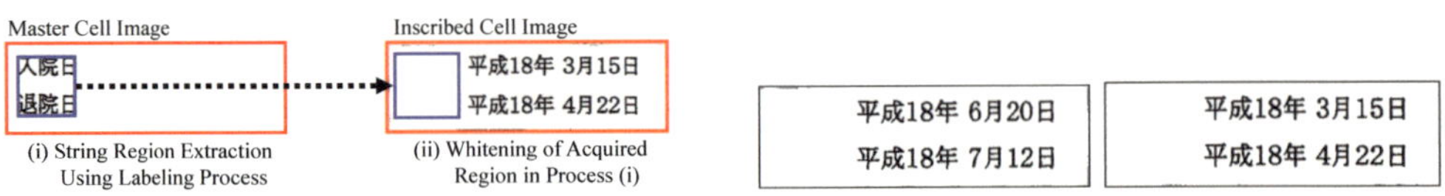

(a)Labeling Process for String Extraction (b)Extraction Result

Fig. 8. Extraction of String Regions (Improved Method)

the shape of dotted lines and schemas. It is supposed that dotted lines and schemas have the following characteristics:

1. The circumscription rectangle size of schemas is larger than that of a single component of dotted lines or character and the shape of schemas is vertically (or horizontally) longer than that of single component of dotted lines or character.
2. Each component of dotted lines is smaller than that of schemas and they are lined up on straight lines.

To express 1, we employ a variance of horizontal and vertical direction S_x and S_y and circumscribed rectangle area A of each connected component. For 2, the number of connected components lined up on straight lines is employed. We call this feature the horizontal (or vertical) connected level L. Figure 9 illustrates the rough image of a horizontal connected level. The center coordinates of each circumscription rectangle are obtained by labeling processing, and the center coordinate of the target rectangle is connected to that of other rectangles with straight lines. In the case that tilts of the lines are within $\pm t$ degrees, it is regarded that these circumscription rectangles distribute on the straight line. In this study, the value of t was set to 0.5 experimentally, because the theoretical detection accuracy is 0.06 degree in the LPP method. The processing for discriminant of vertical dotted lines is not done because tabular form documents used in this study do not have such structures. As a matter of course, the features about discriminate vertical dotted lines can be calculated easily by extending the previous processing.

Figure 10 shows the ideal distribution of the features. In this figure, the connected components of schema images will have large values of S_x, S_y and A as shown in Figure 10(a) and the components of dotted lines will come on the region with a large value of L. But the character components will appear in the region with small values of S_x, S_y and L (Figure 10(b)). It is expected that dotted lines, schemas and characters can be discriminated by using appropriate thresholds to these features.

3.6.2 Extraction of schemas from cell image

To extract schemas from a cell image, we must decide the threshold values for S_x, S_y and A. Since the objective of this section is to extract schemas from the cell, only the threshold values for S_x, S_y and A are used. (The threshold value for L is necessary to discriminate characters and dotted lines.) These threshold values were decided by considering the shape of histograms of each feature. As expected in the above section, the histograms will show bimodal patterns and the threshold values will easily be determined at the bottom of valley

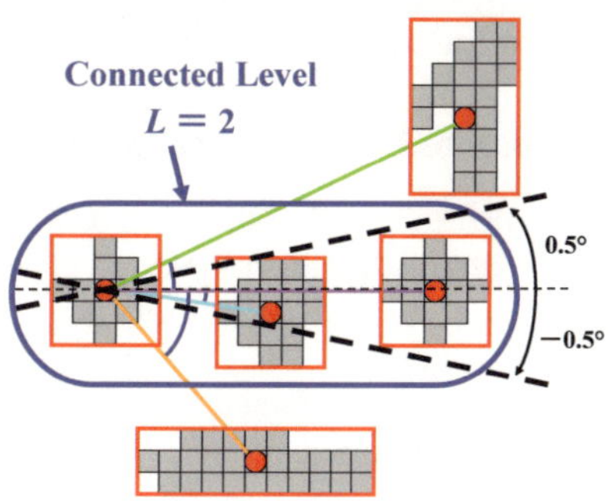

Fig. 9. Horizontal Connected Level L

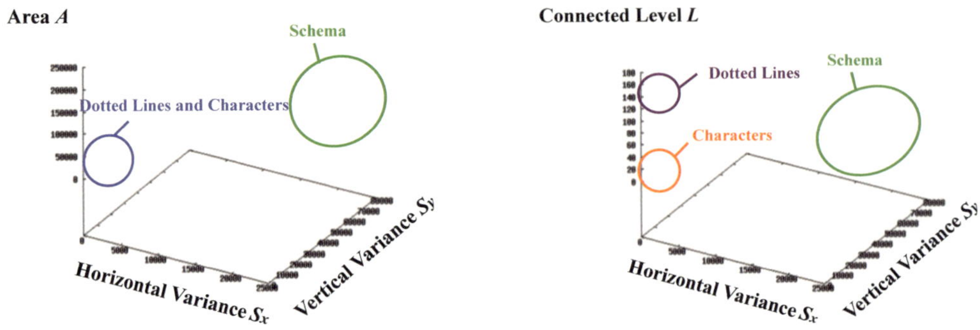

(a) Area A (b) Connected Level L

Fig. 10. Ideal Distribution of Features

between two peaks. To get statistically meaningful histograms we use Sturges' formula, given as:

$$n_c = 1 + \log_2 n_d \approx 1 + 3.32 \log_{10} n_d. \tag{3}$$

Here n_c is the number of classes and n_d means the number of data, respectively. And the threshold value is determined at the bottom of valley between two peaks. With this method, all data having schema characteristics is extracted. In other words, all data having characteristics of dotted lines or characters are not extracted even when they are located in the schema area. These should be recovered.

3.6.3 Extraction of schemas from schema area and recovery

In some cases several schemas are placed closely in a document. In such cases the schema area obtained in the above section might have several schemas which should be divided and extracted from the cell image appropriately. For this we prepare a dividing process in the system using the shape of histogram.

Figure 11(a) and (b) illustrate the outline of the dividing process. As a first step of this process, we obtain a projection histogram of vertical direction for the schema. In the obtained histogram, the part that consists of d_0-continuous elements with zero value is regarded as the boundary of each schema, and the image is divided on the middle point of the part. The same processing is applied to the image for division on horizontal direction. By this processing, schema regions are divided into several mutually independent ones. In this paper, the value of d_0 is given experimentally. Finally, the connected components in the schema, which were classified as characters, are added to the original schema image (Figure 11(c)).

3.6.4 Schema recognition using weighted direction index histogram method

Weighted direction index histogram method (WDIHM) is one feature extraction method. It is often used in handwritten character recognition systems [14–16]. Figure 12 illustrates the rough image of this method. As you can see, the method traces the contour of the character image first, and direction index histograms in each sub-region are generated using chain codes. After this, the spacial weighted filter based on Gaussian distribution is applied to the obtained histograms to generate a feature vector. WDIHM has enough robustness to local shape variations of input character images. As the accuracy of this method is extremely high compared with other character recognition algorithms, this method is employed in many

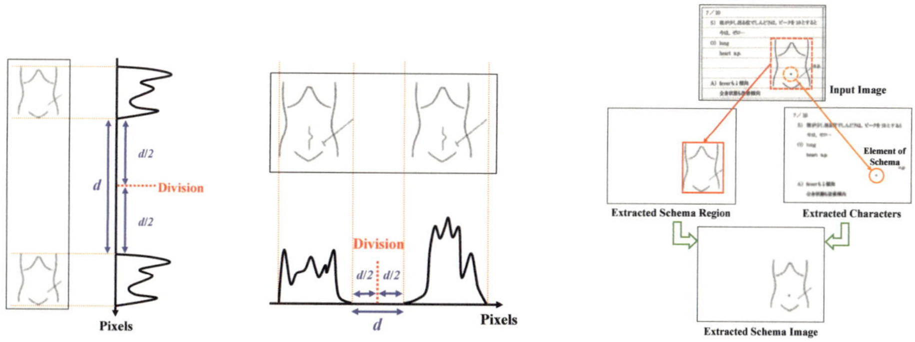

(a) Horizontal Division (b) Vertical Division (c) Extraction of Schema Images

Fig. 11. Division and Extraction of Schema Images from Documents

fields such as commercial OCR software, e-learning systems, factory automation systems and so on [17–20].

Figure 13 shows the outline of schema image recognition method using WDIHM. For schema image recognition, we first have to make a dictionary for recognition. In this method, many images are required to make the dictionary. Since this method divides the input images into some sub-regions and calculates covariance matrix among them for feature vectors, the dimension of feature vector is very large. We used not only basic schema images employed in the hospitals shown in Figure 14(a) but also some additional images, e.g. rotated and shifted ones etc., to make the dictionary (Figure 14(b)). Actually there are more than 120 kinds of schema images used in HIS, but in this study we picked up only five kinds of typical schema images as shown in Figure 14(a) to examine the effectiveness of the proposed method. For the recognition of input schema images, we employ the following discriminant function called Modified Bays Discriminant Function (MBDF)[14, 15].

$$d^l(x) = \sum_{i=1}^{k_1} \frac{\{{}_l\varphi_i^t\,(x - {}_l\mu)\}^2}{{}_l\lambda_i} + \sum_{i=k_1+1}^{n} \frac{\{{}_l\varphi_i^t\,(x - {}_l\mu)\}^2}{{}_l\lambda_{k_1+1}} + ln\left(\prod_{i=1}^{k_1} {}_l\lambda_i \cdot \prod_{i=k_1+1}^{n} {}_l\lambda_{k_1+1}\right) \qquad (4)$$

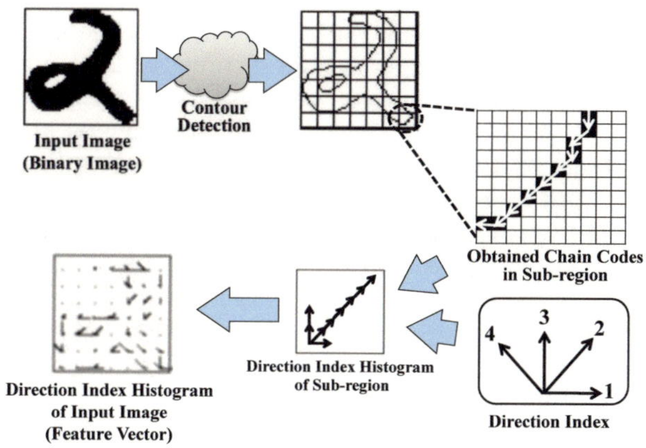

Fig. 12. Rough Image of Direction Index Histogram Method

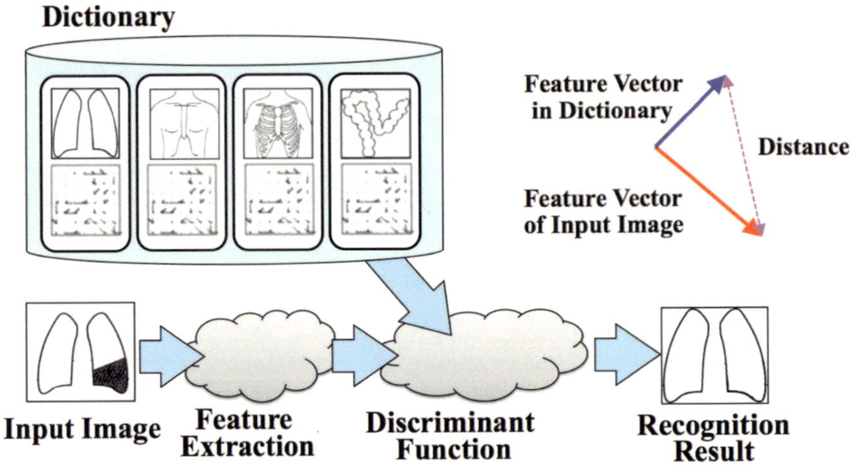

Fig. 13. Outline of Schema Image Recognition Method

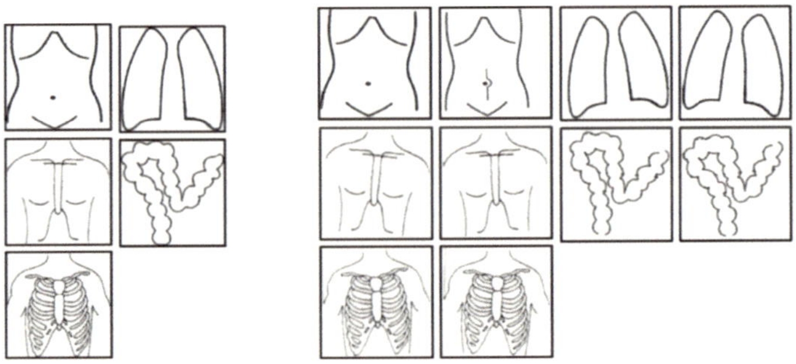

(a) Standard Schema Images (b) Additional Schema Images

Fig. 14. Example of Schema Images for Generating Dictionary

In the above formula, x is the n-dimensional feature vector of the input schema image, and ${}_l\mu$ is the average vector of schema image l in the dictionary. ${}_l\lambda_i$, and ${}_l\varphi_i$ are the i-th eigen value and eigen vector of schema image l, respectively. And k_1 is determined by the number of learning sample $m(1 \leq k_1 \leq m, n)$. These higher-order eigen values are in many cases not used due to the increase of calculation time while contributing little to the improvement of recognition accuracy. But in our case, the higher-order eigen values and vectors will be necessary components to improve recognition accuracy, since the construction of characters (or schema images) are very complex. As the absolute value of higher-order eigen values are very small and the true values of them are difficult to obtain, λ_{k_1+1} are used as the approximation of $\lambda_i(i = k_1 + 1, \cdots, n)$. In this study, the number of sub-regions and the value of k_1 were determined based on the literature [14, 15]. After this process, inscribed annotations are detected by subtracting the input image and the recognition result, i.e. the master image stored in the dictionary. The subtraction result indicates the position of annotations inscribed by medical doctors. To identify the anatomical position of them, we use an anatomical dictionary. The anatomical positions of the annotations are identified after matching between the detected annotations and the dictionary.

4. Experimental results and discussion

4.1 Accuracy of sheet type recognition

To make our system robust in the case of the misalignment of medical records to the scanning machine, we introduce ROI of size $n_{roi} \times n_{roi}$ pixels in 3.4.2 But, if the misalignment error exceeds this range due some reason, say, distortions caused by anthropogenic factors or by a mechanical error of the copying machine, a further improvement will be necessary. We used the following three techniques in the recognition method, and examined their accuracy and the processing time by using 325 sheets.

1. Using Absolute Coordinate System Based on the Top-left Pixel
2. Using Relative Coordinate System Based on the Position of each Node
3. Using Relative Coordinate System Based on the Position of the Top-left and Bottom-right Nodes

Table 1 shows experimental results of sheet type recognition. The table shows that all documents were recognized correctly in cases of relative coordinate systems of 2 and 3. But, when using the absolute coordinate system (case 1), the recognition rate was 96.3%. But the method of case 2 requires a lot of calculation time because of large number of nodes. Since a few thousands paper-based documents are generated in the hospital every day, case 2 might not be a practical solution. From these results, we can conclude the following.

1. The methods using relative coordinate systems are effective for determining the sheet type.
2. From the view point of processing time, we should use as few nodes as possible for sheet type recognition.

Coordinate System Based on...	Recognition Accuracy [%]	Processing Time [msec/sheet]
the Top-left Pixel	96.3	17
the Position of each Node	100	16961
the Position of the Top-left and Bottom-right Nodes	100	17

Table 1. Results of Document Type Recognition

4.2 Result of schema image recognition

4.2.1 Features for schema image extraction

Figure 15 shows an example of distribution of the features extracted from an input image. The obtained distribution of the features was similar to the ideal one as shown in Figure 10. In this experiment, we also applied the extraction method to 6 kinds of printed discharge summary documents in print [21], which have dotted (or broken) lines and schema images. The obtained distributions for these 6 cases were almost same as those of the ideal one. These results indicate that these elements can be divided by using linear discriminant functions with these features in good accuracy.

Figure 16 and 17 are the examples of experimental results from the input images (located at left side in each figure). The result of the extracted ruled lines is shown in the middle, and characters and schemas images are on the right mostly. Figure 17 is a result for an example having plural number of schema images. The extracted dotted lines are not shown in the figures, but the images can easily be acquired by the subtraction of (b), (c) and (d) from the input image (a). To know the effectiveness of the proposed method for cases of handwritten summary documents, we applied the method to such cases. Figure 18 shows an example of the results. Figure 18(a) is a summary for gynecology with some schema images. In this case medical records were written on the sheet with ruled lines. The result shows that each schema can be extracted even for such case of a handwritten summary. But, characters were regarded as ruled lines because they were located on the original ruled lines (Figure 18(b)). In addition, some characters were also extracted with the schema (Figure 18(d)) as the obtained circumscription rectangle has these characters. A method to eliminate them has to be added to the current extraction method.

4.2.2 Accuracy of schema image recognition

Table 2 shows the obtained results of schema image recognition. In this table, each row means the schema type of the input image and each column is that of the recognition result. This table shows that the recognition accuracy of the proposed method was more than 90%.

		Recognition Result					
		a	b	c	d	e	Accuracy
Input Image	a	20	0	0	0	0	100% (20/20)
	b	0	20	0	0	0	100% (20/20)
	c	0	1	19	0	0	95% (19/20)
	d	0	0	5	14	1	70% (14/20)
	e	1	0	2	0	17	85% (17/20)

Table 2. Result of Schema Image Recognition

Figure 19 shows results of success cases of correctly recognized images. These figures were recognized appropriately by using the proposed method even if there are marks, comments, lead lines for explanations in them. These results indicate that the dictionary with various schema images may not be necessary for recognition if input images do not have many annotations. On the other hand, the schema images with large marks or many annotations were not recognized correctly (Figure 20). Table 3 shows the obtained difference values

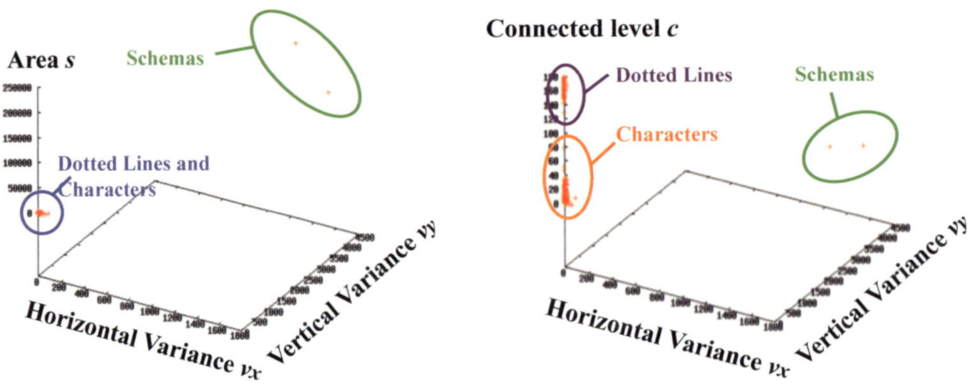

Fig. 15. Example of Obtained Distributions

(a) Input Image (b) Ruled Lines (c) Characters (d) Schema Image

Fig. 16. Example of Extraction Results (1)

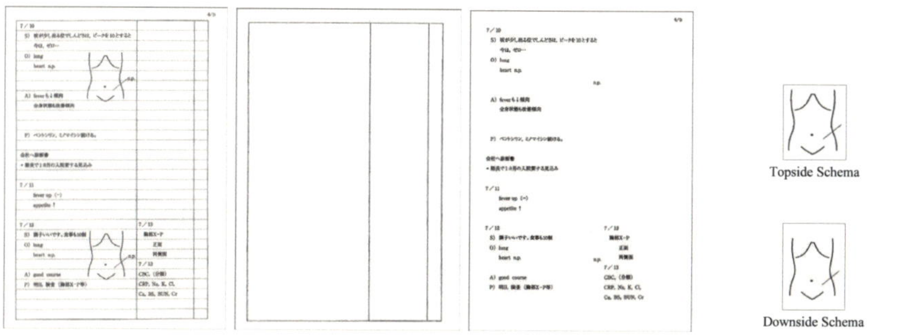

(a) Input Image (b) Ruled Lines (c) Characters (d) Schema Images

Fig. 17. Example of Extraction Results (2)

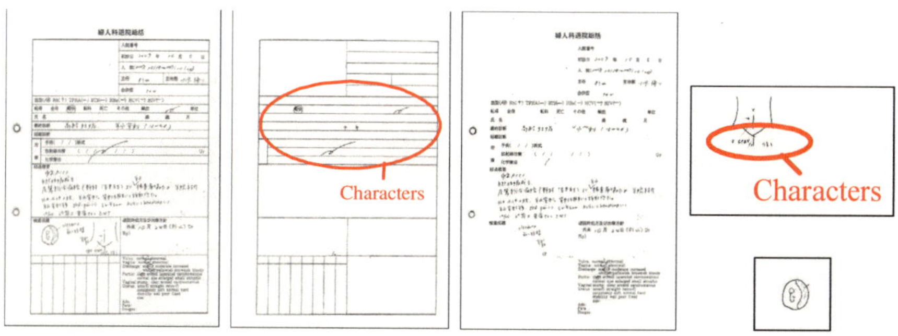

(a) Input Image (b) Ruled Lines (c) Characters (d) Schema Images

Fig. 18. Example of Failure Case

given by the discriminant function. In these cases, the large marks (or lead lines) made the contour shape of the input image change drastically, as a result the distance between the input image and the original schema image was larger than that between the input image and the recognition result. In addition, the proposed method outputs the schema type with the smallest distance as a recognition result. Thus it is difficult to detect schema images not registered in the database. To solve these problems, additional techniques considering the obtained distance values will be required.

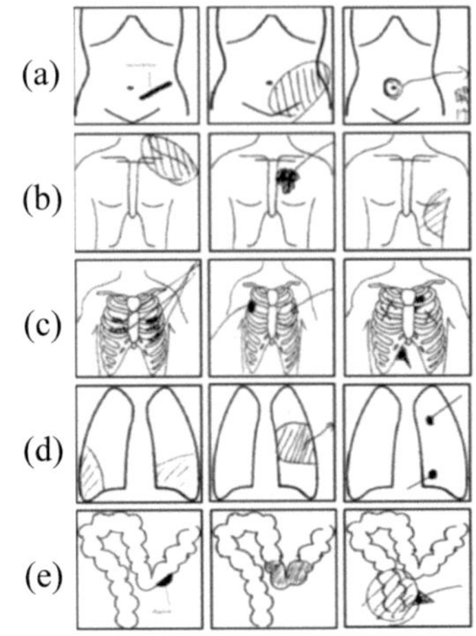

Fig. 19. Result Examples of Schema Recognition (Successful Case)

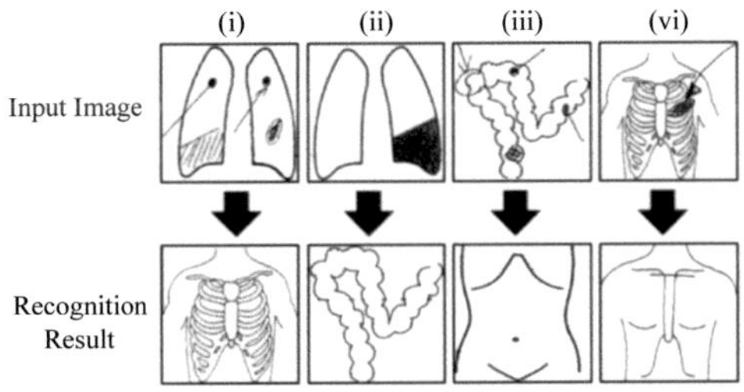

Fig. 20. Result Examples of Schema Recognition (Case of Failures)

Input Image / Distance between...	(i)	(ii)	(iii)	(iv)
Recognition Result and Input Image	1.24	604	1375	-50
Correct Schema Type and Input Image	897	1944	2774	-25

Table 3. Distance Values Given by Discriminant Function

4.3 Generated XML documents

Characters in extracted strings have to be recognized and converted to text data by an Optical Character Reader (OCR) engine. The very strength of our method is that we can define the document type of each frame before the start of recognition of cell images by using the master database and can use any type of OCR engine pertinent to that type. It was found, however, some work is necessary to create interfaces between various OCR engines and our system. At present, we use a commercially available OCR library, developed by "Panasonic Solution Technology, Inc." [22]. The table structure and characters acquired by the proposed method are used to generate an XML file. In this study, an XSL, i.e. defining the table structure of the document, is generated from the acquired node matrix first. The table structure is defined by table tags in XSL. In the next step of the process, an XML document is generated using XSL and converted text data corresponding to the contents of each cell.

Figure 21 and 22 show examples of generated XML files. In the experiments, the table structures of all input images were recognized correctly. In the case of the document with a schema image, the recognition results, i.e. schema type and annotation part, were inserted to the generated XML file (schema tag in Figure 22). In the present experiments, some parts of the characters were misrecognized. These errors may come from the OCR engine itself. To reduce such errors, it would necessary to use an OCR engine pertinent to the scope of the documents analyzed.

4.4 Developed system for resemble case search

As stated in the introduction, the objective of developing our system is to create a system actively used at healthcare sectors, so that a large volume of paper-based medical records can be included in the e-health environment. For this objective it is necessary to show quickly the usability and/or capability of the method for clinical requirements. Though the research is ongoing, we have developed a prototype system to demonstrate what we can do using this system. We developed a system to search similar cases using Microsoft Visual C# .NET. Figure 23(a) and (b) show the photograph and screenshot of the developed system, respectively. In the system, we used a wizard form with icons to improve the usability of the system. When the system is started, then the wizard window appears at the top left of root window and navigates users who are not experts of information systems. The wizard window of the system consists of some components such as "Image Input", "System Configuration" and "Scanning", "Generated XML Viewer" and so on. The image input component supports various input methods. For example, we can input document images from TWAIN devices as well as image files such as Bitmap, JPEG, or PDF files and so on. The system configuration component is so designed as to guide users to set up system parameters easily. When the scanning processes are finished, the structure (and contents) of the input document image are recognized, and a XML file is generated. It takes several tens of seconds before the XML document is generated. The generated XML file is shown in the viewer window (Figure 23(c)). After this, we can search similar cases from the stored documents by using keywords like Figure 23(d). Since the generated XML documents have high compatibility with relational databases, the documents can easily be imported to hospital information systems. If data mining software (or systems) such as data ware house OLAP tools, and so on can be used, these XML documents would be used more effectively for clinical and medical study.

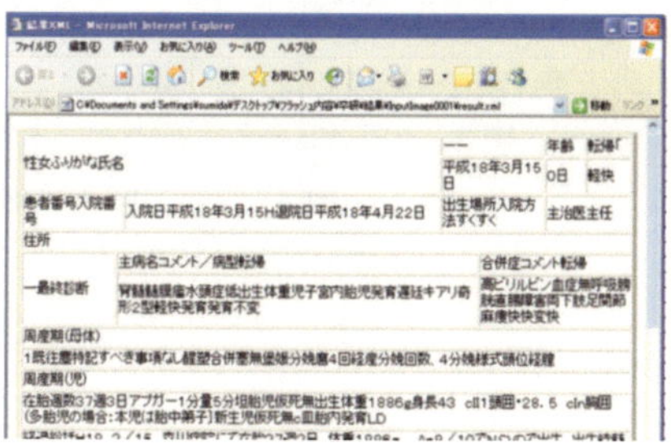

(a) Generated XML Document

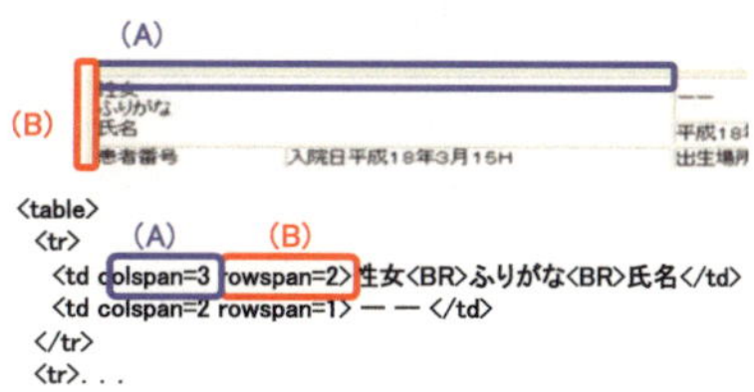

(b) Source of XML File

Fig. 21. Example of Generated XML File (1)

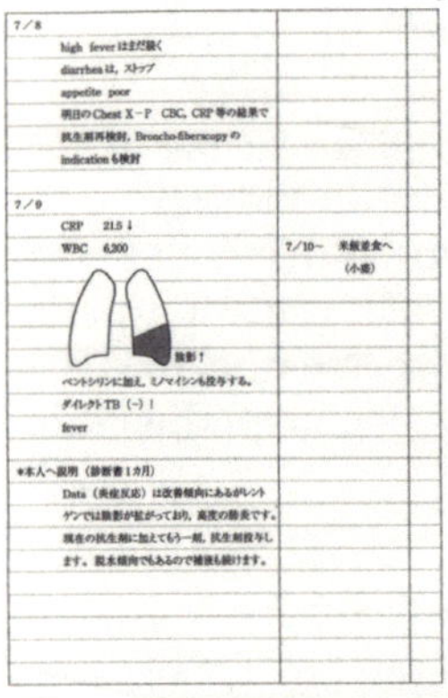

(a) Generated XML Document

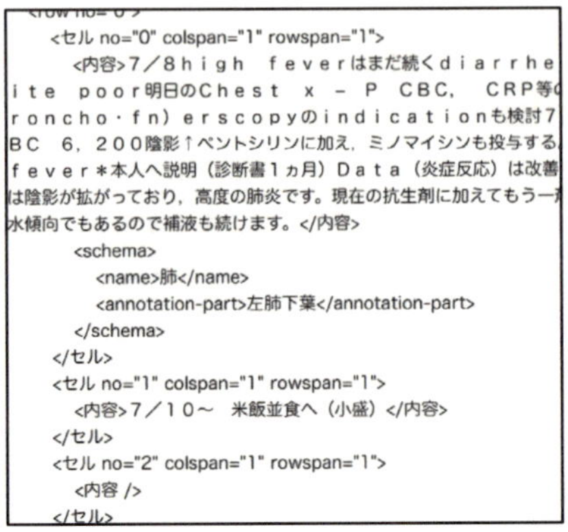

(b) Source of XML File

Fig. 22. Example of Generated XML File (2)

(a) Overview

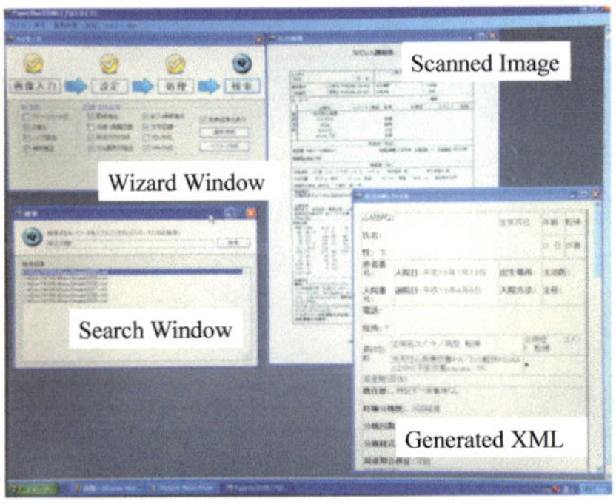

(b) Schreenshot of Main Window

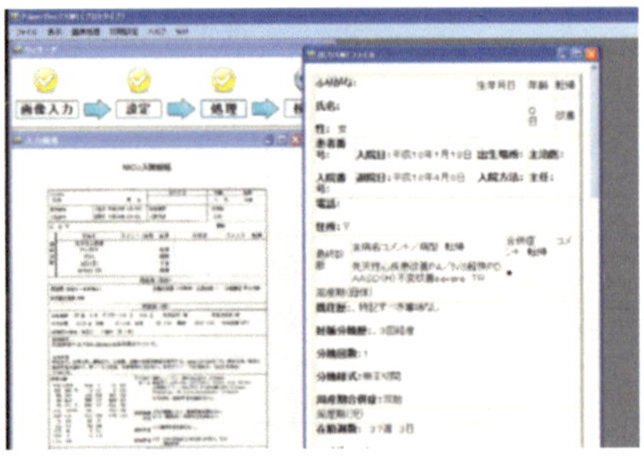

(c) Scanning and XML Viewer

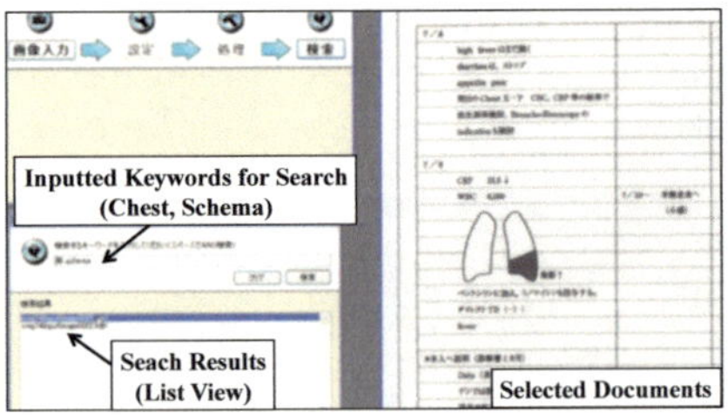

(d) Resemble Case Search

Fig. 23. Developed System

5. Related works

Studies and research for document image analysis systems have been reported [23]-[31]. As related works to ruled line extraction, the detection methods using the Hough transform technique are reported by literature [23]-[27]. Particularly in literature [23] and [24], complex line shapes can be extracted using a pattern-matching method and Hough transform method.

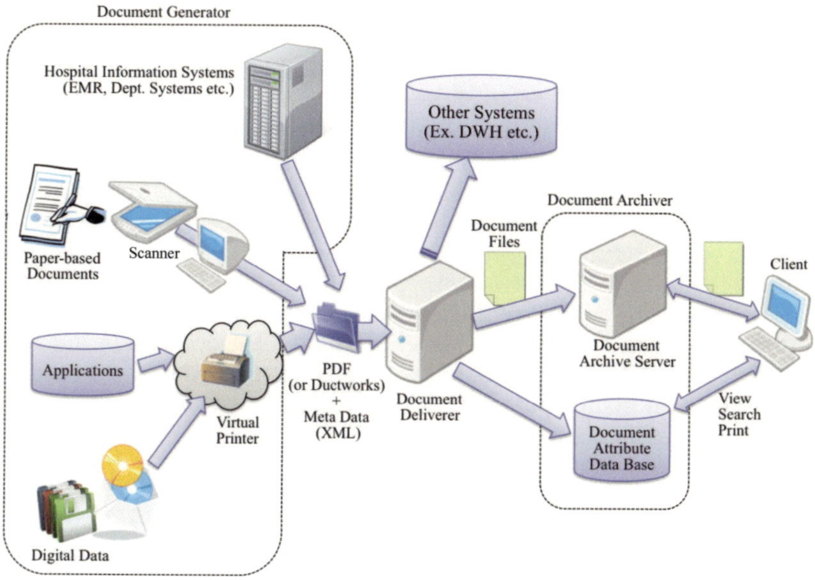

Fig. 24. Basic Structure of DACS

In Literature [25] - [27], authors propose detection methods for character patterns, general curving lines, quadratic curving lines, circular patterns using the concept of [23] and [24], and discuss their effectiveness. These methodologies may have higher extraction accuracy when compared with the proposed method, but they require a large amount of calculation time, because these algorithms are so complex. In practical situation, processing time is the most important factor to evaluate systems. Therefore, it is not realistic to employ them in cases where large number of documents are being processed.

As for related methods for document layout and structure recognition, literature [28] reports the table structure recognition method based on the block segmentation method and literature [29] tries to extract the contents from printed document images using model checking. The method of literature [28], however, depends on the output of commercial OCR systems. On the other hand, our proposed method identifies table types, i.e. document types, using a node matrix and positions of nodes. The node matrix can be acquired easily by using the extracted ruled lines and the lines themselves are obtained by very simple image processing techniques. The proposed method does not depend on an external library in image processing. In the case of [29], only the logical structures in the documents are detected using image analysis but the system is not developed to reuse the information. In a different field, methods to analyze cultural heritage documents are reported by Ogier et al. [30]. In this literature, document analysis techniques are employed to preserve and archiving cultural heritage documents. Literature [31] reports a prototypical document image analysis system for journals. Most of these studies mainly describe the methodology and processing for typical business letters. According to the authors' survey, only a few articles propose document image recognition method for medical documents, such as patient discharge summaries to search similar cases.

In medical fields, many novel information systems have been studied. As one of such examples, we introduce here a new concept and systems to assure lifelong readability for Medical Records in HIS. Figure 24 illustrates the outline of the concept, called Document

Archiving and Communication Systems (DACS), proposed by Prof. Matsumura et al. in 2010 [32]. Since the lifespan of computer systemss is usually very short compared with the need for medical records of a patient, great care is necessary to shift paper-based toward computer based society. DACS is such a system which covers this problem. Because of the very nature of rapid progress of medical science, all the electronic health record system used now will never mature, and, indeed, the system architecture itself is changing. It is sometimes very difficult to retrieve data created by a system previously used. Though electronic health record systems offer us utilities to retrieve any type of data in the database, they loose functionality to grasp many features at a glance which the paper systems had. Prof. Matsumura et al. deliberately introduces the combination of these two concepts. In the DACS, all medical records are not treated as data but as an aggregation of documents. The medical documents generated by the electronic health system are converted to PDF (or JPEG, TIFF, Docuworks) and XML files. By converting the data to such files, the readability of the data are guaranteed, and the meta-data of the documents, e.g. timestamp, patient ID, document type etc., are used as key information of search. After this, these files are delivered to Document Archive Server of DACS, and then system users can view and search the stored documents easily. As a matter of course, the document deliverer of DACS can also deliver the generated files (and XML data) to other systems such as Data Ware House (DWH), and we can use the data for clinical analyses and studies. DACS also supports not only the data stored in HIS but also other data types, e.g. paper-based documents, other applications' data, PDF files generated by other systems and so on. In the case of a paper-based document, the target document is scanned by the optical scanning device and transferred into a PDF file. The meta-data of the documents are also obtained by a scanning sheet with the QR code. This sheet is generated using stored clinical data in the HIS (or input data to the DACS by hand) before scanning. The generated PDF file and its meta-data are delivered by the document deliverer and stored into the database. As you can see, DACS can keep readability of medical records and supports various data types. One of the problems that DACS has now will be the problem of creating meta-data manually. Our method can cover this problem as much of these meta-data are automatically extracted from the images, which would contribute to improve DACS.

6. Toward the future

In this chapter we introduced document image recognition, keyword extraction and automatic XML generation techniques to search similar cases from paper-based medical documents. These techniques were developed for practical use at healthcare sectors, so as to help the incorporation of vast volumes of paper-based medical records into the e-health environment. Good usability and speed, robustness, low running cost and automated execution will be the key requisite for such a system to practically be used, and our system will satisfy many of these requirements. These characteristics of our system mainly come from the use of master information which covers almost all type of medical documents. However, there remain many problems unsolved. One of the largest drawbacks of our system might be the anxiety whether we can get similar accuracy and effectiveness of such documents without tables. As is stated in 3.1 there are many paper based medical documents without tables. But, even in such cases, they are not written randomly in free format. Since medical records are the most important documents for physicians to keep continuity of healthcare, the format itself has been deliberately designed and used. Therefore it is quite plausible that any medical documents without tables will match one of the master information if we can insert frame lines in it. If so, it may not so difficult to improve the algorithm of determining the best suited sheet to include mass or area information.

7. References

[1] H. Harold Friedman, Ed., *Problem-Oriented Medical Diagnosis 5th edition*. Lippincott Williams & Wilkins, 1991

[2] K. Seto, T. Kamiyama, H. Matsuo, "An Object-Modeling Method for Hospital Information Systems," *The 9th World Congress on Medical Informatics*, 52 Pt.2, pp.981–985, 1998

[3] HJ. Lowe, I. Antipov, W. Hersh, CA Smith, M. Mailhot, "Automated Semantic Indexing of Imaging Reports to Support Retrieval of Medical Images in the Multimedia Electronic Medical Record," *Methods of Information in Medicine*, vol. 38, no. 4, pp. 303–307, 1999

[4] H. Kawanaka, Y. Otani, T. Yoshikawa, K. Yamamoto, T. Shinogi, S. Tsuruoka, "Tendency Discovery from Incident Reports with Free Format Using Self Organizing Map," *Japan Journal of Medical Informatics*, vol. 25, no. 2, pp. 87–96, 2005

[5] Y. Otani, H. Kawanaka, T. Yoshikawa, K. Yamamoto, T. Shinogi, S. Tsuruoka, "Keyword Extraction from Incident Reports and Keyword Map Generation Method Using Self Organizing Map," *Proc. of 2005 IEEE International Conference on Systems, Man and Cybernetics*, pp. 1024–1029, 2005

[6] H. Kawanaka, T. Sumida, K. Yamamoto, T. Shinogi, S. Tsuruoka, "Document Recognition and XML Generation of Tabular Form Discharge Summaries for Analogous Case Search System," *Method of Information in Medicine* (Schattauer), vol. 46, no. 6, pp. 700–708, 2007

[7] H. Kawanaka, Y. Shiroyama, K. Yamamoto, T. Shinogi, S. Tsuruoka, "A Study on Document Structure Recognition of Discharge Summaries for Analogous Case Search System," *Proc. of International Workshop on Document Analysis Systems* (DAS2008), pp. 423–430, 2008

[8] N. Otsu, "Discriminant and Least Squares Threshold Selection," *Proc. of 4IJCPR*, pp. 592–596, 1978

[9] N. Otsu, "A Threshold Selection Method from Gray-Level Histograms," *IEEE Trans. Systems, Man, and Cybernetics*, SMC-9, no.1, pp. 62–66, 1979

[10] T. Akiyama, I. Masuda, "A Segmentation Method for Document Images without the Knowledge of Document Formats," *The IEICE Transactions on Information and Systems*, vol. J66-D: pp. 111–118, 1983

[11] T. Tanaka, S, Tsuruoka, "Table Form Document Understanding Using Node Classification Method and HTML Document Generation." *Proc. of third IAPR Workshop on Document Analysis Systems*, pp. 157–158, 1998

[12] Y. Ito, M. Ohno, S. Tsuruoka, T. Shinogi, "Document Structure Understanding on Subjects Registration Table," *Proc. of the fourth International Symposium on Advanced Intelligent Systems*, pp. 571–574, 2003

[13] S. Tsuruoka, C. Hirano, T. Yoshikawa, T. Shinogi, "Image-based Structure Analysis for a Table of Contents and Conversion to XML Documents," *Proc. of Document Layout Interpretation and its Application*, pp. 59–62, 2001

[14] F. Kimura, T. Wakabayashi, S. Tsuruoka, and Y. Miyake, "Improvement of handwritten Japanese character recognition using weighted direction code histogram" *Pattern Recognition*, vol. 30, no. 8, pp. 1329 – 1337, 1997

[15] S. Tsuruoka, M. Kurita, T. Harada, F. Kimura, Y. Miyake, "Handwritten KANJI and HIRAGANA Character Recognition Using Weighted Direction Index Histogram Method," *The Transactions of the Institute of Electronics, Information and Communication Engineers*, vol. 70-D, no. 7, pp.1390-1397, 1987

[16] S. Tsuruoka, H. Morita, F. Kimura, Y. Miyake, "Handwritten Character Recognition Adaptable to the Writer", *Proc. of IAPR Workshop on CT – Special Hardware and Industrial Applications*, pp. 179 – 182, 1988

[17] H. Takebe, "Pattern recognition apparatus and method using probability density function," *United States Patent*, no.7003164 B2, 2006

[18] H. Takebe, Y. Hotta, S. Naoi, "Word recognizing apparatus and method for dynamically generating feature amount of word," *European Patent Specification* (European Patent Office), no.EP0997839, 2005

[19] S. Tsuruoka, N. Watanabe, N. Minamide, F. Kimura, Y. Miyake, M. Shrindhar, "Base line correction for handwritten word recognition," *Proc. of the Third International Conference on Document Analysis and Recognition*, vol.2, pp. 902 – 905, 1995

[20] S. Hirose, M. Yoshimura, K. Hachimura, R. Akama, "Authorship Identification of Ukiyoe by Using Rakkan Image," *The Eighth IAPR International Workshop on Document Analysis Systems*, pp. 143 – 150, 2008

[21] All Japan Hospital Associations, Ed., *Text Book for Generation of Standard Medical Records and their Administration*. Jiho Inc., 2004

[22] Panasonic Solution Technologies Co., Ltd. Color OCR Library. Color OCR Library: "Yomitori Kakumei" SDK, http://panasonic.co.jp/

[23] D. Casasent, R. Krishnapuram, "Curved Object Location by Hough Transformations and inversions," *Pattern Recognition*, vol. 20, no. 2, pp. 181-188, 1987

[24] R. Krishnapuram, D. Casasent, "Hough Space Transformation for Discrimination and Distortion Estimation," *Computer Vision, Graphics and Image Processing* vol. 38, no. 3, pp. 299–316, 1987

[25] D. Pao, H.F. Li, R. Jayakumar, "Detecting Parametric Curves Using the Straight Line Hough Transform," *Proc. of 10th International Conference on Pattern Recognition*, pp. 620-625, 1990

[26] K. Fujimoto, Y. Iwata, S. Nakata, "Parameter Extraction of Second Degree Curve from $\theta - \rho$ Hough Plane," *The IEICE Transactions on Information and Systems*, vol. J74-D2, no. 9, pp.1184–1191, 1991

[27] J. Yan, T. Agui and T. Nagao, "A Complex Transform for Extracting Circular Arcs and Straight Line Segments in Engineering Drawings," *The Trans. of the Institute of Electronics, Information and Communication Engineers*, vol. 75, no.8, pp.1338–1345, 1992

[28] T. G. Kieninger, "Table Structure Recognition Based on Robust Block Segmentation," *Proc. Document Recognition V, SPIE*, vol. 3305, pp. 22-32, 1998

[29] M. Aiello, "Document Image Analysis via Model Checking," *AI*IA Notizie*, vol.1, 200–2, 2002

[30] J.M. Ogier, K. Tombre, "Madonne: Document Image Analysis Techniques for Cultural Heritage Documents," in Digital Cultural Heritage, *Proceedings of 1st EVA Conference*, pp. 107–114, 2006

[31] G, Nagy, S. Seth and M. Viswanathan, "A Prototypical Document Image Analysis System for Technical Journals," *IEEE Computer*, vol. 25, no. 7, pp. 10-22, 1992

[32] Y. Matsumura, N. Kurabayashi, T. Iwasaki, S. Sugaya, K. Ueda, T. Mineno, H. Takeda, "A Scheme for Assuring Lifelong Readability in Computer Based Medical Records", *MEDINFO 2010* C.Safran et al. (Eds.) , IOS Press, pp. 91 – 95, 2010

5

Open Source Software Development on Medical Domain

Shinji Kobayashi
Ehime University
Japan

1. Introduction

The expansion of information technology (IT) in daily tasks and computerization has had multiple impact in our lives. This is particularly illustrated in the benefits of electronic healthcare records (EHR), from both the perspective of the healthcare provider and the patient. IT has been shown to improve efficiency and safety for healthcare delivery(Halamka et al., 2005).

With the advent of the Internet, many patients are eager to obtain information about their health instantly. Health related words are popular terms on the Internet search key words on the web (Eysenbach & Kohler, 2003). Quite a number of Net-savvy patients look up their possible conditions before meeting the physician.

For governments, efficiency of the healthcare policies is a big concern, because total expenditure for health care has been rising year by year (OECD, 2011). It is reasonable idea that information technology will improve efficiency in medicine, as in the other domains. President Obama of the US declared to invest to propagate EHR to improve health care quality and efficiency with massive Budget (Clinton, H. R. et al., 2006).

However, even with all the positive implications of EHR, many healthcare organizations have yet to implement them. This is not due to skepticism about their benefits but mainly due to financial reasons. Inadequate capital for purchase and maintenance cost are the significant barriers to many organizations (AK et al., 2009). Issues such as difficulty committing to a particular vendor and concerns about compatibility of the chosen vendor's system with existing and future systems have to be considered before implementing EHR.

This global problem also affects Japan. It is estimated that to implement an EHR system in a Japanese hospital will cost approximately USD 10,000 per hospital bed. If this was scaled up to full HER implementation for all medical organizations in Japan (of which there are about 150,000), the Japan Medical Association (JMA) estimated this to cost roughly USD 180 billion over a 10 year period. Given that the size of the Japanese medical market is about USD 300 billion per year, this technology is not readily affordable in Japan without a significant reduction of costs. One approach to reducing the high cost of clinical information system is to integrate various existing clinical systems. A major barrier to this solution is the lack of established standardized data communication protocol and consequently communication among different systems is problematic. Another potential solution to reducing the high costs of implementing IT systems in health care is the use of Open Source Software (OSS).

OSS movement around medicine has gained momentum in this decade. A technical report has been described about this medical OSS movement (Morrison et al., 2010). International Medical Informatics Assotiation (IMIA) launched OSS SIG and has a website to share information as well providing the OSS available for download. In this chapter, we discuss about the movement and its background, introduce major of the and illustrate the future of the software technology in the medical domain. More information is available at IMIA OSS SIG site (www.medfloss.org/).

2. Open Source Software (OSS)

Open Source Software can be defined as computer software for which the human readable source code is made available under a copyright license (or arrangement such as the public domain) that meets the Open Source Definition (Open Source Initiative, 1997–2005)[1]. This includes free distribution of the software, the inclusion of the source code in the program, and permitted modifications and derived works which can be distributed under the same terms as the license of the original software. In addition, the license itself should not be specific to a product, must not restrict other software and must be technology neutral. In essence this permits users to use, change, and improve upon the software as well as allowing it to be redistributed in modified or unmodified form. This in turn has considerable commercial and technical benefits.

The availability of OSS source codes allows engineers to avoid reinventing the wheel and to concentrate instead on developmental efficiency. Proactive use of OSS promotes a low cost and short delivery time of software and this has, for example, been beneficial in the development of software for the Internet.

A particularly attractive appeal of OSS is that an organization (user) gains confidence for future availability and full ownership of its data and customizability of its software by avoiding 'vendor lock-in'. Organizations can freely adapt OSS to their personal needs performing any necessary customization themselves or by employing a third party.. This is in marked contrast to proprietary software where the organization is dependent on the vendor's willingness to perform any customization, usually has little control over how quickly they perform the customization and will inevitably pay a substantial fee for it. The organization would also not have any control over a vendor's decision to change data format or even structure.

2.1 Open source and standards

It is no doubt that the Internet has become widespread rapidly and accompanied with great innovations. It was suggested that one of the reasons that the Internet succeeded was that the synergy between open source software and open standard had promoted the movement (Kenwood, 2001). This synergy has also driven innovation in the medical domain(Reynolds & Wyatt, 2011).

With respect to the implementation of standards, Health Level 7 or HL7-compliant OSS is abundant throughout the world. Mirth is well designed platform to handle HL7 standards

[1] OSS is also called as FLOSS (Free/Libre/Open Source software). FLOSS is more correct term for use, but in this chapter OSS is used on behalf of FLOSS

(Table 1)(Brauer, 2008). Mirth connect supports multiple standards, HL7 v2.x, HL7 V3, XML, X12, EDI, DICOM, NCDP, and delimited text.

Project name	Mirth
Description	Interoperability solution for health care
Platform	Java, ESB
License	MPL license Ver 1.1
Project site	http://www.mirthcorp.com/

Table 1. Technical overview of Mirth

The openEHR Project has standardized these programs according to their unique modeling method and has released them as the ISO/EN 13606 standard (The openEHR Foundation, n.d.). The openEHR project gathered more than 1500 developers and clinicians from 58 countries as of October 2011. The development platform utilized ranges from Eiffel, Java, and Ruby. OSS and open standard products have improved interoperability of the Internet, and can similarly improve the interoperability of medical systems.

3. OSS in medicine

A wide range of OSS solutions are already in use in healthcare. Many of these are technical tools and business applications, e.g. Linux, Apache, LibreOffice.org, and so on, but a large number of healthcare domain specific OSS also exists. As of October 2011, there are 572 healthcare related OSS available for download from SourceForge. Most of them are developed by small groups, but some major projects are maintained by industry and commercial support is available. International collaboration has been also grown, motivated in some communities which share similar problems in healthcare.

In this section, major medical OSS projects are shown with description. If you are interested in the topics, please join their community.

3.1 EHR

Hospitals have adopted information systems to manage clinical practice. Commonly, a hospital needs integrated EHR to administer clinical information from subsystems for departments, such as laboratory data, pharmacy, radiology section etc. As of other enterprise domain, proprietary vendor systems are also dominant in medical domain, but OSS is getting a larger share in this field today. In this section, major EHR projects are shown for example below.

3.1.1 OpenEMR

OpenEMR is one of the most popular OSS in medical domain, and was developed by a not-for-profit company which was founded in 2005 by a medical doctor and owner of a small primary care facility in North Carolina. It supports medical practice management, electronic medical records, prescription writing and medical billing (Table 2)(Fig 1) (OpenEMR Project, n.d.). OpenEMR is freely customisable, becase it based on widely used platform built on PHP to construct web application and MySQL database.

It supports multiple languages, and are used in the United States, Puerto Rico, Australia, Sweden, Holland, Israel, India, Malaysia, Nepal, and Kenya. OpenEHR was also certified

Project name	OpenEMR
Description	Electronic medical record and medical practice management
Platform	PHP, MySQL
License	GPL
Project site	http://www.oemr.org/

Table 2. Technical overview of OpenEMR

by ONC (Office of the National Coordinator of Health Information Technology) as complete ambulatory EHR (Office of the National Coordinator for Health Information Technology, n.d.).

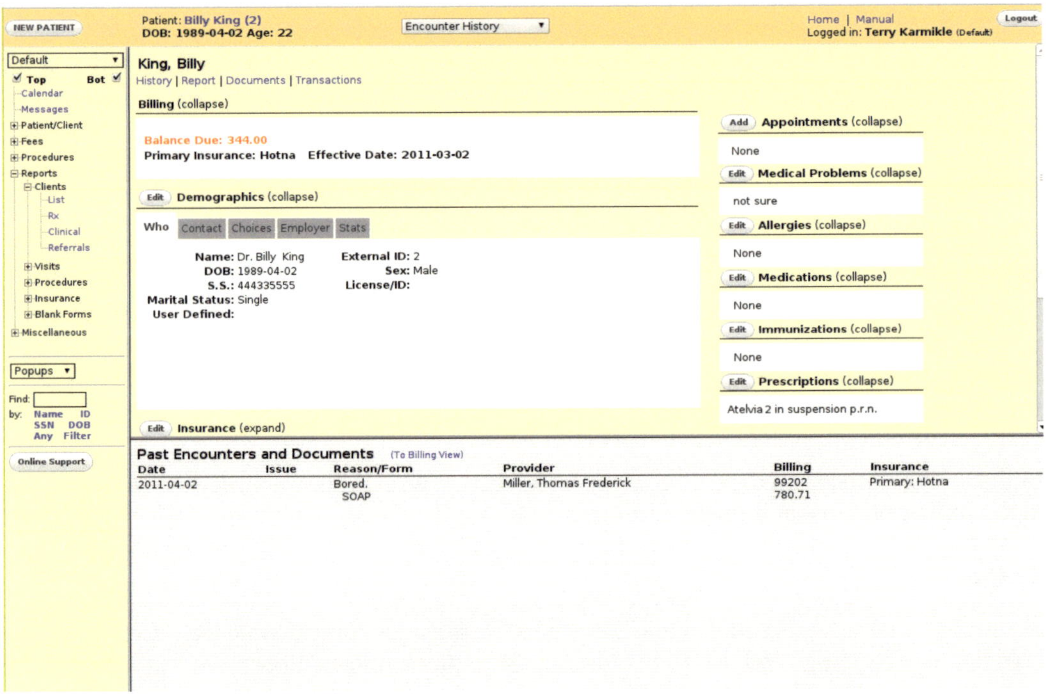

Fig. 1. Screenshot of OpenEMR

3.1.2 OpenVistA

VistA is an integrated comprehensive clinical information system supporting clinical, administrative, financial, and infrastructure functions (Table 3)(Veterans Health Administration, n.d.). Its components include a graphical user interface, computerized order entry system, bar-coded medication administration, electronic prescribing and clinical guidelines. It was developed by the Departments of Veteran Affairs in the United States to serve the more than 4 million military veterans cared for in its 150 hospitals and 700 clinics. It is mature enough and very versatile to be configured to fit any type of health care organization, from clinics and medical practices to nursing homes and large hospitals.

OpenVistA is an open source software project based on VistA technology. OpenVistA has been adopted for use by several other health institutions in America as well as hospitals in other countries, e.g. Egypt, Germany, and Mexico. However, Technology of Vista is not based on modern computer language or platform. It is controversial that health care system should use novel technology or stable technology, but you have to consider that engineers who skilled in MUMPS are available or not for your project.

Project name	OpenVistA
Description	Electronic health record for all clinical field, based on veteran's hospital information system
Platform	MUMPS, Delphy/Kylix
License	Public domain, GPL
Project site	http://www.oemr.org/

Table 3. Technical overview of WorldVistA

3.1.3 OpenMRS

OpenMRS is a community-developed, open source, electronic medical record system platform. It has been developed by community, led by a collaborative effort of the Regenstrief Institute (Indiana University) and Partners in Health (Boston Philanthropic Organization).

OpenMRS is focused on building and managing health systems in the developing world, where AIDS, tuberculosis, and malaria afflict the lives of millions (Table4) (Fig. 2)(OpenMRS Project, n.d.).

Prevention and surveillance of infectious disease benefits from an OpenMRS system. OpenMRS has been supported by the Google Summer of Code from 2007. OpenMRS uses MySQL databases, Java, Spring framework, Microsoft InfoPath for its forms development.

Project name	OpenMRS
Description	Infection control system for developing countries
Platform	Java, Spring framework, Microsoft InfoPath
License	OpenMRS Public License 1.1
Project site	http://openmrs.org/

Table 4. Technical overview of OpenMRS

3.1.4 PatientOS

PatientOS project has aimed to produce the highest quality, free enterprise-wide healthcare information system, and been designed from the onset to be a hospital information system (Table 5)(Fig. 3). The software architecture, design patterns and framework has been built for the complexities and challenges of an enterprise-wide information system. PatientOS supports not only human hospitals, but also veterinary care hospitals (Fig. 4).

Local business support for PatientOS is available in US, Canada and India.

3.1.5 GNUmed

The GNUmed project provides EMR in multiple languages to assist and improve longitudinal care, specifically in ambulatory settings (i.e. multi-professional practices and clinics) (Table

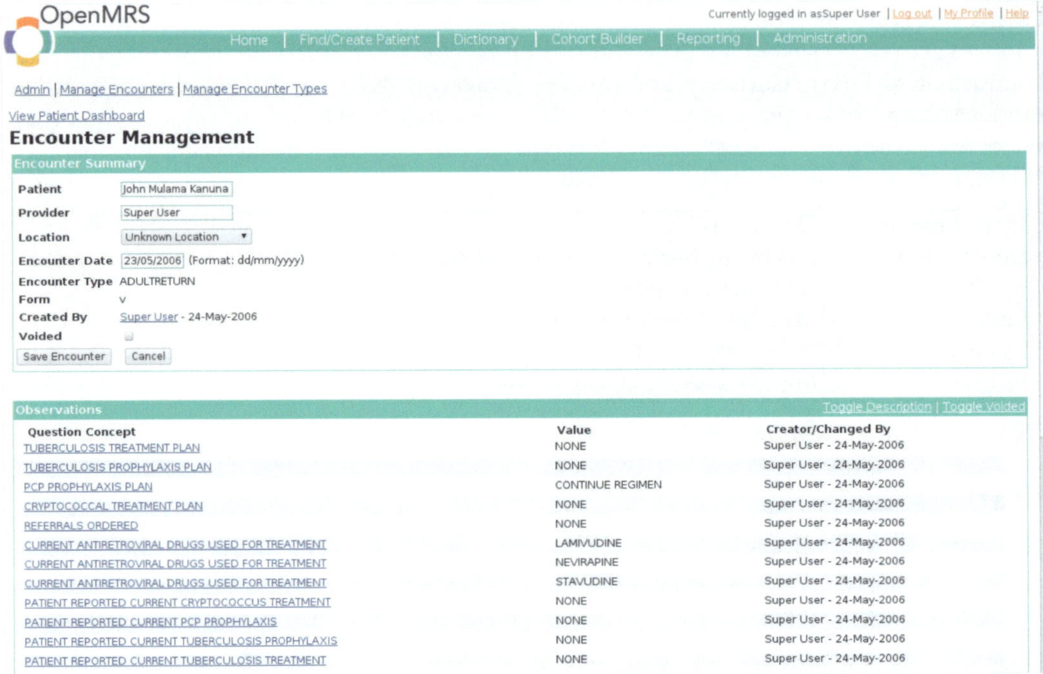

Fig. 2. Screenshot of OpenMRS

Project name	PatientOS
Description	Infection control system for developing countries
Platform	Java, JBoss, Myrth
License	GPLv3
Project site	http://www.patientos.org/

Table 5. Technical overview of PatientOS

6). It is made available at no charge and is capable of running on GNU/Linux, Windows and Mac OS X. GNUmed cleanly separates the medical aspects (record keeping) from the administrative aspects (billing, storage) of a medical practice. Thereby it allows GNUmed to be internationalized to different jurisdictions.

Project name	GNUmed
Description	EMR, specifically in ambulatory settings
Programming language	Python
License	GPL
Project site	http://www.gnumed.org/

Table 6. Technical overview of GNUmed

3.1.6 FreeMED

FreeMED is an OSS electronic medical record and practice management system which has been developed since 1999 (Table 7)(Surhone et al., 2010). It was first developed by Jeffrey Buchbinder in the United States for general practitioners. It evolved to have an international

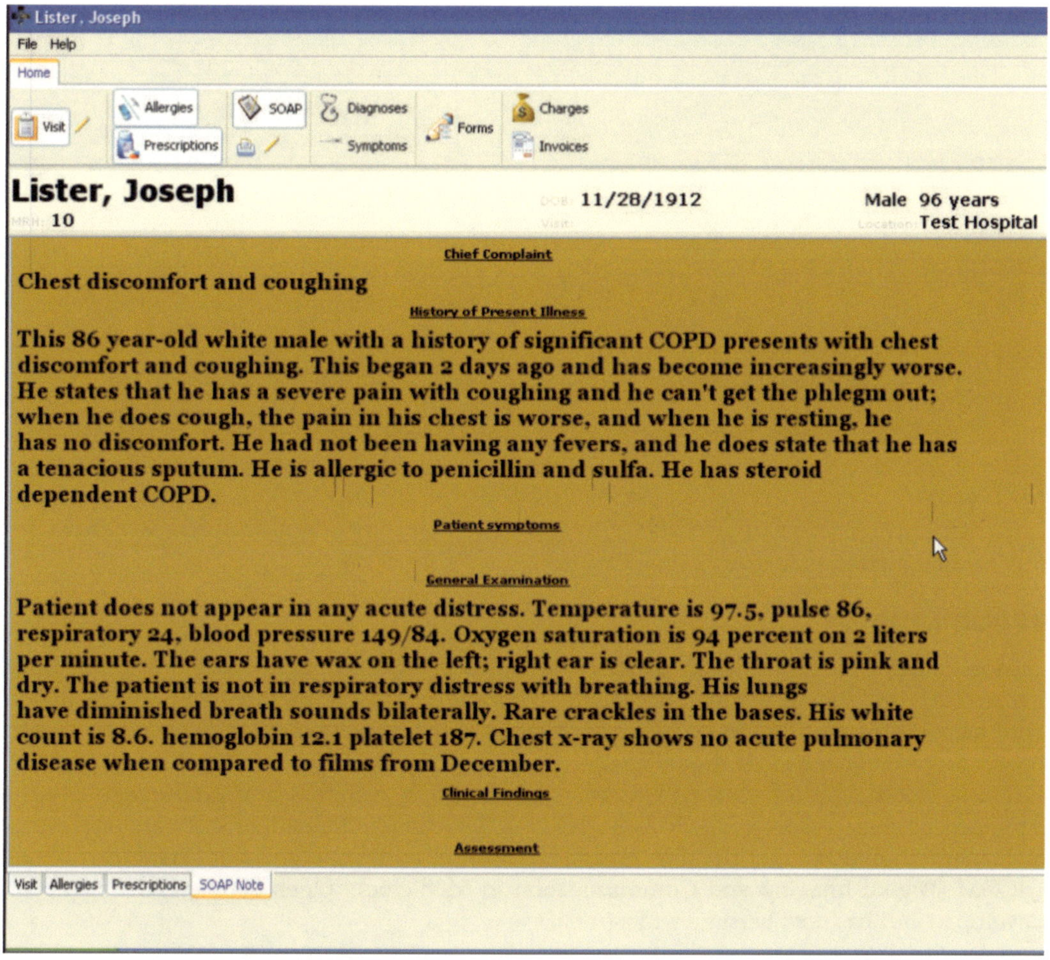

Fig. 3. Prescription form of PatientOS

development group and has been translated into a variety of languages. The platform was so called LAMP (Linux, Apache, MySQL and PHP), but now being refactored to J2EE for scalability. FreeMED is currently hosted by FreeMED Software Foundation, which is a non-profit corporation. Primary goal of FreeMED is the betterment of the open source software community and the world in general through promoting development and adoption of FreeMED and other open source medical software projects. Commercial support is available For FreeMED.

Project name	FreeMED
Description	EMR for general practitioner clinics
Programming language	PHP, MySQL, (Re-factoring to J2EE)
License	GPL
Project site	http://freemedsoftware.org/

Table 7. Technical overview of FreeMED

Fig. 4. Pet registration form of PatientOS

3.2 Digital imagings

Clinical imaging is necessary for modern physicians to make diagnosis. Digital imaging have improved portability of clinical image and enhanced quality of pictures that are calculated with the aid of computers. A picture archiving and communication (PACS) system has been developed to manage such digital images from various modality, such as X-ray, CT, MRI, PET and so on. Typical systems had been developed by vendors of digital image devices equipped as an accessory of devices. Today, PACS become independent software on devices to manage digital images, because standardization is widely accepted to many devices as DICOM (Digital Imaging and Communication in Medicine). Open source PACS has been developed and has now become widespread.

3.2.1 OsiriX

OsiriX is a popular OSS for medical imagery viewer (Rosset et al., 2004)(Table 8, Fig. 5). OsiriX was developed on Mac OS X by Dr Antoine Rosset and Dr Osman Ratib, in the department of radiology and medical computing of Geneva (Switzerland). OsiriX can also display DICOM standard format images from most of common modalities (ultrasound, CT, MRI, PET, etc). OsiriX is works mainly on Mac OS X, but also provide clients for iOS, such as iPad or iPhone and Windows clients can viewed image via a web server extension.

If you use large amount of digital images, additional 64 bit package might be necessary, but it is proprietary, too. However, for personal use, OsiriX basic package is very useful for physicians and even for radiologists.

3.2.2 dcm4che

dcm4che is a powerful and robust OSS DICOM and medical standard server (Warnock et al., 2007)(Table 9). It is a collection of open source applications and utilities for the healthcare enterprise. These applications have been developed in Java.

Project name	OsiriX
Description	Clinical image viewer for Mac OS X
Platform	Objective C, Cocoa framework
License	LGPL
Project site	http://www.osirix-viewer.com/

Table 8. Technical overview of OsiriX

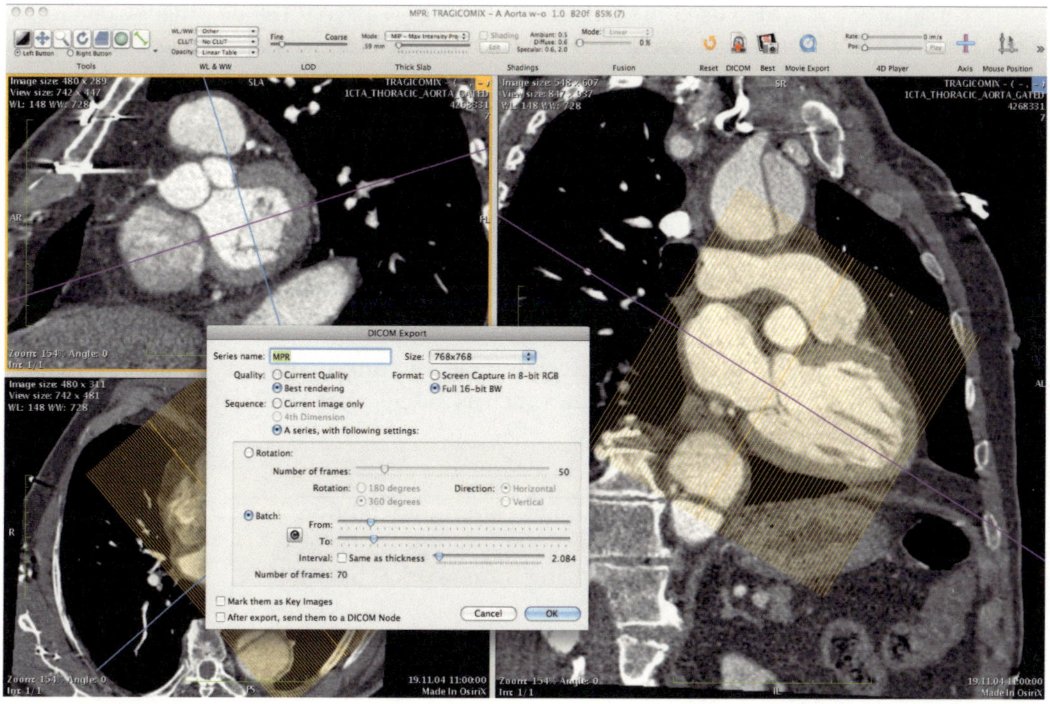

Fig. 5. Screenshot of OsiriX

Also contained within the dcm4che project is d (the extra 'e' stands for 'enterprise'). dcm4chee is an Image Manager/Image Archive (according to IHE; Integrating the Healthcare Enterprise). The application contains DICOM, HL7 services and interfaces that are required to provide storage, retrieval, and workflow to a healthcare environment. dcm4chee is pre-packaged and deployed within the JBoss application server. By taking advantage of many JBoss features (JMS, EJB, Servlet Engine, etc.) and assuming the role of several IHE factors for interoperability, the application provides many robust and scalable services to provide standardized messages related to clinical imaging works including HL7 and IHE-XDS.

Project name	Dcm4che
Description	DICOM server, archive and manager
Platform	Java, JBoss
License	MPL/GPL/LGPL triple license
Project site	http://www.dcm4che.org/

Table 9. Technical overview of Dcm4che

3.3 Research in biomedicine

Biomedical science also benefits from OSS. Bioinformatics has launched a number of OSS to build tools for their research (Dennis, 2004). Bioinformatics, which is a new frontier of biology, was a key technology to achieve Human Genome Project (Stein, 1996). At first, bioinformatics library was developed by Perl, but now many computer languages are available for bioinformatics and most of them are OSS. Many OSS tools are utilized for biomedical research, even if they are not targeted to biomedicine. R is a open source statistical environment for universal use, but is also used in biomedical statistics widely(R Development Core Team, 2005).Thus, OSS for biomedical research is an active domain. Some major projects are shown below for example.

3.3.1 OpenClinica

Medical research projects are supported by OpenClinica, a web-based platform for managing clinical studies(Table 10)(Akaza Research, n.d.). It is an industry-led software for capturing and managing clinical trial data. It allows users to build their own studies, design electronic Case Report Forms (eCRFs), and conduct a full range of clinical data capture and management functions. It also supports enterprise edition as hosting or already deployed form.

OpenClinica is designed to be used in diverse types of clinical studies. It supports Good Clinical Practice (GCP), regulatory guidelines such as 21 CFR Part 11, and is built on a modern architecture using leading standards.

Project name	OpenClinica community edition
Description	Clinical research support platform
Platform	Java, Spring framework/Hibernate
License	LGPL
Project site	https://community.openclinica.com/

Table 10. Technical overview of OpenClinica

3.3.2 ImageJ

ImageJ is a digital image processing tool for biological laboratories (Table 11)(NIH, n.d.). It was inspired from NIH Image on Macintosh. It can display, edit, analyze images of multiple formats, such as TIFF, GIF, JPEG, BMP, DICOM, FITS and raw. It can process pixel-value statistics to analyze magnification of the data. Many plug-ins are available for specialized processing.

Project name	ImageJ
Description	Laboratory image processing
Platform	Java
License	Public domain
Project site	http://rsbweb.nih.gov/ij/

Table 11. Technical overview of ImageJ

3.3.3 NetEpi

NetEpi, which is short for Inter **Net** -enabled **Epi** demiology, is a suite of OSS tools for epidemiology and public health practice which makes full use of the Internet (Table 12). NetEpi Collection is a data collection and management tool for use in communicable disease outbreaks and other epidemiological investigations and studies. It is written in Python and uses only open source software components and infrastructure, including the PostgreSQL database.

Project name	NetEpi
Description	Tools for epidemiology and public health
Platform	Python
License	MPL 1.1
Project site	http://code.google.com/p/netepi/

Table 12. Technical overview of NetEpi

4. Medical OSS in Japan

Japanese medical practice is generally subsidized by public health insurance programs. To receive reimbursement, doctors need to submit details of medications prescribed and treatments administered to their patients. To meet the government's accounting rules a health insurance computing system called *'Receipt Computer'* was developed during the 1970's and released in the 1980's. This software was expensive to deploy, costing as much as US$ 50,000 even in very small clinics or hospitals. Nevertheless, it was installed in 90% of clinics and hospitals in Japan as it could meet the complex bureaucratic accounting procedures. The high cost of the software inevitably placed a financial strain on clinics. In addition all the data entered in the receipt computer was locked into the vendor's proprietary software and could not be utilized for any other purpose or with any other systems without paying the vendor additional fees for integrating it.

To address the high costs of commercial software and to avoid any dependency on a specific vendor or technology, the JMA decided to provide its members with an OSS based information and communication infrastructure. In 2000, it presented an OSS project known as ORCA (On-line Receipt Computer Advanced) with two major goals (Japan Medical Association, 2001). The first was to provide a networked system with software for submitting claims for government reimbursement (named as 'JMA standard receipt computer') and related applications at low or no cost to JMA members. The second was to use the knowledge and experience from the project to inform healthcare policymakers about the potential of OSS for other aspects of medical management in Japan, particularly for electronic healthcare records.

All the components of the JMA standard receipt computer are OSS (Table 13). The platform is Debian GNU/Linux and Ubuntu Linux, using PostgreSQL for database system. JMA provides standardized terminology databases about disease, drug, operation, and contraindication of drug combination. MONTSUQI is a middle ware designed for this system to monitor transaction of modules to database system. This system has its own rich client implemented with customized gtk 1.2, because Japanese needs input method for Japanese characters, i.e. kanji, hiragana, and katakana. Web environment cannot switch input method on demand in the forms field . MONPE is a printing environment that can design complex receipt form with many ruling lines. At first, OpenCOBOL was developed for ORCA project,

Product Name	Description
PostgreSQL	Relational database management system.
MONTSUQI	Transaction monitor
MONPE	Report printing environment
OpenCOBOL	COBOL compiler
Debian GNU/Linux, Ubuntu Linux	OS environment

Table 13. Components of JMA standard receipt software

because the developer of the ORCA needed qualified COBOL compiler. OpenCOBOL is now widely used for migration of legacy system to Linux system(The OpenCOBOL Project, n.d.). The ORCA project also released the other related products as OSS(Japan Medical Association, 2000). Ikensho, one of the products of the ORCA project, is a reporting system for care insurance system for the government. Today, nearly 20,000 medical providers in Japan are using Ikensho, and the number of participants is increasing. According to the ORCA website in Oct 2011, 11,395 clinics and hospitals (about 11 percent of share) have adopted JMA standard receipt computer The software is free and can be installed by individuals themselves or by JMA-authorized vendors in which case, a fee is payable.

The Medical Open Software Council was established 2004to investigate potential applications of OSS in the medical field in Japan,. OpenDolphin was developed as a client part of the regional health care system and is now independently utilized in many clinics in Japan(MINAGAWA, n.d.). OpenDolphin has a standardized connectability to JMA standard receipt computer via CLAIM protocol(MedXML Consortium, n.d.). This is one of the reference implementation of CLAIM protocol. NOA is an EMR system that was formerly developed by Dr Ohashi for his clinic use and released as OSS for public use(OHASHI, n.d.). Dr Ohashi, is a gynecologist and has developed his EMR system for more than twenty years.

More and more medical OSS has been developed in Japan. One of the key areas where OSS may play a role is standardization of medical data transaction protocols, as described previously. In Japan, there are few vendors of medical information systems, limiting competition and driving up the cost of information systems. The limited number of vendors also creates other problems such as 'data lock-in' state, in which the hospital cannot use information entered within its system in intuitive ways as it is limited by the functionality and features provided by the vendor. In addition, 'vendor lock-in'may also occur, in which an organization cannot change vendors because their present vendor will not provide them with the necessary information about their system to allow data migration to take place. These problems do not occur with OSS and users consequently avoid any 'lock-in state'.

As OSS resources become more commonly used in the medical field, barriers to new vendors should be reduced, and more vendors will be attracted to the medical field. The increased competition should break the oligopoly of vendors in Japan and lead to greater diversity and lower cost of medical IT systems. At present, each organization may operate slightly differently from other organizations, and clinical information systems usually have to be customized for individual organizations, which increases the initial cost. With greater uses of OSS systems the diversity of available clinical information systems will increase and therefore be easier adapted to the needs of new organization without the need for extensive customization.

4.1 Medical OSS in Asia/Africa

Developing countries in Asia/Africa share many problems in health care. Infectious disease control is one of the most severe problems, which is the target for OpenMRS. Many African countries and WHO have supported OpenMRS development as an effective political action.

Another problem is education for young engineers to develop software for medicine. The United Nations University International Institute for Global Health (UNU-IIGH) in Kuala Lumpur, Malaysia has a short training course to teach OSS development and operation[2]. UP Manila, the national telehealth centre of Philippines, has also lead medical OSS movement in Asia.

Community Health Information Tracking System (CHITS) is a web-based electronic medical record developed by the University of the Philippines College of Medicine for government health facilities in the country (Fig. 6). It runs on a Linux system using Apache, MySQL, and PHP. Developed by Dr Herman Tolentino in 2003, CHITS is now expanding to more sites in the Philippines. It contains all the important programs utilised by the Philippine Department of Health and the Philippine Health Insurance Corporation.

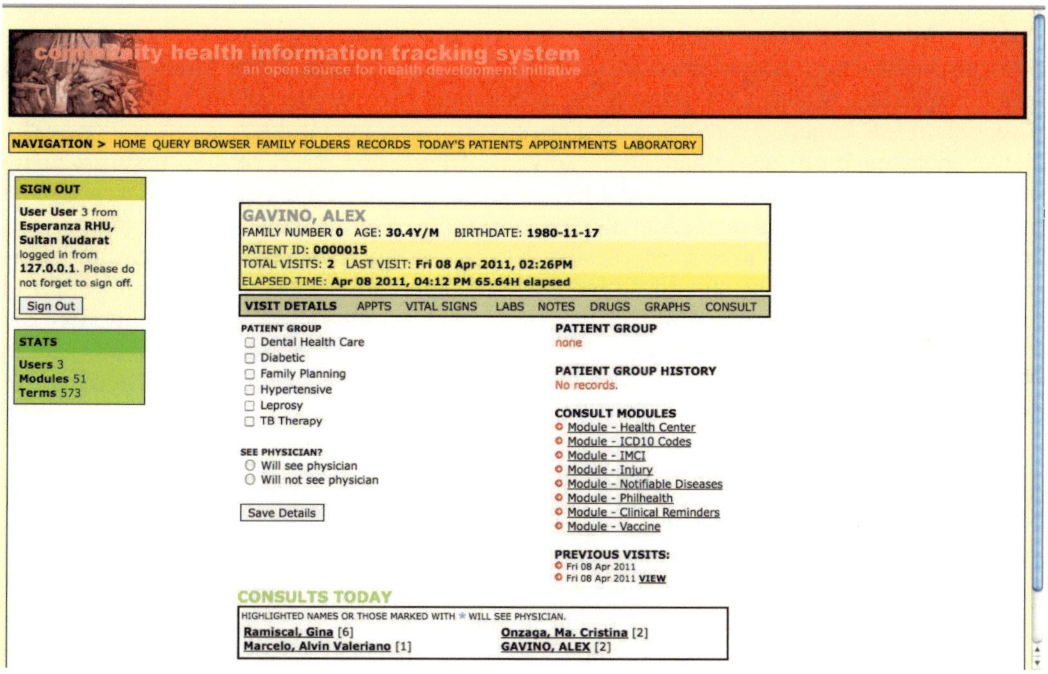

Fig. 6. Screenshot of CHITS

The International Open Source Network ASEAN+3 (www.iosn.net) was established by UNDP as a center of excellence for free and open source software in the region. It conducts conferences and trainings on FLOSS for health through the UP Manila National Telehealth Center (www.telehealth.ph). Some of the FLOSS topics had been on geographic information systems for disasters and OpenMRS.

---

[2] http://iigh.unu.edu/?q=node/85

5. Discussion

OSS offers great promise for realizing the vision of ubiquitous, low-cost, and quality EHR systems to support healthcare. The absence of license fees and the removal of dependency on a single vendor remove some of the most significant barriers to the implementation of EHRs.In addition, the absence of common data standards which makes it difficult to integrate systems or change from one EHR system to another, may also be addressed by OSS.

Although OSS clearly has many attractions, potential drawbacks must also be considered. As OSS development depends mainly on volunteers and usually provides its products *'as is'*, some people are skeptical about its security and availability. However, comparisons of OSS with proprietary software have been favorable (Raymond, 1997). For example, the analysis of source codes for the Linux kernel has been reported to have fewer bugs (Coverity Inc., 2004), and be more reliable than proprietary software (Miller et al., 1995; 1990). OSS has also been shown to respond more quickly than proprietary software in releasing patches to identified vulnerabilities. Clinical information systems must have a high level of security to maintain patient privacy. OSS can theoretically be made more secure than proprietary software because it can receive input from many developers (Coverity Inc., 2004; Miller et al., 1995; 1990; Raymond, 1997).

As described earlier, the potential of OSS has been recognized in the medical field, and many healthcare related OSS projects have achieved success (Japan Medical Association, 2000; OpenEMR Project, n.d.; OpenMRS Project, n.d.; Veterans Health Administration, n.d.). However, many problems remain to be solved. The development of OSS requires many developers with numerous skills and ideas in order to produce a good product, and as a consequence OSS projects recruit developers worldwide. Unfortunately, worldwide projects are rare in medicine, because each country has its own unique medical system and thus software cannot readily be shared without specific adaptations and a literal translation of the language. When language is not a barrier, the practice is exactly the same throughout the world, e.g. viewing radiology images, OSS can be readily used with minimal or no adaptation (NIH, n.d.; Rosset et al., 2004; Warnock et al., 2007). Furthermore, despite differences in medical systems, the work flow at hospitals does not differ markedly among countries, making it possible to produce a unified worldwide medical application. To accomplish this, a worldwide medical project should separate common and local components (e.g. accounting, insurance claims, etc.) and standardize their interoperability.

Even OSS is superior in terms of the quality of software, medical organization still needs vendor's support to maintain information systems. To qualify the support of vendors, JMA label OSS vendors which has enough skill to support ORCA systems. The authenticated vendors are listed in the JMA web site. At first, unskilled vendors confused medical organizations, but the labeling program has improved service of vendors and eliminated wrong vendors from the market of medical information systems. While many medical organizations have reaped the benefits of OSS with the labeling of skillful vendors, some medical providers cannot be supported in some area, mainly in the Japan countryside . The offices of OSS vendors are mainly located in urban areas, because they can get access to many other jobs as well. OSS support vendors are increasing in number, but their skillsare quite varied and their distribution area uneven. For every medical organization to have OSS benefit, more and more OSS vendors should be cultivated. This means, medical OSS market should grow enough to sustain OSS vendors. The ORCA project has been shown to be one of the most successful Medical OSS projects; suggesting that this labeling program might be appropriate to be developed in other countries as well.

OSS is sometimes used for purposes other than those intended by the developers. Although OSS has not been developed specifically for clinical use, some OSS has been adapted for the clinical situation. Similarly, OSS that has been developed for medical applications may also be used in other fields as OpenCOBOL (The OpenCOBOL Project, n.d.) or CGI.pm (Stein, 1996). OSS should be enriched not only for clinical use but also for use by the entire OSS community, as human intellectual property.

6. Conclusion

Even in medical field, OSS has the potential to improve both clinical operations and the interoperability of the medical systems. A number of promising OSS projects in the medical field may benefit both medicine and human intellectual property.

7. Acknowledgments

I appreciate Dr Alvin Marcero, Mr Randy Joseph Fernandez, Mr Thomas Karopka and Dr Nurhizam Saphie for their insightful advice.

8. References

AK, J., CM, D., EG, C., K, D., SR, R., TG, F., A, S., S, R. & D., B. (2009). Use of electronic health records in u.s. hospitals, *New England Journal of Medicine* 360: 1628–1638.

Akaza Research (n.d.). OpenClinica, `http://www.openclinica.org/`.

Brauer, J. (2008). Mirth: Standards-based open source healthcare interface engine, *Open Source Business Resource* .

Clinton, H. R. & Obama, B. (2006). Making patient safety the centerpiece of medical liability reform, *NEJM* 354: 2205 – 2208.

Coverity Inc. (2004). Analysis of Linux kernel, `http://linuxbugs.coverity.com/linuxbugs.htm`.

Dennis, C. (2004). Biologists launch 'open-source movement.', *Nature* 431: 494.

Eysenbach, G. & Kohler, C. (2003). What is the prevalence of health-related searches on the world wide web? qualitative and quantitative analysis of search engine queries on the internet, *AMIA Annu Symp Proc.*, pp. 225 – 229.

Halamka, J., Aranow, M., Ascenzo, C., Bates, D., Debor, G., Glaser, J., Goroll, A., Stowe, J., Tripathi, M. & Vineyard, G. (2005). Health care it collaboration in massachusetts: The experience of creating regional connectivity, *J Am Med Inform Assoc.* 12(6): 596–601.

Japan Medical Association (2000). ORCA Project, `http://www.orca.med.or.jp/`.

Japan Medical Association (2001). JMA IT Declearation, `http://www.orca.med.or.jp/orca/sengen/declaration.html`.

Kenwood, C. A. (2001). A Business Case Study of Open Source Software, *Technical report*, The MITRE Corporation.

MedXML Consortium (n.d.). Clinical Accounting InforMation (CLAIM) Specification Version 2.1a Type B PRELIMINARY, `http://www.medxml.net/E_claim21/default.html`.

Miller, B., Koski, D., Lee, C. P., Maganty, V., Murthy, R., Natarajan, A. & Steidl, J. (1995). Fuzz revisited: A re-examination of the reliability of UNIX utilities and services, *Technical report*.

Miller, B. P., Fredriksen, L. & So, B. (1990). An empirical study of the reliability of UNIX utilities, *Communications of the Association for Computing Machinery* 33(12): 32–44. URL: *http://citeseer.ist.psu.edu/miller90empirical.html*

MINAGAWA, K. (n.d.). OpenDolphin Project, http://www.digital-globe.co.jp/.

Morrison, C., Iosif, A. & Danka, M. (2010). Report on existing open-source electronic medical records, *Technical Report 768*, University of Cambridge Computer Laboratory.

NIH (n.d.). ImageJ, http://rsb.info.nih.gov/ij/.

OECD (ed.) (2011). *OECD Health Data 2011*, OECD. URL: *www.oecd.org/health/healthdata*

Office of the National Coordinator for Health Information Technology (n.d.). Onc complete ambulatory ehr certified, "http://onc-chpl.force.com/ ehrcert/ EHRProductDetail?id=a0X30000003mNwTEAU".

OHASHI, K. (n.d.). NOA Project, http://www.ocean.shinagawa.tokyo.jp/NOA_PROJECT/.

Open Source Initiative (1997–2005). The open source definition, http://www.opensource.org/docs/definition_plain.php.

OpenEMR Project (n.d.). OpenEMR, http://www.openemr.net/.

OpenMRS Project (n.d.). OpenMRS, http://openmrs.org/.

R Development Core Team (2005). *R: A language and environment for statistical computing*, R Foundation for Statistical Computing, Vienna, Austria. ISBN 3-900051-07-0. URL: *http://www.R-project.org*

Raymond, E. (1997). The Cathedral and the Bazaar, http://www.catb.org/~esr/writings/cathedral-bazaar/.

Reynolds, J. C. & Wyatt, C. J. (2011). Open source, open standards, and health care information systems, *J Med Internet Res* 13(1): e24. URL: *http://www.jmir.org/2011/1/e24/*

Rosset, A., Spadola, L. & Ratib, O. (2004). Osirix: an open-source software for navigating in multidimensional dicom images., *J Digit Imaging* 17: 205–16.

Stein, L. (1996). How Perl Saved the Human Genome Project, http://www.bioperl.org/GetStarted/tpj_ls_bio.html.

Surhone, L., Timpledon, M. & Marseken, S. (2010). *Freemed*, VDM Verlag Dr. Mueller AG & Co. Kg. URL: *http://books.google.com/books?id=2NOwcQAACAAJ*

The OpenCOBOL Project (n.d.). OpenCOBOL, http://www.OpenCOBOL.org/.

The openEHR Foundation (n.d.). The openEHR Project, http://www.opehr.org/.

Veterans Health Administration (n.d.). Veterans Health Information Systems and Technology Architecture (VISTA), http://www.va.gov/vista_monograph/.

Warnock, M. J., Toland, C., Evans, D., Wallace, B. & Nagy, P. (2007). Benefits of using the dcm4che dicom archive., *Journal of digital imaging : the official journal of the Society for Computer Applications in Radiology* 20 Suppl 1: 125–9. URL: *http://www.pubmedcentral.nih.gov/articlerender.fcgi?artid=2039778*

6

Communication Architecture in the Chosen Telematics Transport Systems

Mirosław Siergiejczyk
Warsaw University of Technology, Faculty of Transport, Poland

1. Introduction

The term telematics comes from French *télématique,* and emerged at the beginning of the seventies as a combination of the words telecommunications (*télécommunications*) and computer science (*informatique).* At the end of seventies it started to be used in English. Nineties made it more widespread in Europe, when the European Union had introduced telematics development programmes to various sectors. It is one of those terms, which are by-products of scientific progress, namely in this case, tremendous advance of transportation and information technologies. The term is predominantly used to describe structural solutions integrating electronic communication with information collection and processing, designed to cater for a specific system's needs. It also pools different technical solutions, which use telecommunications and IT systems (Wawrzyński W., Siergiejczyk M. et al., 2007, Wydro K. B. ,2003).

Telematics can be defined as telecommunications, IT, information and automatic control solutions, adapted to address physical systems' needs. Those solutions derive from their functions, infrastructure, organisation, and processes integral to maintenance and management. In this case, a physical system consists of purpose-built devices, and comprises administration, operators, users and environmental considerations.

Technical telematic solutions use electronic communication systems transmitting information. Among those systems are WAN (Wide Area Network) and LAN (Local Area Network) networks, radiowave beacons, satellite systems, data collection systems (sensors, video cameras, radars, etc.) and systems presenting information both to administrators (e.g. the GIS system) and to users (variable message signs, traffic lights, radio broadcasting, WAP, WWW, SMS).

The very essence of telematics is data handling, i.e. collection, transmission and processing. Data collection entails gathering multivariate data from sensors and the environment through purpose-built devices. The data are then transmitted over dedicated transmission mechanisms - assuring reliability and good transmission rates - to the processing centres. In case of data transmission and processing, one should pay attention to issues of signal usefulness and its functional intent. Furthermore, an important feature of telematics-based applications is their capability to effectively integrate different subsystems and make them interoperable. Apart from various applications of telematics (medical telematics, environment telematics and other), its broadest application area is transport.

The following chapter discusses data exchange architecture in transport telematic systems. The issues concerning the structure and a means enabling information exchange between different parts (elements) of transport telematic systems (means of data stream transmission) were presented across four subsections.

The second part of the chapter delves into the very essence of transport telematic systems. The concept of a transport telematic system is outlined and the transport telematics itself is situated among other fields of knowledge and technologies. Information flows in telematic systems were then analysed, concentrating with due diligence on transmission of telematics-based information. Functions of transport telematic systems were defined, as a service intended for a diverse range of target audiences directly or indirectly connected with transport processes of people and/or goods. Delivering those services requires building data transmission networks between entities using telematic systems to provide transport services

The third part of the chapter discusses the fundamental nature of communication architecture as well as defines and determines the structure and a means enabling information exchange between different parts (elements) of a system (means of data stream transmission). Based on literature analysing data exchange in Intelligent Transport Systems, such architecture was illustrated in an integrated urban traffic/public transport management system. Another example of telematics-based data flow is data exchange between highway management centres and highway telematic systems. Communication architecture of highway telematic system was presented along with schematically depicted data transmission in a highway management centre.

The subsequent section concerns the issues of building a teleinformatic infrastructure enabling rail transport services. General architecture of rail infrastructure manager's telecommunications network was discussed, and services provided by that network characterised. IT standards required to deliver integrated rail transport IT systems were discussed as well. Wired and wireless communication networks were presented. Teleinformatic services dedicated for rail transport were analysed.

The final part of the chapter discusses the issues of teleinformatic networks used in air traffic management systems. Higher number of aircrafts within individual sectors, is only acceptable should concurrently data transmission systems, informing about situation in individual sectors of airways be improved. Basic issues related to migration of X.25 networks to networks using the IP protocol in their network layer were presented. The concept includes the AFTN, OLDI and radar data transmission networks alike. One of the most important surveillance data distribution systems - ARTAS - was also described. Finally, presented was the possibility of deploying SAN networks - characterised by integrated architecture - in order to enable exchange of construction data, planned and real airspace restrictions.

2. Information flows in telematic systems

2.1 Transport telematics

The field concerning application of telematics in transport systems is called transport telematics. It comprises integrated measuring, telecommunications, IT and information systems, control engineering, their equipment and the services they provide.

Said equipment and services are provided as telematics-based applications, i.e. purpose-built tools. Example of such an isolated application is a road weather information system, which informs users e.g. about crosswind.

Transport telematics marked its presence in Polish publications in mid-nineties. Already back then, efforts were made to identify conceptual range and field of applications of transport telematics (Wawrzyński W., 1997). Consequently it was defined as a field of knowledge and technical activity integrating IT with telecommunications, intended to address transport systems' needs.

Transport telematics is a field of knowledge integrating IT and telecommunications, intended for needs of organising, managing, routing and controlling traffic flows, which stimulates technical and organisational activity enabling quality assurance of transit services, higher efficiency and safety of those systems (Wawrzyński W., Siergiejczyk M. et al., 2007)

Cooperating individual telematic solutions (often supervised by a superior factor e.g. an operator supported by purpose-built applications), create Intelligent Transport Systems (ITS). Convergence of telecommunications and IT, right through to Intelligent Transport Systems has been presented schematically in figure 1.1.

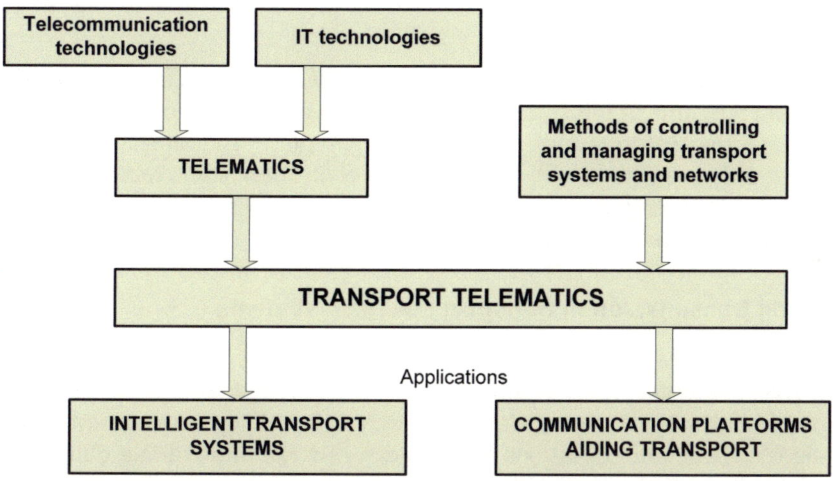

Fig. 1.1. Transport telematics amongst related fields of knowledge and technology

The name Intelligent Transport Systems was accepted at the very first world congress held in Paris, 1994, in spite of proposal made by International Organization for Standardization of RTTT (*Road Traffic and Transport Telematics*). Regardless of the name, those systems create architecture, designed to aid, supervise, control and manage transport processes and interlock them. Transportation Management Systems, integrating all modes of transport and all transit network elements within a given area, are also referred to as ATMS (*Advanced Traffic Management Systems*) (Wydro K. B. ,2003).

Key functionalities of telematic systems are information handling functionalities. Namely its collection, processing, distribution along with transmission, and its use in decision-making processes. They are both the processes carried out in a pre-determined fashion (e.g.

automatic traffic control) and incident-induced processes (decisions of dispatchers and real-time information supported, independent infrastructure users) (Klein L.A., 2001).

Telematics-enabled physical infrastructure - called intelligent systems - can vary in function and dimensions. However, not only the range and number of elements constitute the size of a telematic system. First and foremost the quantity and diversity of information fed through and processed in the system matters, followed by the number of entire system's domains of activity. In a broad sense, intelligent transport systems are highly integrated measuring (detector, sensor), telecommunications, IT, information and also automatic solutions. Intelligent transport integrates all kinds and modes of transport, infrastructure, organisations, enterprises, as well as maintenance and management processes. Used telematic solutions link those elements, enable their cooperation and interaction with environment, users in particular. Telematic solutions can be dedicated for a specific type of transport (e.g. road transport) and operate within a chosen geographic area (e.g. a local administrative unit). They can also integrate and coordinate a continental or global transport system.

Such solutions normally have an open architecture and are scalable: if required they can be expanded, complemented and modernised. Their aim is to benefit users through interaction with individual system elements assuring safer journeys and transit, higher transport reliability, better use of infrastructure and better economic results plus to reduce environmental degradation.

The fundamental feature of telematics-based applications is the capability to disseminate and process vast amounts of information adequate to a given function, adapted to consumer needs - users of that information, specific for right place and time. Information can be communicated either automatically or interactively, upon user request. An important feature of telematics-based applications is their ability to effectively integrate different subsystems and cause them to operate in a coordinated fashion.

2.2 Information transmission in transport telematic systems

One of crucial properties of telematic systems is broadcasting and transmitting information, i.e. its flow. Distribution of telematic information is strictly linked to telecommunications, i.e. transmission of information over a distance through different signals - currently, often electric and optic signals. Telecommunications services can provide multivariate data: alphanumeric data, voice, sounds, motion or still pictures, writing characters and various measuring signals, etc. The information chain is the salient aspect of telematic information distribution in terms of telecommunications. In essence, the chain transmits multivariate messages from transmitter to receiver, thus concentrates on two data exchange points. However, the fact the transmission took place matters, as opposed to the way the information was transmitted. The way of transmitting information matters in case of a communication chain, which is part of an information chain. In case of a communication chain, important is data transmission from transmitter to receiver without data identification. Important here is the message conversion to transmittable signal and the transmission medium. During transmission, the signal is exposed to interferences, thus often becomes distorted. Hence it is crucial, that the signal transmitted to receiver is the best reproduction of original signal. The transmission medium is called communication channel which is usually a wire (twin-lead, coaxial), optical fibre or radio channel (Siergiejczyk M., 2009).

Telematics-based systems interact with many other systems and environment, and can encompass many constituent subsystems. Hence the aforementioned elements have to interchange information (figure 2.1). In order to facilitate dataflow, required are different types of transmission media, without which data distribution would not be possible. Transmission media are used for both quick and reliable communication with widespread systems, demanding tremendous amounts of data to be long-distance transmitted, and short-distance transmission of basic control messages or measuring data from sensors. Therefore, in case of systems on the table, transmission media and transmission mechanisms play an important role.

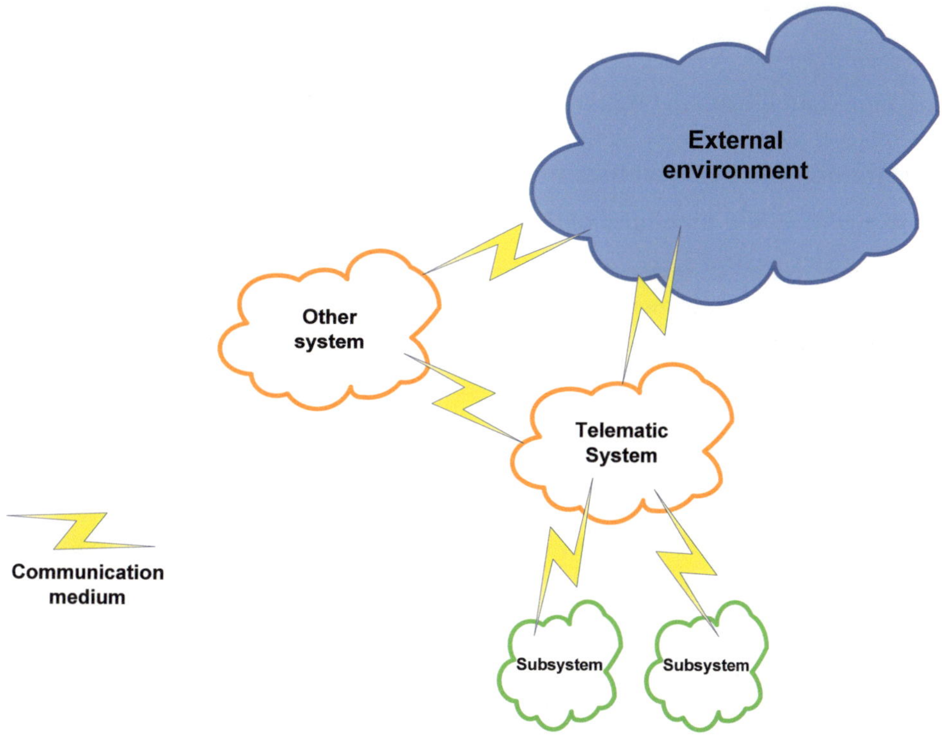

Fig. 2.1. Telematic data exchange

The focal point of the entire telematic system is the traffic operations centre (management centre). Flowchart in figure 2.2 illustrates telematics-based information flow.

Different methods and transmission media of data have to be used due to characteristics of information transmitters and receivers. Both the method and medium depend on used devices and their technological advancement, channel capacity requirements, power supply, etc. Moreover, significant factors include weather conditions, likelihood of electromagnetic interferences, whether elements are mobile or fixed, working conditions, software and telecommunications-imposed requirements. One of the most important factors are the set-up and maintenance costs of chosen medium and the method of transmitting telematics-based information.

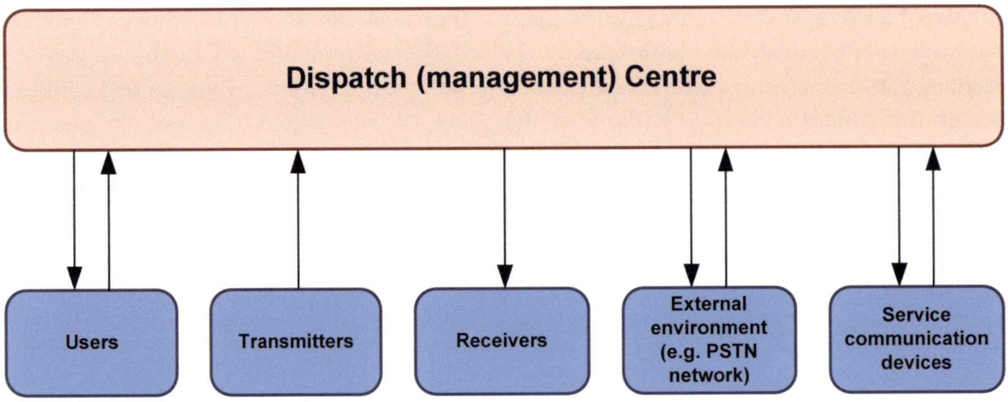

Fig. 2.2. Flowchart illustrating telematics-based information flow

3. Communication architecture in road transport telematic systems

3.1 Determination and functions of transportation architecture of telematic systems

Transport architecture of transport telematic systems defines and determines the structure and a means enabling information exchange between different parts (elements) of a system (means of data stream transmission). It concerns two mutually complementing facets, distinguished by different operating principles: assurance of a means enabling point-to-point data transmission; assuring reliability of transmitting and interpreting telematics-based information.

The issue of assuring a means enabling point-to-point data transmission and ensuring the chosen means are valid in terms of costs, maximum distortions or signal latency, concerns description and definition of communication mechanisms. They correspond to the first four OSI (*Open System Interconnection*) model layers, namely physical layer, data link layer, network layer and transport layer. The communication platform has to be independent of used technologies and specific products to a maximum extent. In order to do that, envisaged are e.g. physical dataflow analysis in most representative example systems. On that basis, the most representative telecommunications needs can be recognised in a telematic system, including necessary interfaces. Spelling out such typical telecommunications needs is an important advantage of transportation infrastructure. Ever-changing telecommunications technologies impede developing technologically independent architecture, up-to-date over longer time horizons. However, put forward overview of typical dataflow, will remain valid as long as the most representative system image does not substantially alter. Thus, said methodology lays the grounds for analysing loosely telecommunications-related issues in ITS systems.

Apart from strictly telecommunications-related issues, one has to bear in mind the problem of ensuring reliability of telematics-based information transmission and its correct interpretation. It is a problem of standards, which would guarantee to communicating parties reliable and efficient data exchange. In reality though, a system's capability to provide services relies to a great extent on data, which the system can process within a time unit. Thus, not only the type of data processed by a system matters, but also their level of detail available for designing a service or other operation needed by a telematic system. Other technical issues, such as data storage, storage location should not be ignored as well. That solution can cause the need for a diversified way of data exchange, and consequently e.g. different message display standards (Siergiejczyk M. ,2009).

The communication part of a telematic system, determines links between environments of transport and telecommunications. Due to rapid development of telecommunications, telematic systems designers have a wide selection of means at their disposal, enabling them to accommodate needs induced by variable implementation circumstances. Communication architecture does not hint though, on particular systems of technologies, instead merely identifies technology-based capabilities. Four types of media were listed here, all suitable to transmit information in transport telematic solutions. Those are the following telecommunications systems (Wawrzyński W., Siergiejczyk M. et al., 2007):

- wired (stationary point to stationary point connectivity);
- long-distance wireless (stationary point to mobile point connectivity);
- dedicated short-distance (stationary point to mobile point connectivity);
- between mobile in-vehicle terminals (mobile connectivity).

It is worth pointing out, that there are numerous transmission techniques used for communication between stationary points. E.g. proprietary or leased communication channels can be used to operate traffic control subsystems. With intended other applications, they can be microwaves, spread spectrum radio systems or local radio networks.

Structure of physical architecture envisaged subsystems of the Control Centre (Management and Supervision) connected with a wired network. It allows every subsystem to collect, integrate and disseminate information to other subsystems in line with mutually accepted communication and coordination rules, positively affecting operational effectiveness of those subsystems. Depending on range and coverage, there are two types of wireless communication. The first is long-range wireless communication, stipulating means used in case of services and applications, where information is sent over long distances and regional full coverage is required, providing constant network access. Further distinction concerns one-way and two-way communication, as it influences the choice of technology (e.g. radio transmission is possible with one-way communication). Short-range wireless communication is the second type, used to send information locally. There are two types, vehicle-to-vehicle and DSRC (*Dedicated Short Range Communications*). The former is used i.a. for collision avoidance systems, whereas DSRC – for electronic toll collection, access authorisation etc. Generally, it is fair to say that the analysis of traffic assignment and required data feed rates, and the analysis of available transmission techniques lead to the conclusion, that commercially available wired and wireless networks are capable of accommodating current and future transmission needs in terms of telematics-based information.

3.2 Communication architecture in road transport

The KAREN (*Keystone Architecture Required for European Networks*) framework architecture introduced by the European Union, implies support mechanism for information exchange between different system elements. Such exchange should comply with the following:

- the mechanism should enable data transmission between relevant parties and be sustainable in terms of cost, accuracy and transmission latency;
- assure correctness of data transmission and interpretation.

Both those conditions require:

- introduction of detailed analysis of definitions and descriptions of communication connections in main interfaces of physical transport subsystems;
- defining necessary communication protocols.

Physical structure of a system i.e. elements identification, which i.a. exchanged data are classified under Physical Architecture in KAREN. Identified were five main types of elements and characterised were requirements concerning data exchange between such elements (KAREN, 2000, Wawrzyński W., Siergiejczyk M. et al. ,2007, Wydro K. B., 2003):

- *Central* – the place which is used to collect, collate and store traffic data and to generate traffic management measures, or fleet management instructions (e.g. Traffic Control Centres, Traffic Information Centres or Freight and Fleet Management Centres);
- *Kiosk* - a device usually located in a public place, providing traveller information (e.g. tourist information, often self-service)
- *Roadside* – the place where detected are traffic, vehicles and pedestrians, tolls collected and/or traffic management measures taken, and/or information are provided to drivers and pedestrians;
- *Vehicle* - a device that is capable of moving through the road network and carrying one or more people (e.g. bicycles, motorcycles, cars, Public Transport Vehicles) and/or goods (any form of road going freight carrying vehicle);
- *Traveller* – a person driving or using a vehicle.

Because communication with environment requires systemic description of that environment, its active elements are defined as terminators. A terminator can be a person, system or a unit, from which data would be received and which are sent requests. Especially, they can be:

- road infrastructure („roadside");
- emergency system;
- external service providers;
- measuring systems;
- multi-modal transport structure;
- travellers.

Figure 3.1 illustrates example data exchange in an integrated traffic and road transport management system. In order to describe data exchange, the following have to be distinguished:

- communication channel, i.e. physical data transmission medium;
- location, data source and sink, i.e. place where data originates or is received;
- physical interfaces, i.e. system elements enabling data exchange.

Systemic characteristics of data exchange processes requires dividing that area in two:

- internal communication, comprising data exchange between system's diversely located elements,
- system-terminator communication.

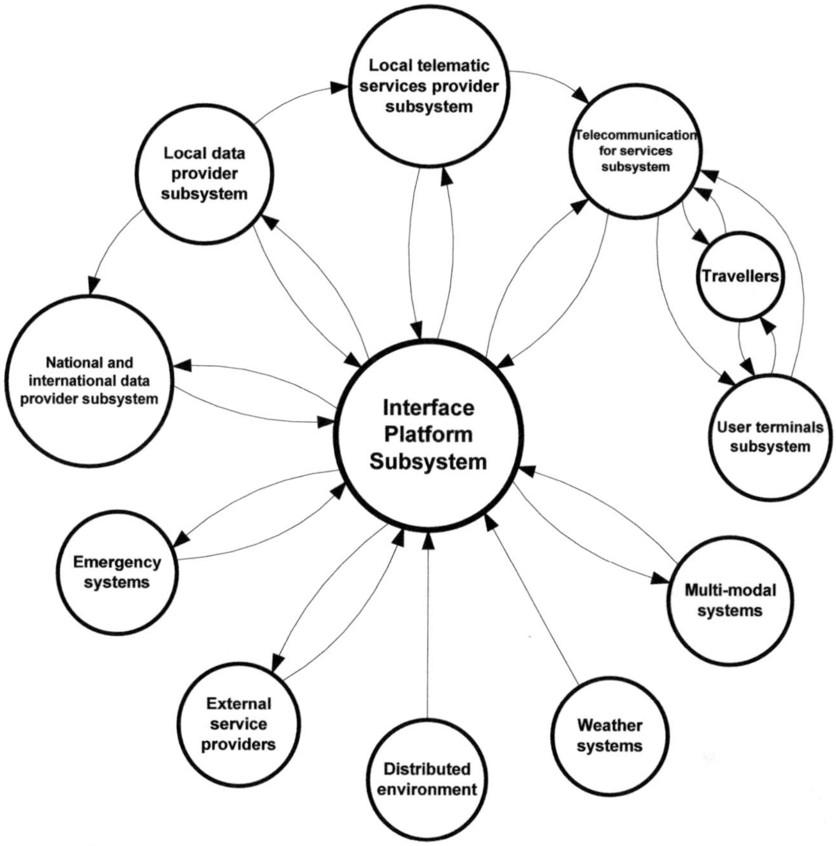

Fig. 3.1. Data exchange in an integrated traffic and road transport management system (Wydro K. B., 2003)

3.3 Communication structure of highway telematic systems

Another example of telematics-based data flow is data exchange between highway management centres and highway telematic systems. Highway management centres are centrepiece and the most important elements of highway telematics infrastructure (Highway Management Center/ Traffic Management Center). A centre receives any data from telematic systems located along a highway, and manages as well as operates those systems. Using dedicated devices and software, variable message signs and cameras placed along supervised section can be controlled. The centre can also process emergency calls and have systems for collecting and analysing weather data. It also carries out functions of comprehensive highway monitoring systems and provides information to users (drivers) (Wawrzyński W., Siergiejczyk M. et al., 2007).

Among highway management centres' functions are:

- traffic management;
- weather and traffic conditions monitoring;
- road surface monitoring;
- emergency situations management (accidents) and emergency calls processing;
- providing information to travellers both before and during the journey;
- visual highway monitoring and adequate reactions;
- maintenance services management.

An important aspect concerning highway management centre is its location. Centres are located about every 60 km. The reasoning behind such practice is to assure maximum distance of an accident from the nearest centre to be less than 30 km. Close proximity from centres of maintenance and emergency services additionally further the case. Nevertheless, in some cases big highway traffic monitoring and surveillance centres form, whose range reaches up to several hundred kilometres. Also important is for the centre to be located in heavily populated areas and on their periphery due to availability of highly qualified staff and infrastructure elements.

Usually, the infrastructure of a modern highway management centre combines routers, servers, LAN workstations, high resolutions screens with dedicated controllers and drivers, peripheral devices and other network devices and an array of telecommunications connections. Most crucial is the router, which is charged with receiving, transmitting and routing packets in the network. Servers can support routers, and what is more, they are equipped with high capacity hard disks enabling video recording. They also support local network workstations and execute automated processes of telematic systems. Dedicated servers are also used to process pictures captured by surveillance cameras, which replaced thus far used analogue devices (multiplexers, video splitters). On centre's walls hung are high resolution screens, which display CCTV footage, feed from different applications, maps showing position of highway patrol vehicles etc.

An important element of management centre's architecture, are workstations performing the function of a dispatch station operated by qualified staff. Powerful PCs equipped with computer monitors and keyboards are used. A reliable operating system is also crucial. Dedicated console or station built-in workstations are also often used. Using specialist software, an operator can monitor and analyse data from weather stations and roadside sensors. Moreover, thanks to the Internet current weather in the country can be previewed – the system automatically generates alerts and takes action, thus aiding human decisions. Using the workstation, an operator can manage messages displayed on variable message signs, RDS/DAB (*Radio Data System/ Digital Audio Broadcast*) system messages and operate a parking guidance system. Chosen stations can process emergency calls from the highway communication system without having to use dedicated dispatch stations. After the call is answered, the number of column issuing the report is displayed on the computer screen. The conversation is held by using headphones with microphone connected to a computer and saved to the hard drive. The number of stations processing emergency calls should be sufficient to assure instant connection with the dispatcher.

In order for the highway management centres to function efficiently, data transmission has to be assured (figure 3.2). Communication with telematics-based highway systems is crucial (emergency communication, traffic-related weather forecasts, video surveillance) as is data

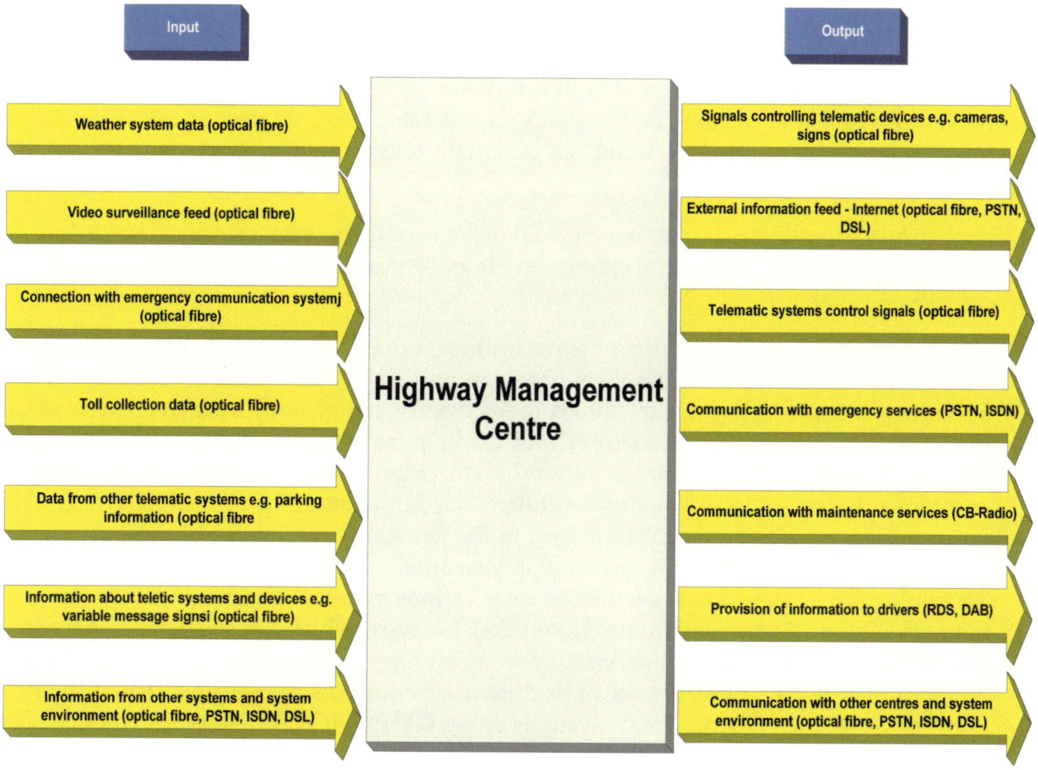

Fig. 3.2. Data transmission in highway management centres

exchange with other management centres, which currently is enabled by optical fibre running along a highway. Subsequently, signals are converted, decoded and read by dedicated applications (Siergiejczyk M., 2009).

Communication with emergency services is also important, which has to be direct. Connection is established instantly upon operator's call. The PSTN (*Public Switched Telephone Network*) telephone network is used for that purpose, and more modern systems use the ISDN network (*Integrated Services Digital Network*) with the "hot line" service. To communicate with regional maintenance service the CB (*Citizen-Band*) radio communication is used (long-range antenna fitted to rooftops).

4. Communication infrastructure in rail transport

4.1 Introduction

Railway operators almost always have used means of communication to provide efficient rail services. It is clear, that communication have been a tool, which to a great extent streamlined rail traffic management. Along with rail network development and technical advancement of telecommunications, those tools seem to have penetrated the transit process and are deeply embedded in rail transport. E.g. rail traffic control. Currently, the introduction of TCP/IP- enabled *(Transmission Control Protocol/Internet Protocol)* networks have contributed to deploying telecommunications services in the processes of transport and customer (passenger) service. Examples are data centres, recovery data centres, and virtual private networks dedicated for individual railway sectors or even applications (train tracking, consignment tracking, online tickets booking etc.). Those services increase the competitiveness of rail carriers and railway companies. The above-mentioned example services could not be provided without an adequate telecommunications network (in this case TCP/IP-compliant networks).

Building a telecommunications network is a process, which once started - according to experience - has to be constantly continued. It is "induced" by several facts (Gago S., Siergiejczyk M. , 2006):

1. Telecommunications infrastructure is meant to last many years, e.g. telecommunication cables (both conventional and optical fibre) are used for several dozens of years.
2. Such long usage of optical fibre cables (over twenty years) will cause over that period telecommunication services to evolve and develop, as it was seen in case of telephone networks. Originally, telephone networks provided only voice broadcast services, subsequently joined by telefax and ultimately complemented by the ISDN networks (voice broadcast and data transmission). In the nearest future, voice broadcast services will be provided only through convergent networks - *„voice over packet"*.
3. Technological advancement of telecommunications networks causes new generation networks NGN (Next Generation Networks) to form, which are capable of handling every telecommunications service. In a different domain, the technological advancement leads to creation of optical internet networks supporting DWDM *(Dense Wavelength Division Multiplexing)* systems using GMPLS *(Generalised Multiprotocol Label Switching)* protocol, i.e. so called IP over DWDM.
4. Requirements of telecommunications systems (teleinformatic, telematics) users are ever-increasing in terms of provided services, illustrated by words
   - now,
   - everywhere,
   - free of error,
   - safely.

Due to those reasons, core telecom network designers have to accommodate the following:

- quantitative and territorial network expansion,
- qualitative network development i.e. possible technological advancement in terms of teletransmission, switchgear and managing devices,
- advancement in terms of creating and introducing new teleinformatic services to the network e.g. database services (CDN - *Content Delivery Network*, SAN - *Storage Area Network*) etc,
- implementation of ever newer and better secure data exchange and processing systems.

Physical telecom/teleinformatic/telematics rail network (hardware) should be built in such a way, to accommodate current and future services demanded by users:

- Telecommunications,
- Teleinformatic,
- Telematics.

The role of communication devices is accurate data transmission over specified time from transmitter to receiver. Both transmitter and receiver can be people, devices, different IT, telematics and information systems etc. In modern, digital telecommunications, application systems decide on transmitted data interpretation. Data can be interpreted as part of voice, video, control signal etc.

4.2 Systems and telecommunications services of the infrastructure manager

Systems and devices necessary for efficient controlling, routing and managing railway traffic, using telecommunications technology can be classified as follows:

1. Railway traffic controls.
- station equipment,
- wire equipment,
- regional equipment (remote control and dispatch),
- level crossing traffic safety equipment,
- CCTV equipment for monitoring level crossings,
- CCTV equipment for end-of-train detection,
- train control equipment.

2. Telephone service communication equipment.
- traffic control communication:
  - announcement communication,
  - train radio communication,
  - station communication,
- dispatch communication,
- conference communication.

3. Telematics-based devices (systems) concerning safety and comfort of people and goods.
- train emergency systems,
- signalling devices:
  - fire alarms,
  - anti-theft system,
  - burglar alarm,
- traction substation control devices,
- railroad switch warming devices,
- non-traction energetics control devices (station and platform lighting etc.),
- CCTV equipment for monitoring immobile and mobile railway stock.

4. Communication devices and systems related to traffic and company management.

4.3 Wired communication systems

Telephone network

Thus far, the role of communication related to traffic and company management was played by:

- general-purpose telephone network available for virtually every employee. It is a means for the employees to communicate internally and with entities outside the railway,
- telephone traffic network, for traffic-related communication, i.e. employees directly dealing with train traffic, traffic safety assurance e.g. so called train radio cammunication,

- telephone dispatch network assisting train control and management, almost exclusively used by dispatchers,
- teleconference phone network assisting operational company management.

The services provided by the aforementioned networks are still going to be useful and used in transport and company management processes.

Data transmission networks

Railway companies operate generally nationwide. Their management is computer-aided. Data required by those systems have to be collected nationwide also. In order to do that, a data transmission network is needed. Quality_of_service of data transmission has to cater for particular applications. Factors, taken into account in service quality evaluation are first and foremost the BER (*Bit Error Rate*) and data transmission latency. Preferred currently are TCP/IP-compliant convergent networks. Via that network, not only conventional data transmission services can be provided but also other teleinformatic services, which were created over the course of telecom, IT and media services convergence e.g. e-business, e-commerce, e-learning, CDN, SAN etc.

4.4 Wireless communication networks

Analogue radio communication

Wireless communication systems operating in 150 MHz band are currently used for railway needs. That band, divided into adequate number of channels is used for a range of different radio transmission technologies and applications, intended both for train control (train radio communication) as well as managing individual applications in different railway sectors (switch control radio communication, maintenance, Railroad Police etc.). Analogue communication is technically and morally outdated and increasingly expensive (due to channels in 25 kHz steps, however a change is planned to 12.5 kHz steps and in the technology itself).

GSM-R digital cellular network system

Under Polish conditions, the GSM-R system is going to be the direct successor of the aforementioned wireless communication system. The GSM-R system is a wireless convergent network, which enables voice broadcast and data transmission services. Both those services are commonly used in European railway companies, which have already implemented those systems. The technology of deploying that system without having to disrupt transport, requires introduction of additional, detailed temporary procedures. That temporary period can take least a few years.

GSM-R networks are already operational worldwide, including European countries. In the nearest future, the GSM-R is planned to be built in Poland as well. Currently used at Polish Railways communication uses 150 MHz band which reached its maximum capacity, hence does not meet today's technical requirements, norms and standards, and lacks the necessary functionalities. The quality of connection is unsatisfactory. Major difficulties start to show upon crossing the country border. Consequently, either the train radiotelephone or the locomotive has to be replaced for one, which supports the type of communication used in the given country. The UIC *(French: Union Internationale des Chemins de fer)*, or International Union of Railways envisaged predominantly the unification of European train communications systems by deploying the EIRENE project (*European Integrated Railway radio Enhanced Network*) (UIC EIRENE FRS, 2006). Implementation of GSM-R translates into tangible financial benefits for the railway industry. Railway line capacity improves substantially, border crossing time shortens to minimum. Concurrently, the service quality improves (e.g. by introducing consignment monitoring). There is a possibility to deploy applications capable of: automatic barriers control at level crossings, direct video feed from unattended railway crossings to the train driver, or voice messages communication over platform speakers. By using those solutions, train traffic safety increases considerably. Implementation of railway-dedicated mobile communication system will be the milestone for Polish railway transport, allowing it at the same time to technologically catch up Western Europe.

GSM-R is a digital cellular network system dedicated for railway transport. It provides digital voice communications and digital data transmission. It offers expanded functionalities of the GSM system. It is characterised by infrastructure located only in close proximity to rail tracks. In order to counteract electromagnetic interference, the 900 MHz frequency was used. GSM-R is intended to support deployed in Europe systems: ERTMS (*European Rail Traffic Management System*) and ETCS (*European Train Control System*), which is charged with permanent collection and transmission of rail vehicle-related data, such as speed and geographic location. GSM-R as part of ETCS mediates in transmitting information to the train driver and other rail services. By deploying the above-mentioned systems, train traffic safety increases considerably, real-time vehicle diagnostics is possible along with consignment and railroad car monitoring. Moreover, railway line capacity at individual lines substantially increases due to accurate determination of distance between trains (Bielicki Z., 2000).

Three fundamental types of cells are used in GSM-R systems. They were illustrated in figure 4.1 The first (1) are cells, which are assumed to cover only the railway line area. They are characterised by elongated shape and small width. The second (2) are cells covering station areas and partially railway lines. They are usually circular or elliptic. The third (3) are large cells, covering railway areas such as sidetracks, railway building complexes etc. Every type of cell supports all types of radiotelephones. Size and shape of cells can be altered by adjusting telepowering or using omnidirectional antennas, either broadband or linear. The GSM-R system is intended for railway applications only, thus the coverage does not exceed railway areas.

Data transmission in GSM-R provides four fundamental groups of services: text messages, main data transmission applications, automated faxes and train control applications. Text messages can be distributed in two ways: point-to-point between two users or point-to-multipoint to many users simultaneously. Data transmission service concerns remote on-board and traction devices control, automatic train control, railway vehicle traffic monitoring and passenger oriented applications. Passenger-oriented services can feature schedule information, weather information, Internet access. Known from public solutions, GPRS and EDGE packet transmission services were introduced to the GSM-R network. GSM-R normative documents stipulate minimum data transmission rate of 2.4 kbit/s. Moreover, railway communication network gives an option of implementing packet data modes such as GPRS or EDGE. Those standards were discussed in the previous chapter. In the GSM-R system, both the infrastructure and data transmission mode bear no difference to those used in public cellular networks.

Infrastructure of railway mobile communication, in principle resembles the one used in public GSM networks, however, in order to provide rail services they had to be complemented with certain elements: group call register (known also from GSM Phase 2+), functional addressing register, dispatcher centre and elements supporting the ATC (*Automatic Train Control*). GSM-R system elements communicate with each other via Signalling System No 7 (SS7) (Siemens, 2001).

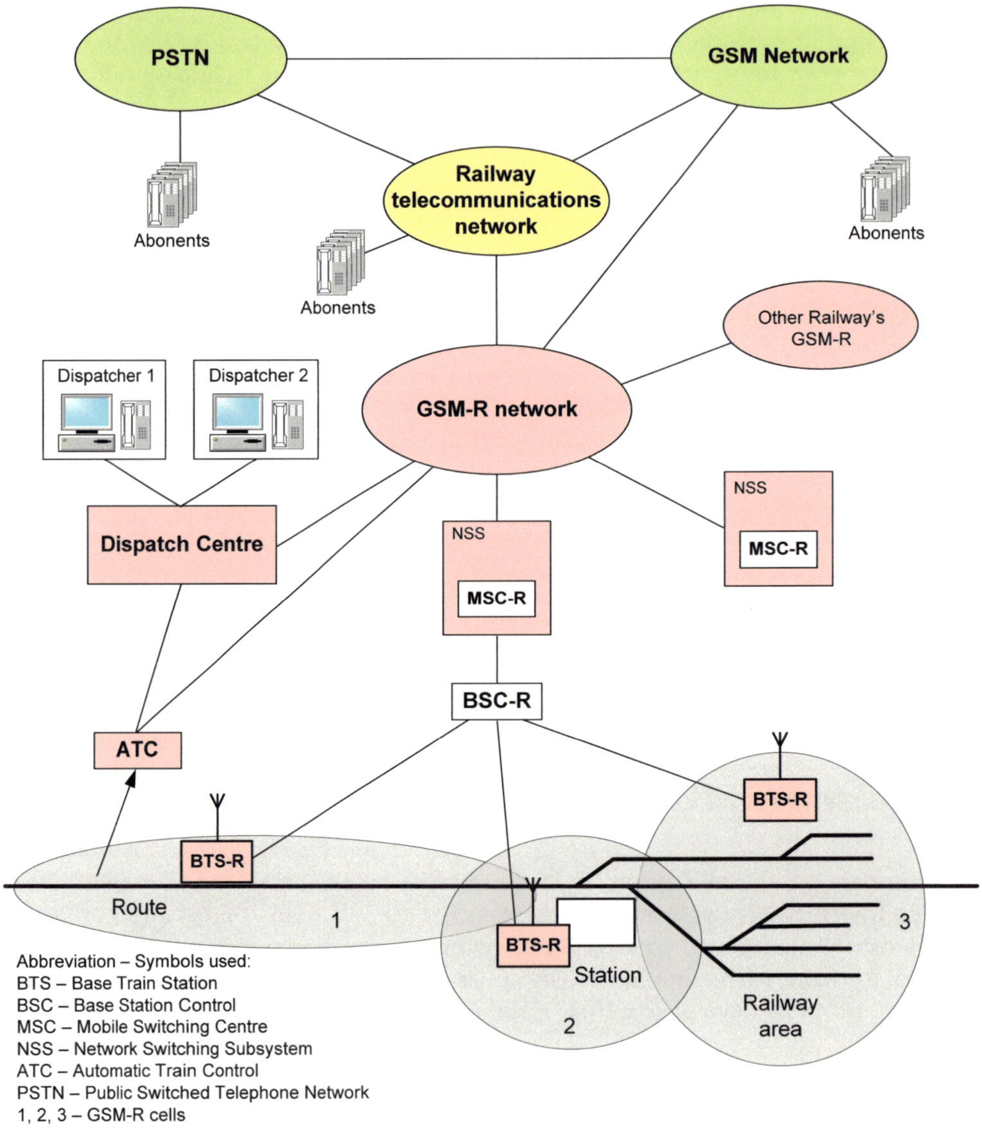

Fig. 4.1. Diagram of GSMR network at Polish Railways

Among the most important GSM-R services are (Urbanek A., 2005):

- point-to-multipoint communication, i.e. voice broadcast call

- functional addressing , where functional numbers are given to each user, by which they are identified based on their function;
- voice group call, point-to-multipoint, call set-up over a duplex connection,
- high-priority calls, which are quickly set-up. Set-up time should not exceed one second. The eMLPP (enhanced Multi-Level Precedence Pre-emption) mechanism prioritises the calls;
- position locating through transmitting short ID numbers of the base station, where the train currently is;
- emergency call. Those are calls of highest possible priority. They are made in case of an emergency.
- short message service known from public GSM networks have been deployed in railway network to i.a. transmit encoded messages, imposing execution of different actions related to railway vehicle control;
- Direct Mode communication enabling communication without a fixed mobile system infrastructure.

GSM-R can also handle diagnostic data transmission: data collection from measuring instruments located in various parts of railway vehicle, collected data bundling and transmission of collected diagnostic data over the GSM-R network to Maintenance Centre.

4.5 Teleinformatic services for railway transport

Teleinformatic and telematic services related to:

- traffic control,
- train control,
- company management,
- collaboration with carriers

Along with those services' parameters should give guidelines for building telecommunication networks catering for needs of companies operating in the railway transport sector, both the physical layer i.e. optical fibre cables and the data link layer i.e. transmission systems (e.g. SDH, Ethernet). As experience would suggest, there is currently - in every aspect - no better transmission medium than the optical fibre (broadband - several THz, low attenuation etc.). Solely on those grounds, an investor deciding to build a network of optical fibre cable should use that medium to a maximum extent. Due to Railway Company characteristic applications, broadly defined terminal devices are included in data transmission process, thus protocols of network and transport layers of the aforementioned ISO/OSI model (e.g. IP, TCP, UDP protocols) will be also used.

According to TSI requirements: "the originator of any message will be responsible for the correctness of the data content of the message at the time when the message is sent. (...) the originator of the message must make the data quality assurance check from their own resources (...) plus, where applicable, logic checks to assure the timeliness and continuity of data and messages". Data are of high quality, if they are complete, accurate, error free, accessible, timely, consistent with other sources and possess desired features i.e. are relevant, comprehensive, of proper level of detail, easy-to-interpret etc.

The data quality is mainly characterised by:

- accuracy,
- completeness,
- consistency,
- timeliness.

Accuracy

The information (data) required needs to be captured as economically as possible. This is only feasible if the primary data, which plays a decisive role in the forwarding of a consignment, a wagon or a container, is only recorded, if possible, on one single occasion for the whole transport. Therefore the primary data should be introduced into the system as close as possible to its source, e.g. on the basis of the consignment note drawn up when a wagon or a consignment is tendered for carriage, so that it can be fully integrated into any later processing operation.

Completeness

Before sending out messages the completeness and syntax must be checked using the metadata. This also avoids unnecessary information traffic on the network.

All incoming messages must also be checked for completeness using the metadata.

Consistency

The owner of the data should be clearly identified. Business rules must be implemented in order to guarantee consistency.

The type of implementation of these business rules depends on the complexity of the rule. In case of complex rules which require data from various tables, validation procedures must be implemented which check the consistency of the data version before interface data are generated and the new data version becomes operational. It must be guaranteed that transferred data are validated against the defined business rules.

Timeliness

The provision of information right in time is an important point. Every delayed data looses importance. As far as the triggering for data storage or for message sending is event driven directly from the IT system the timeliness is not a problem if the system is well designed according to the needs of the business processes. But in most of the cases the initiation of sending a message is done by an operator or at least is based on additional input from an operator (e.g. an update of train or railroad car related data). To fulfil the timeliness requirements the updating of the data must be done as soon as possible also to guarantee, that the messages will have the actual data content when sending out automatically by the system. According to TSI the response time for enquiries must be less than 5 minutes. All data updates and exchange must be done as soon as possible. The system reaction and transmission time for the update should be below 1 minute.

Currently almost all teleinformatic services have to be protected against:

- data modification,
- data destruction,
- data interception.

Due to its core activity, Infrastructure Manager has to prioritise data security issues. All data concerning controlling, monitoring, and management of train traffic have to be protected at each layer of the ISO/OSI model. Perhaps train control devices and systems are equipped with autonomous security systems, nonetheless data transmission process has to be secured. Other systems e.g. company management aiding systems should also be protected, because they contain critical company data, e.g.:

- financial data,
- development plans,
- pricing plans,
- network topology,
- device authentication data etc.,

or companies are legally obliged to protect them - e.g. personal data.

Telecommunication services, which are and will soon be provided to the Infrastructure Manager, can be listed as follows:

- telematic services (control, monitoring),
- telephone services,
- data transmission services,
- information services,
- multimedia services (e.g. videoconference).

Competition, clients and technical advancement induce informatisation of the Infrastructure Manager i.e. deployment of ERP, CRM class systems or other, aimed at improving company competitiveness. Company informatisation has its share in reducing overheads through so called database services. They require the data to be constantly available and always up-to-date. In order to assure both, IT devices are needed e.g. servers and teleinformatic networks.

Among database services, which are set to become tools used in a company acting in capacity of Infrastructure Manager are:

- Data Centre - various databases e.g. clients database, assets database, employee database etc. Databases have to be systematically updated.
- Recovery Data Centre - recovery databases, which have to be synchronised with the main database.
- Content Delivery Network - servers, databases containing information for:
  - clients,
  - employees,
  - business partners.

In those cases, data access through telephone is limited to relevant groups of interest.

- Storage Area Network - well-protected memory resources warehouses placed in adequately adapted rooms. Those warehouses store data, which are available exclusively to data owners.
- Industry portal - contains information about a company's commercial activity in terms of completed tenders for services or supply of materials and devices. Companies, which would like to offer their services to or collaborate with the PKP PLK company, can

advertise through that portal. Their offers may concern e.g. supply of materials, provision of services, prices, ads etc.

- B2B e-commerce. This service allows buying, selling and payments online.
- Contact Centre - is a touchpoint, an interface of a service provider - in this case PKP PLK - with the client. Currently, this service has strong growth dynamics worldwide.
- E-learning - a service useful in training staff, allowing to communicate e.g. rationale behind board's or senior employees' decisions.
- Virtual Private Network - virtual application-dedicated networks. This service substantially increases application security, at least because of limited access (only authorised users/entities can access the application).

Generally all the above-mentioned services can be provided through adequately designed, TCP/IP-compliant convergent network equipped with powerful hardware. Adequately designed and equipped TCP/IP network is capable of assuring equally adequate security:

- infrastructure security (connection and node redundancy with specific switch-over times in physical, connection and network layers),
- data security - thanks to relevant devices (BER appropriately low, below 10^{-12} - practically of $10^{-15}\div10^{-17}$ order), IPSec type protocols, TLS etc., and using appropriate encryption of key size up to 256 bits.
- data traffic security - thanks to adequate architectures and protocols (Diffserv, MPLS, RSVP -*Resource reSerVation Protocol* enabling traffic engineering e.g. multiple priority queue management.

5. Communication networks in air traffic management systems

5.1 Introduction

Air transport is one of those transport sectors, which experience dramatic growth in provided transport services. Increased demand for both people and goods transport causes air operations volume to grow by over a dozen percent year-on-year.

For many years, a solution to the airspace capacity problem have been on agenda of air traffic engineers. The underlying assumption, however, is that no action they undertake, can cause decrease in air traffic safety and high probability of air collisions. Hence a higher number of aircrafts within individual sectors, is only acceptable should concurrently data transmission systems, informing about situation in individual sectors of airways be improved.

The ever-increasing air traffic volumes, entails the necessity to modify existing air traffic management systems. The changes on the table are of organisational and procedural nature, and involve modifications to existing ICT-aided management systems, used to assure smooth and safe air traffic. Commercial aviation is possible thanks to aeronautical fixed telecommunication networks, as they enable data exchange between groundcrew, without which aviation could not operate. It is the groundcrew, between which over 90% of information related to flight safety is exchanged. Collection of atmosphere and airport-related information, services availability, imposed restrictions and subsequent teletype message transfer is possible due to aeronautical fixed telecommunication networks. Flight plan reporting and processing, air traffic control coordination are merely a part of the entire torrent of information (Sadowski P., Siergiejczyk M., 2009).

The notion of aeronautical communication is mostly associated with air-ground communications. In reality, an equally important and even more extensive are ground data networks. In order to assure a safe flight, all services need to communicate with each other, namely: aeronautical information service, weather station, air traffic controllers, and many other airspace users. Network technology heavily influenced the way information is being exchanged today in air transport. That is because computer networks enable creating, expanding and modernising ground systems assuring smooth and safe air traffic. Development of aeronautical telecommunication networks aims to integrate networks and services operating as parts of national air traffic control systems, and in the future to extend those solutions to airborne aircrafts.

5.2 Telecommunication networks in air traffic management

The X.25 protocol was a widely used communications protocol in aviation. It was used in backbone networks transmitting teletype messages - AFTN, SITA, OLDI *(On Line Data Interchange)* systems, radar data transmission systems (ASTERIX over X.25) and aircraft charging systems used by the *Central Route Charges Office* (CRCO).

The The AFTN (*Aeronautical Fixed Telecommunications Network*) network uses an old technology - telex. The AFTN messages transmission protocol is a set of rules, which guarantees consistency of exchanged data and provision of information to receivers according to hash tables. This protocol derives from obsolete (still used in aviation and marine NAVTEX system, delivering meteorological information) ITA2-based teletype transmission mechanisms. All air traffic control services are main AFTN users, who predominantly request information about filed flight plans and flight status (take-off, delay, landing), emergency situations and issues teletype messages concerning take-off, delays and landing. Meteorological offices provide AFTN with TAF and METAR teletype messages, using information from other offices themselves. NOTAM offices generate NOTAM and SNOWTAM teletype messages. Briefing offices feed NOTAM, SNOWTAM, TAF and METAR information to the pilots. Airline operators often have their own operating divisions, which use the same information as briefing offices do. Civil aviation and the air force authorities also own AFTN terminals. The CFMU (*Central Flow Management Unit*) - European air traffic management system, which issues slots - is predominantly communicated with via AFTN (Sadowski P., Siergiejczyk M., 2009).

A modernised version of AFTN, which breaks with the telex tradition, is the CIDIN (*Common ICAO Data Interchange Network*). Development of that solution had begun already during the 80's, however, it is being implemented into commercial use now - CIDIN was implemented in Warsaw in May 2002. From the AFTN end-user perspective, introduction of CIDIN entailed swapping an old computer terminal for a more modern one, equipped with characteristic liquid crystal display. Real changes came in form of data transmission method. CIDIN brings civil aeronautical network closer to the standard, internet user have long been familiar with. The previously used standard was the telex protocol, however, currently the network is based on either TCP or IP X.25. It resulted in considerably higher data transmission capacity and reliability - max capacity is currently 64 kbps. Both in Poland and most countries in the world, the standard is 9600 bps - completely sufficient at current network usage intensity.

The OLDI (*On Line Data Interchange*) system is responsible for communication between neighbouring traffic control areas. Precisely speaking - interconnected air traffic control systems. It replaced voice information exchange concerning control hand-off over aircrafts en route (EUROCONTROL/IANS, 2006). The system leans on exchanging i.a. ABI (*Advanced Boundary Information*) teletype messages - informing the ATC (*Air Traffic Control*) system about an aircraft approaching the handover point.

Due to low data transmission error level, it could be used for connections characterised by low technical parameters. The protocol's drawback was its feature - connectivity. Prior to data transmission, connection between communicating devices had to be established by using a dedicated connection.

Due to current development of local and wide area network infrastructure and used high-reliability transmission media, Air Traffic Management (ATM) systems are being introduced with datagram data transmission technologies. Wide area networks can be built as multi-component structures thanks to the IP protocol. Those structures are built using different technologies - both standard and very unconventional. That flexibility is possible due to developed network protocol stacks (TCP/IP), which is supported by the majority of hardware and software platforms.

The above-mentioned actions cause the X.25 protocol to be withdrawn from many aviation applications in favour of the IP protocol. Another powerful fact acting to disadvantage of the X.25 protocol, is that manufacturers of hardware (X.25 switches) supporting the protocol discontinued their sale and the technical support for X.25 solutions will have been unavailable by the end of the XXI century's first decade (EUROCONTROL/IANS, 2006).

Because aeronautical data transmission is inherent to ATM, the above-mentioned factors affect considerably air traffic management systems (ATM). Thus, many key for ATM systems will be subject to modification in the future, in a bid to adapt them to IP data exchange technology. Among the systems, which first should undergo modification are:

- surveillance data distribution systems: ARTAS, RMCDE (*Radar Message Conversion and Distribution Equipment*), ASTERIX-compatible radar stations (*All Purpose Structured Eurocontrol Surveillance Information Exchange*),
- aeronautical teletype message distribution and airport planning systems
- existing: AFTN, CIDIN, WPPL,
- implemented at PAŻP (*Polish Air Navigation Services Agency*): TRAFFIC (PANSA, 2008),
- weather information distribution systems,
- air traffic control systems: PEGASUS_21 (PANSA, 2009),
- airspace management system: CAT (*Common Airspace Tools*) (PANSA, 2008),
- aircraft charging system: CRCO.

5.3 The concept of IP protocol migration and implementation into ATM systems

In 2001 at EUROCONTROL the IPAX working group was set-up to develop a plan of IP protocol migration and implementation into ATM systems. It was charged with adapting industrial standards of packet (IP) data transmission to data exchange standards in ATM/CNS systems (*Air Traffic Management / Communication Navigation Surveillance*). IPAX group's action plan included:

- transition from X.25 network layers to IP with its integral security mechanisms,
- modification of existing applications and systems so they would be compliant with secure IP networks (developing interfaces of existing systems with IP networks),
- maintaining application interfaces for operational users in order to protect investments put into ATM systems.

One of the earliest modifications made in relation to X.25 protocol replacement with the IP protocol, was the change implemented into the OLDI (*On-Line Data Interchange*) system. The OLDI system has been operating using the X.25 protocol, which was implemented with a higher layer protocol - FDE (*Flight Data Exchange*). Due to X.25 layer replacement with the IP layer, the higher layer protocol was also reimplemented. In order to adapt the OLDI system to packet data transmission, the FDE protocol was replaced by the FMTP protocol (*Flight Message Transfer Protocol*) (EUROCONTROL, 2008).

ANSP (*Aeronautical Service Provider*) centres across Europe are envisaged to ultimately be introduced with that change. Its deployment overlaps with requirements stipulated by the FDE/ICD (*Flight Data Exchange/Interface Control Document*) and it is the fundamental requirement of the COM-04 objective contained by the ECIP (*European Convergence and Implementation Plan*) document. During transition to FMTP, Eurocontrol will support FDE-based solutions (OLDI over X.25) until OLDI over TCP/IP is activated Europe-wide (see figure 5.1.).

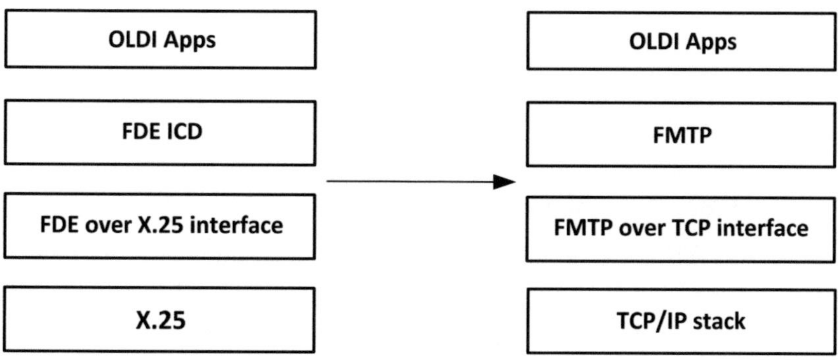

Fig. 5.1. FMTP implementation into OLDI system

The other large-scale change is modification of aeronautical teletype message distribution system - AFTN/CIDIN ground-ground network. That network is currently the main medium for flight plan forwarding and exchange of airport planning related data. That change aims to migrate the X.25 technology - used for establishing inter-centre backbone connections - to IP technology using AMHS (*ATS Message Handling System*) gateways. The IPAX group set about deploying that solution in PEN (Pan European Network). The task aims to build a global IP network supporting data exchange between air traffic management systems.

The system intended to replace the AFTN/CIDIN network uses the X.400 protocol implemented in IP networks. X.400 and AFTN network will be linked over the transition period via gateways converting teletype messages format between protocols - AMHS/AFTN GATEWAYS (Sadowski P., Siergiejczyk M., 2009). In figure 2.2 illustrates AMHS/AFTN network architecture.

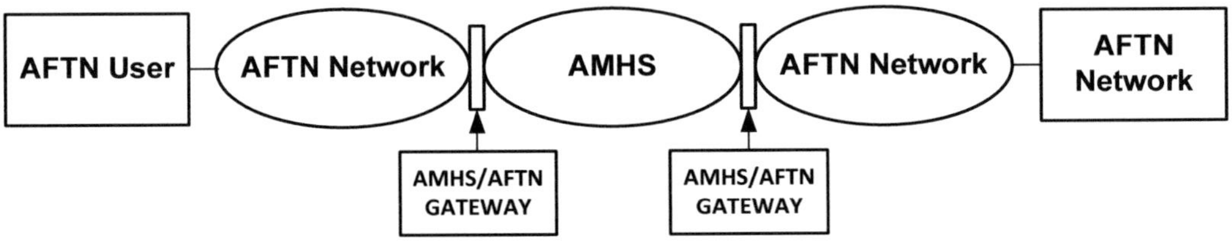

Fig. 5.2. AMHS/AFTN network architecture

In order to assure continuous operation and interoperability of two heterogeneous systems, AMHS/AFTN gateways have to have the following functionalities:

- two-way teletype message conversion,
- AFTN and AMHS teletype messages mapping and redirection
- connection to external AFTN/CIDIN centres and AMHS gateways,
- syntax validation and error correction,
- teletype message tracking and network traffic logging,
- API (Application Interface) for interoperability with other IT systems.

The AFTN protocol has many limitations. AFTN network adaptation to IP standards - and in higher layers to X.400 - yields a range of benefits, amongst which are i.a.:

- binary message forwarding,
- unlimited message size (1800 characters per AFTN message).

5.4 IP protocol in surveillance data distribution

ARTAS (*Advanced Radar Tracker and Server*) is a system designed to establish an accurate air traffic picture and to distribute the relevant surveillance information to community of user systems. It is a surveillance data distribution system using tracks (radar data reports about aircraft position). The ARTAS system has a distributed architecture, composed of co-operating subsystems, called ARTAS Units, which form a consistent estimate of air traffic situation, based on radar data reports. Radar data are collected from ARTAS Unit-connected radars (primary and secondary) either through the RMCDE (*Radar Message Conversion Distribution Equipment*) devices or directly. ARTAS Units and RMCDE devices are connected to the LAN/WAN network and can communicate over

TCP/IP protocols. ARTAS Units were implemented with the following functionalities (EUROCONTROL/IANS, 2007):

- tracker – processes radar data and presents the most current, air traffic situation, based on radar data reports,
- server – provides track and radar data to online users, and forwards radar data to the tracker.
- system manager – administers the ARTAS system.

ARTAS connections require constant data stream transmission, hence PVCs (*Permanent Virtual Circuits*) are used. Assuring continuity of data transmission is a significant issue. Routing mechanisms ensure possibly low redundancy. System nodes are connected by many alternative routes. In addition, every radar station has at least two connection points with the core network. Communication is established through access networks, which are independent for each node. Illustrated in figure 5.4 is the communication architecture between ARTAS Unit modules – ARTAS surveillance data distribution system.

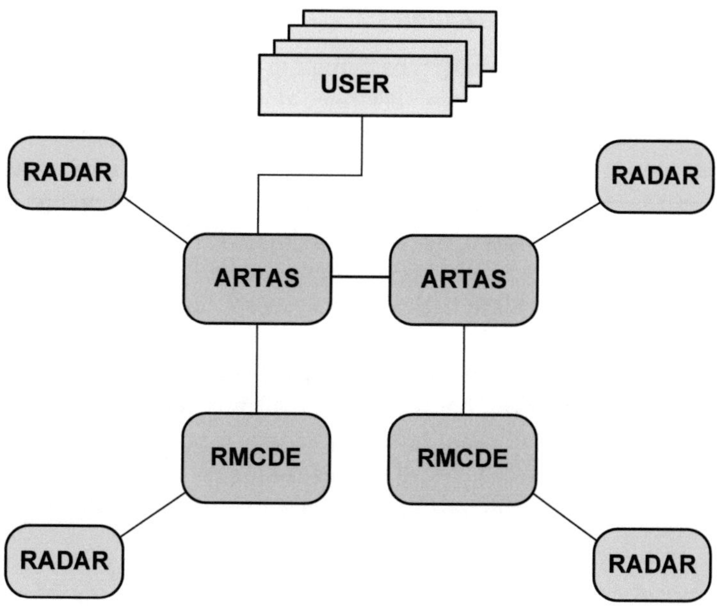

Fig. 5.3. ARTAS architecture

ARTAS modules communicate via a LAN/WAN network. ARTAS-connected users communicate with the modules also via TCP/IP protocols. ARTAS Units - kilometres from each other - are connected to a wide area network, and communicate via TCP/IP protocol stack.

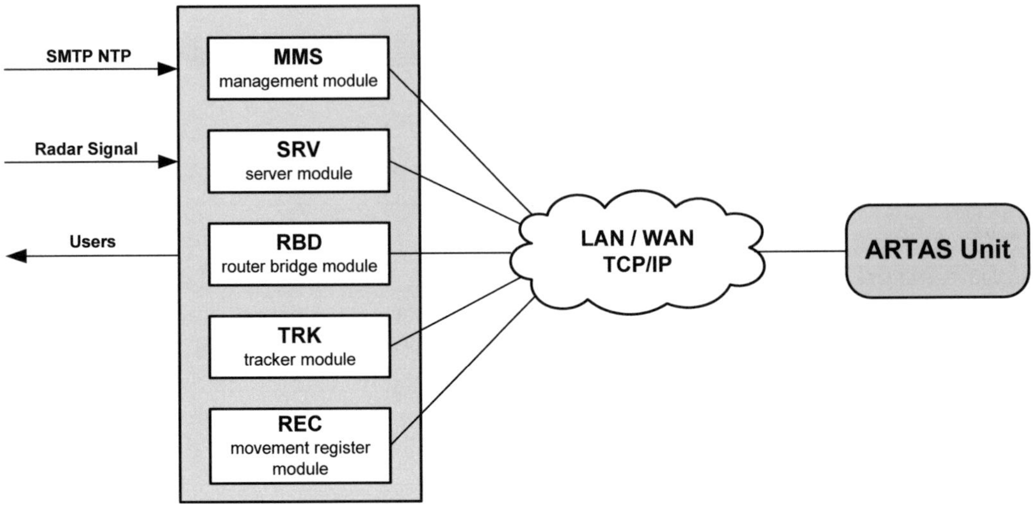

Fig. 5.4. ARTAS modules

5.5 Fibre channel over IP in civil aviation

SAN networks are centrepiece of creating backup data centres and efficient backup systems, due to high-volume data transactions between devices composing the solution. The technology central to implementation of SAN networks is the Fibre Channel protocol. It is a high-speed, serial dedicated interface connecting servers and mass-storage devices. Fibre Channel is a hybrid protocol i.e. network and channel protocol, defined as open ANSI and OSI standard. The channel is a closed and predictable mechanism transmitting data between a limited number of units. A typically set-up channel usually requires very little input for subsequent transfers, thus providing high efficiency. Very little decisions are made over the course of data transmission, enabling the channels to be established by the physical layer. The most popular channel protocols are SCSI (*Small Computer System Interface*) and HPPI (*High Performance Parallel Interface*). Networks are relatively less predictable. They adapt to changeable environment and can process many nodes, however, establishing communication channels between those nodes requires more decisions, resulting in significantly higher latencies compared to channel transmission (Sadowski P., Siergiejczyk M., 2009).

Fibre Channel model consists of 7 layers. Layer models (commonly known seven-layer ISO/OSI model) enable single layer operation, independently of the layer immediately beneath. Fibre Channel's layers meet ISO/OSI model specification and are divided into two groups: physical and signalisation layers (0-2) - FC-PH and Upper Layers (3-4) (Janikowski A. (2002).

FCIP (*Fibre Channel over IP*) is a mechanism tunnelling the FC (*Fibre Channel*) mechanism used in SAN (*Storage Area Networks*) in IP wide area networks. Such solution enables communication between scattered data centres, using secure network infrastructures (using

SSL, IPSec etc. mechanisms). FCIP protocol causes rapid development of wide area data exchange and storage networks, increasing at the same time capabilities and efficiency of built systems. Due to range of existing IP networks, FCIP enables building global data storage systems. In figure 5.5 is presented SAN architecture of ARMS and TRAFFIC systems.

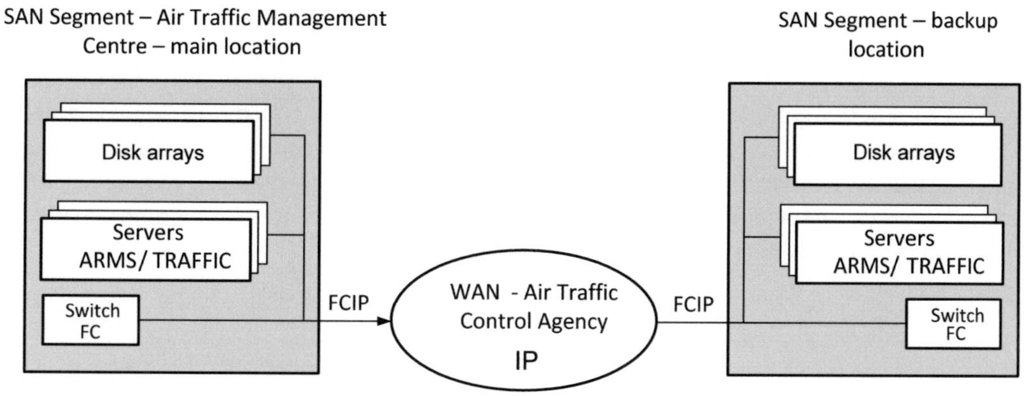

Fig. 5.5. SAN architecture of ARMS and TRAFFIC systems

Advantage of SAN/FCIP-enabled data transmission systems is first and foremost low cost of establishing connections over long distances and IP-native data encryption. Disadvantages of FCIP-enabled systems include data transmission latencies due to IP networks' characteristics and that transmission disruptions (connection malfunction) cause SAN network segments' segmentation.

Architecture design of SAN (fabric - segment of the SAN network) ARMS and TRAFFIC systems envisages interoperability enabling exchange of construction data, planned and real airspace restrictions. One of functional and technical requirements (PANSA, 2008). is the concept of a backup data storage centre, both for transactional and archival databases. That requirement is met with the Fibre Channel SAN architecture with data matrix relocated by the FCIP protocol outside the Air Traffic Management Centre. The concept of a backup data storage centre intended for an Air Traffic Management Agency is presented in figure 5.5.

Reconfiguration of existing systems, so they would use IP networks for data transmission, is aimed at achieving global interoperability of air traffic management systems. Unification of aeronautical data processing and exchange technologies is necessary to reach that objective. That process will have positive bearing on data processing time and will eliminate irregularities, which cause delays and inconsistency of air operations. Interoperable data exchange technologies used in ATM systems, will render feasible airspace unification programmes in Europe (SES - Single European Sky) and globally. The global AFTN message exchange network is a salient example. Its migration to AMHS standards, maintaining old infrastructure elements, enables forwarding teletype messages about planned air operations. In dramatic cases they originate from technologically out-dated teletype terminals and are fed to highly advanced AMHS systems.

6. Summary

An important issue facing transport in general is information exchange between supply chain actors. Enabling that information to be transmitted, requires creating data (information) exchange touch points (interfaces) and determining access privileges and methods for different entities participating in transport processes.

The ever-expanding range of applications for telematic systems poses - thus far difficult to evaluate - a potential, future risk to undisturbed functioning of transport telematic systems. The telematics-induced "networkisation" and integration of computer systems present a tangible and ever-increasing threat of both novel attacks taking advantage of network access and deliberate damage to critical system elements. Further development of telematics should take place in line with the "Fail-Safe" rule.

Systematic implementations of telematic technologies cause telematic systems to become a viable consideration for development of multimodal transport. A potentially limiting factor here can be the trend to use a single transport system in transport planning. However, one of the biggest obstacles impeding further development of transport telematics is the technology integration of different systems. This problem is driven by fast-paced innovation and mostly inadequate standardisation.

Touch points of different systems have to be normalised, functions and services standardised and costs analysed, all in a bid to allow such integration. It can stifle, however, development prospects for transport telematics. The solution comes in form of a gradual standardisation system, compatible at each stage. Benefits reaped from deployment of transport telematic systems could not be quantified, until their impact and results are recognised. Also, a line has to be drawn between telematics-related benefits for transport, environment, economy and the society, hence providing reasons for detailed economic analysis scrutinising implementation of transport telematic systems.

Providing telematic services supporting transport tasks and processes is one of fundamental tasks of transport telematic systems. The quality of telematic services in transport depends on network integrity, understood as the offered service being independent of the access method and the communications protocol. Regardless of how information is transmitted to the user, the service provided has to maintain constant parameters. Service quality of a telematic service should remain the same at different locations. Thus, a need arises to create and analyse functional-operating models in terms of availability and continuity of telematic services in transport.

The other problem obstructing further development of transport telematics is the typically long time of implementing the system. Deployment time often exceeds the total time needed to develop a new technology. Hence, as practice shows, a system might become technologically outdated by the time it is mature enough for practical applications. Effective technologies, however, should not be replaced by newer solutions if telematics was to develop. Many sectors manage to continue using obsolete, but proven technologies to their advantage, because a transition to new technologies would be too financially strenuous (e.g. flight and railway security).

7. References

Bielicki Z. (2000). Pan-European Communications. New signals no. 4. KOW, ISSN 1732-8101 Warsaw, Poland

EUROCONTROL (2008). Eurocontrol guidelines for implementation support (EGIS) Part 5 Communication & Navigation Specifications Chapter 13 Flight Message Transfer Protocol (FMTP). Eurocontrol, Belgium

EUROCONTROL/IANS (2006). Training activities COM-DATA. Eurocontrol Luxemburg.

EUROCONTROL/IANS (2007). Training activities: ARTAS, Eurocontrol Luxemburg

European Parliament and Council (2001). Directive 2001/16/EC of the 19 March 2001 on the interoperability of the trans-European conventional rail system.

Gago S., Siergiejczyk M. (2006). Service convergence in railway-dedicated IP networks. "Telecommunications and IT for Railway". Polish Chamber of Products and Services for Railway (CD), January 2006, Szczyrk, Poland

Janikowski A. (2002). Fibre Channels outlined. NetWorld no. 3. IDG PH, ISSN 1232-8723, Warsaw, Poland

KAREN (2000). Foundation for Transport Telematics deployment in the 21st Century. Framework Architecture for ITS. European Commission Telematics Applications Programme (DGXIII/C6). Brussels.

Klein L.A. (2001). Sensor Technologies and date requirements for ITS. Publisher Artech House ITS Library, ISBN 1-58053- 077-X, Boston, USA, London, England

Ochociński K. (2006). Technical Specifications for Interoperability for Telematic Applications for Freight (TSI TAF). SIRTS and CNTK seminar, 07.2006, Warsaw, Poland

PANSA (2008). System TRAFFIC. Functional and Technological Specifications (FTS), Warsaw, Poland

PANSA (2009). Materials provided by the Polish Air Navigation Services Agency. Warsaw, Poland

Pogrzebski, H. (2005). Functions of the TAF-TSI specification – planning procedure and train preparation. TTS Rail Transport Technology. R. 11, no. 11. EMI-PRESS, ISSN: 1232-3829, Lodz, Poland

Sadowski P., Siergiejczyk M. (2009). IP networks for air traffic management systems. Telecommunication Review and Telecommunication News no. 8-9. ISSN 1230-3496. Sigma NOT PH, Warsaw, Poland

Siemens (2001). GSM-R Wireless Communication. New Signals no. 29, KOW, ISSN 1732-8101, Warsaw, Poland

Siergiejczyk M. (2009). Exploitation Effectiveness of Transport Systems Telematics. Scientific Works of Warsaw University of Technology. Transport Series. Issue No. 67. Publisher: OW PW. ISSN 1230-9265, Warsaw, Poland

Siergiejczyk M., Gago S. (2008). Teleinformatic platform for data transmission in cargo transport. Logistics no. 4. Publisher: Institute of Logistics and Warehousing , ISSN 1231-5478, Poznan, Poland

UIC EIRENE FRS (2006). Functional Requirements Specification. PSA167D005-7 International Union of Railways, Paris, France

UIC Leaflet No. 407-1 (2009). Standardised data exchange between infrastructures for international trains. International Union of Railways, Paris, France

Urbanek A. (2005). GSM-R Rail communication. NetWorld no. 1. IDG PH, ISSN 1232-8723, Warsaw, Poland

Wawrzyński W. (1997). Transport telematics - conceptual range and fields of application. Transportation Digest no. 11. ISSN: 0033-2232, Warsaw, Poland

Wawrzyński W., Siergiejczyk M. et al. (2007). KBN 5T12C 066 25 grant final report. Telematics-enabled transport - methods of using telematics in transport. Project manager: Prof. W.Wawrzyński, PhD Eng., Warsaw January.

Wydro K. B. (2003). Dataflow analysis in Intelligent Transport Systems. Research and development paper. Communications Institute Publishing House, Warsaw, Poland

7

Critical Role of 'T-Shaped Skills & Incentive Rewards' as Determinants for Knowledge Management Enablers: A Case of Indian Study

Abdul Hafeez-Baig and Raj Gururajan
School of Information Systems, Faculty of Business and Law, University of Southern Queensland, Toowoomba, Queensland, Australia

1. Introduction

Knowledge management (KM) plays an important role for organisations. It involves activities such as creating, acquiring, sharing and managing knowledge at individual and organizational levels (Alavi & Leidner, 2001). Knowledge and knowledge management are both multi-faceted concepts and activities, and strongly related to cultural background (Bock et al., 2005). In this context, Srinivas (2009) indicates that the theories of knowledge management generated—based on western cultural background—are not necessarily applicable to eastern cultures such as India.

Currently, KM is providing a better understanding of its success factors; and KM approaches are more focused to address particular challenges such as securing knowledge from experts leaving an organisation (Heisig, 2009). However, issues and factors that enable or facilitate an organisation to further enhance its knowledge management are essential elements in the decision making process of managers and executives (Lee & Choi, 2003; Gan, 2006; Khalifa & Liu, 2003; Emelo, 2009). The enablers for organisations in implementing their knowledge management systems were proposed and discussed in the literature (Lee & Choi, 2003; Yu et al., 2004; Robbins et al., 2001). However, most of the studies focused on only few factors. Therefore, building a theoretical framework to understand these factors and their influences is necessary to form a new starting point for comprehensive understanding (Heisig, 2009). Additionally, researchers indicated that a majority of these factors/enablers were based on western countries—which is different from the Asian context (Chaudry, 2005; Srinivas, 2009). In a rapidly developing country such as India, where the management system in organisations is markedly different to that of western styles, the question of 'whether the enablers still influence the implementation of knowledge management systems in the same way?' is still under debate. This research issue is significant because cultural issues appear to influence aspects of management decision making. Our review of the literature also indicated there is very limited information regarding KM in the Indian context.

As the seventh largest country and the second most populous country in the world, economic reforms since 1991 have transformed India into one of the fastest growing economies (ERS, 2009). The Indian subcontinent is identified with its commercial and cultural wealth in much of its long history (Oldenburg, 2007). Four major religions, Hinduism, Buddhism, Jainism and Sikhism originated here, while Zoroastrianism, Judaism, Christianity and Islam arrived in the first millennium CE and shaped the region's diverse culture. India is a republic consisting of 28 states and seven union territories, with a parliamentary system of democracy. It has the world's twelfth largest economy at market exchange rates and the fourth largest in purchasing power (2009). Long traditions, combined with an advanced educated pool of managers and strong yet conservative management practices, indicate that KM enablers might be different for India. Thus, this study posed the question, 'What are the enablers for implementing knowledge management systems in India?'

In this study, a theoretical model for KM enablers was constructed in order to reach a more comprehensive understanding of the research issue. This model is based on a review of the literature and a multiple case study with 80 organisations in four Indian cities. These cities are located in metropolitan and regional areas with various population sizes, social structures and history. Subsequently, the initial model developed was examined by a survey in the same cities with larger samples. This is explained further in the following sections.

2. Literature review[1]

The detailed literature review provided herein consists of three sections. In the first section, the basic concepts and definitions of knowledge, knowledge management, and knowledge management systems are provided. In the second section, the organisational outcomes that may be influenced by implementing knowledge management systems are presented. Subsequent to this, the enablers of knowledge management systems are gathered and discussed as the foundation for the theoretical model proposed in this study.

2.1 Knowledge management & KMS

Although knowledge and knowledge management are complex and multi-faceted concepts (Alavi & Leidner, 2001), knowledge management has become increasingly important in today's highly competitive business environment. For example, knowledge assets of organisations have played a crucial role in this shift and are viewed as being increasingly important in knowledge management (Yelden & Albers, 2004). Further, in the knowledge-based view of the firm, knowledge is the foundation of a firm's competitive advantage and, ultimately, the primary driver of a firm's value (Bock et al., 2005; Gan, 2006). Researchers have provided definitions to better understand the concepts of knowledge and knowledge management. For example, knowledge management has been defined as the process of capturing, storing, sharing, and using knowledge (Davenport & Prusak, 1998). KM is also the systematic and explicit management of knowledge-related activities, practices, programs and policies within the enterprise (KM, 1997), or the art of creating value to organisations by leveraging intangible assets (Sveiby, 1997). Accordingly, knowledge is defined as a justified belief that increases an entity's capacity for effective action (Alavi & Leidner, 2001; Huber, 2001). Knowledge can be further viewed as a state of mind; an object; a process; a condition of having access to information; or a capability (Alavi & Leidner, 2001).

---

[1] The theme of literature and methodology adopted in this study is similar to authors' previous publications in the KMS domain.

To manage knowledge assets more effectively, knowledge management systems are the IT-based platform designed for facilitating KM by providing larger databases, more powerful computation ability, higher performance data structures, and smarter query techniques (Weber et al., 2001). Knowledge management systems (KMS) refer to a class of information systems applied to managing organisational knowledge. It is defined as IT-based systems developed to support and enhance the organizational processes of knowledge creation, storage/retrieval, transfer and application (Alavi & Leidner, 2001; Li & Tsai, 2009). The main function of KMS is to guide employees in obtaining useful information from knowledge bases and make existing experiences freely available to other employees of an organisation (Abdullah et al., 2005). The final goals of KMS are to employ many different techniques to represent knowledge, with the aim of enhancing the decision-making capability of human decision-makers (Cowie et al., 2009). According to recent studies (Li & Tsai, 2009), KMS have proven to be efficient and effective in organising large volumes of high-complexity knowledge.

Some studies have explored various aspects of KMS. For example, several aspects of KMS should be taken into consideration in implementing KM in an organisation (Li & Tsai, 2009), namely: (1) how to transfer tacit knowledge to explicit knowledge; (2) how to retrieve desired knowledge from knowledge bases; (3) how to visualize knowledge; and (4) how to create more valuable knowledge by reuse. Furthermore, with the rapid development of wireless technologies, new research issues are gaining prominence. For example, in a mobile and networked environment, solutions regarding how to provide up-to-date, context specific information to whom and where, is appropriate (Cowie et al., 2009). Another example is how to use mobile clinical support systems to address different intelligent decision support such as knowledge delivery on demand, medication advice, therapy reminders, preliminary clinical assessment for classifying treatment categories and providing alerts regarding potential drugs interactions and active linking to relevant medical conditions (Cowie et al., 2009). These requirements, emanating from new technological developments, have fostered the study of KMS to a new stage. One important research issue is how knowledge management systems influence the outcomes of organisations.

2.2 KM and organisational outcomes

Knowledge management promotes efficiency and optimal use of resources to achieve organisational goals. This awareness is creating new interest in KM solutions that have the potential to improve business performance (Lamont, 2009). For example, there are numerous cases where international companies have demonstrated that by successfully applying KM it will improve organisational competitiveness and performance (Wong & Aspirwall, 2006). In a fast-changing environment, knowledge processes are the most precious resources in sustaining and enhancing long-term organisational competitiveness (Song, 2002).

Determining key outcomes of implementing KMS in organisations appears to be difficult. These outcomes include achieving organisational efficiency, competitive advantage, maximising organisational potential and better management of knowledge assets (Gan, 2006). The first organisational outcome which can be enhanced by implementing KMS is competitive advantage. A firm's competitive advantage depends first and foremost on its knowledge: on what it knows, how it uses what it knows, and how fast it can know something new (Prusak, 1997). For example, to ensure continued competitive advantage, organisations need to fully understand both their customers and competitors (North et al., 2004; Al-Hawamdeh, 2002). Customers are an integral component of the organisation's intellectual capital and is the reason for the organisation's existence (Stewart, 1997). To ensure that an organisation effectively leverages this intellectual capital with regard to their customers, information technology solutions such as customer relationship management (CRM) are useful to manage whatever knowledge of customers the organisation possesses (Probst et al., 2000). Another organisational outcome that can be enhanced is to maximise organisational potential by implementing KMS. For knowledge-intensive organisations, the main driver in maximising the value of its research and development endeavours and investments is through recycling and reusing experiments and results obtained (Al-Hawamdeh, 2002). Companies such as 3M and BP maximised organisational potential from effective knowledge management to achieve successes in their respective competitive industries (Cortada & Woods, 1999).

A KMS also assists an organisation to manage knowledge assets in a comprehensive way. Knowledge has become a central focus of most organisations these days. As a result, managing knowledge assets—finding, cultivating, storing, disseminating and sharing them—has become the most important economic task of employees in any organisation (Stewart et al., 2000). Notwithstanding the above outcomes, studies increasingly indicate that organisational outcomes could be enhanced by implementing knowledge management systems (Lamont, 2009). Therefore, an understanding of the obstacles and enablers of implementing KMS may be helpful as the starting point in further understanding this issue.

2.3 Obstacles and enablers of implementing KMS

Previous studies indicated that when organisations implement their knowledge management systems, some obstacles and enablers exist in the process. For example, many firms actively limit knowledge sharing because of the threats associated with industrial espionage, as well as concerns about diverting or overloading employees' work-related attention (Constant et al., 1996). Once knowledge sharing is limited across an organisation, the likelihood increases that knowledge gaps will arise, and these gaps are likely to produce less-than-desirable work outcomes (Bock et al., 2005). Despite the fact that organisations may reward their employees for effective knowledge management practices, this may create obstacles for knowledge management. One example is that some organisations provide pay-for-performance compensation schemes, which may also serve to discourage knowledge sharing if employees believe that knowledge sharing will hinder their personal efforts to distinguish themselves relative to their co-workers (Huber, 2001). Further, there are major challenges in promoting the transfer and integration of explicit and tacit knowledge between channel members, including: lack of recipient's cognitive capacity; lack of the sender's credibility; lack of motivation of the sender or the recipient; the existence of an arduous relationship between the sender and recipient; and causal ambiguity due to the complexity of knowledge (Frazier, 2009; Szulanski & Jensen, 2006).

Recent studies have attempted to provide guidelines and successful experiences to reduce obstacles. For instance, there are four areas that need to be focused on when implementing knowledge management systems. These areas include (Emelo, 2009): understanding who the knowledge sources are; measuring where and how knowledge flows; facilitating knowledge to flow more rapidly and freely; and reinforcing knowledge with supportive relationships. Additionally, a review of the literature reveals that there are many enablers that are known to influence knowledge management practices (Gan, 2006). These enablers can be broadly classified into either a social or technical perspective. The social perspective of knowledge management enablers plays an important role and has been widely acknowledged (Smith, 2004). These enablers are further discussed below.

One enabler is collaboration, which is considered an important feature in knowledge management adoption. It is defined as the degree to which people in a group actively assist one another in their tasks (Lee & Choi, 2003). A collaborative culture in the workplace influences knowledge management as it allows for increased levels of knowledge exchange—a prerequisite for knowledge creation. This is made possible because a collaborative culture eliminates common barriers to knowledge exchange by reducing fear and increasing openness in teams (Gan, 2006). Another enabler is mutual trust. It exists in an organisation when its members believe in the integrity, character and ability of each other (Robbins et al., 2001). Trust has been an important factor in high performance teams as explained in organisational behaviour literature. The existence of mutual trust in an organisation facilitates open, substantive and influential knowledge exchange. When team relationships have a high level of mutual trust, members are more willing to engage in knowledge exchange. A further important enabler is learning. It is defined as any relatively permanent change in behaviour that occurs as a result of experience (Robbins et al., 2001). In organisations, learning involves the dynamics and processes of collective learning that occur both naturally and in a planned manner within the organisation (Gan, 2006). In addition to the above, leadership is often stated to be a driver for effective knowledge management in organisations (Khalifa & Liu, 2003). Leadership is defined as the ability to influence and develop individuals and teams to achieve goals that have been set by the organisation (Robbins et al., 2001). Adequate leadership can exert substantial influence on organisational members' knowledge-creation activities. The presence of a management champion for the knowledge management initiative in order to set the overall direction for knowledge management programmes—and who can assume accountability for them—is crucial to effective knowledge management (Yu et al., 2004).

Organisational incentives and rewards that encourage knowledge management activities amongst employees play an important role as an enabler (Yu et al., 2004). Incentives are mechanisms that have the ability to incite determination or action in employees within an organisation (Robbins et al., 2001). Rewards, on the other hand, can be broadly categorised as being either extrinsic or intrinsic. Extrinsic rewards are positively valued work outcomes that are given to the employee in the work setting, whilst intrinsic rewards are positively valued work outcomes that are received by the employee directly as a result of task performance (Wood et al., 1998). Research supports the view that both intrinsic and extrinsic rewards have a positive influence on knowledge management performance in organisations (Yu et al., 2004).

Organisational structure plays an important role as it may either encourage or inhibit knowledge management. The structure of the organisation impacts the way in which organisations conduct their operations and, in doing so, affects how knowledge is created and shared amongst employees (Lee & Choi, 2003). One enabler to KM is the level of non-centralisation. This refers to the degree to which decision making is non-concentrated at a single point, normally at higher levels of management in the organisation (Robbins et al. 2001; Wood et al. 1998). The concept of centralisation includes only formal authority—that is, rights inherent in one's position. An organisation is said to be highly centralised if the top management makes the organisation's key decisions with little or no input from lower level employees (Robbins et al., 2001).

Another structural enabler is the level of non-formalisation. It refers to the written documentation of rules, procedures and policies to guide behaviour and decision-making in organisations (Wood et al., 1998). When an organisation is highly formalised, employees have little discretion over what is to be done, when it is to be done and how they should do it, resulting in consistent and uniform output (Robbins et al., 2001). However, formalisation impedes knowledge management activities. This is because knowledge creation requires creativity and less emphasis on work rules, thus, the range of new ideas that emerge from a highly formalised structure is limited. Most teams are composed of individuals who operate from a base of deeply specialised knowledge (Davvy, 2006). These individuals need mechanisms to translate across the different 'languages' that exists in organisations (Ford & Staples, 2006). This brings rise to the need for employees with T-shaped skills—that is, skills that are both deep and broad (Leonard-Barton, 1995). Employees who possess T-shaped skills not only have a deep knowledge of a particular discipline (e.g. financial auditing), but also about how their discipline interacts with other disciplines (e.g. risk analysis, investment analysis and derivatives). Iansiti (1993) states that the deep knowledge in a particular discipline is aptly represented by the vertical stroke of the 'T', whilst knowledge of how this discipline interacts with other disciplines is represented by the horizontal top stroke of the 'T' (Iansiti, 1993).

Lastly, but no less important an enabler, is IT infrastructure. It plays an important role in knowledge management. Technology infrastructure includes information technology and its capabilities which are considered to assist organisations to get work done, and to effectively manage knowledge that the organisation possesses (Holsapple, 2005). The information technology infrastructure within an organisation can be broadly categorised into hardware technologies and software systems. It has been found that information technology infrastructure plays a crucial role in knowledge management as it allows for easy knowledge acquisition and facilitates timely communication amongst employees. Information technology infrastructure also speeds up the pace of knowledge creation and assists in the process of building organisational memory (Okunoye & Karsten, 2002). These aspects were investigated in this study for their applicability in the Indian context.

3. Qualitative phase of the study[2]

In this research study a qualitative data collection approach was used to explore the initial views and opinions of the Indian professional towards knowledge management and to complement the development of the instrument for the quantitative survey technique section of this research study. The specific qualitative technique adopted was a case study

[2] Some findings of this research have previously been published by the authors.

approach to identify the enablers of knowledge management for businesses implementing KMS. While a common practice in an exploratory study is to adopt a mixed-method approach, as both (qualitative and quantitative) complement each other, it is a common strategy in the domain of information systems discipline as well. It is believed that such a strategy has strengthened the findings of this research study by reaffirming the findings of the qualitative approach. Findings of the qualitative approach have already been published previously by the authors.

There were four Indian cities included in this study to collect the data, namely, Chennai, Coimbatore, Madurai and Villupuram. Based on the history and location of these Indian cities and their economic structure, population, history, culture and social values, organisations from these cities were subsequently selected. Both qualitative and quantitative data was collected only through the four studies mentioned above. This research adopted a five point Likert scale to measure the views and opinions of Indian businesses toward knowledge management systems. In this study, 100 participants were selected in each of the cities mentioned above, and participants were randomly selected through the managers' recommendations in the domain of KMS implementation with primary focus enablers of KMS. The next section of this paper provides the data analysis and discussion of the quantitative data collected through the survey technique.

3.1 The proposed theoretical model

Based on the literature review and the results of the Indian case study, the following theoretical model was constructed in Figure 1 for further investigation. The concepts of these factors have been discussed in Section 2.3.

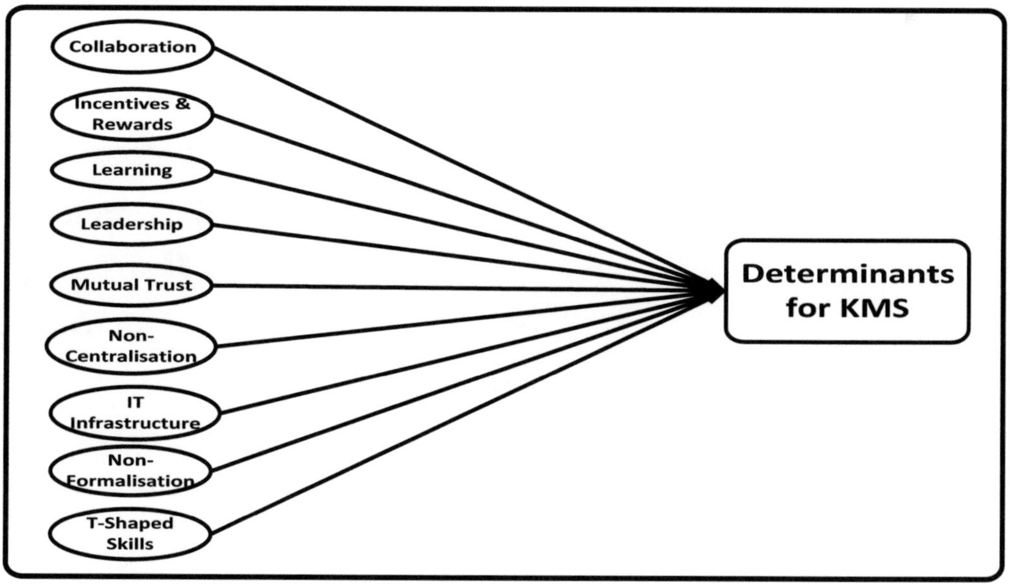

Fig. 1. Proposed theoretical model for the enablers of KMS in India

In order to understand the nine determinants identified through the literature review in the context of knowledge management, the Cronbach's Alpha reliability test was firstly conducted through SPSS for all the nine items used in the survey instrument. Table 1 below shows the value of 0.991, as per Hair et al. (2006); this represents a high level of reliability.

Cronbach's Alpha	N of Items
.991	9

Table 1. Reliability Statistics for nine determinants of KM

Once the reliability of all the determinants was ascertained, a correlation analysis among the nine determinants was conducted to further understand the relationship among these determinants of KM. A Pearson Correlation indicated a moderate level of significant correlation for all the determinants; and the values of r ranged from 0.27 to 0.50 for the enablers of KM. Furthermore, to understand the associations of each enabler of KM in the Indian environment, multiple regression analyses were conducted between the independent variables, Collaboration, Mutual Trust, Learning, Leadership, Incentive Rewards, Centralisation, T-Shape Skills, and ICT. In the equation, the variable 'Enablers of KM' was considered a dependent variable. Multiple regression analyses showed that the nine determinants have the potential to explain the phenomena of knowledge sharing in the Indian business environment ($R = 0.62$, and $R2 = 0.39$, $df = 6.4$, $p < .05$). However the 'Beta' and 't' values indicated that only the variables 'Incentive Rewards' and 'T-Shape Skills' were significant ($p < .05$), and all other variables were not significant ($p > .05$). The initial model in Figure 1 was refined as per the multiple regression analysis and is shown in figure 2 below.

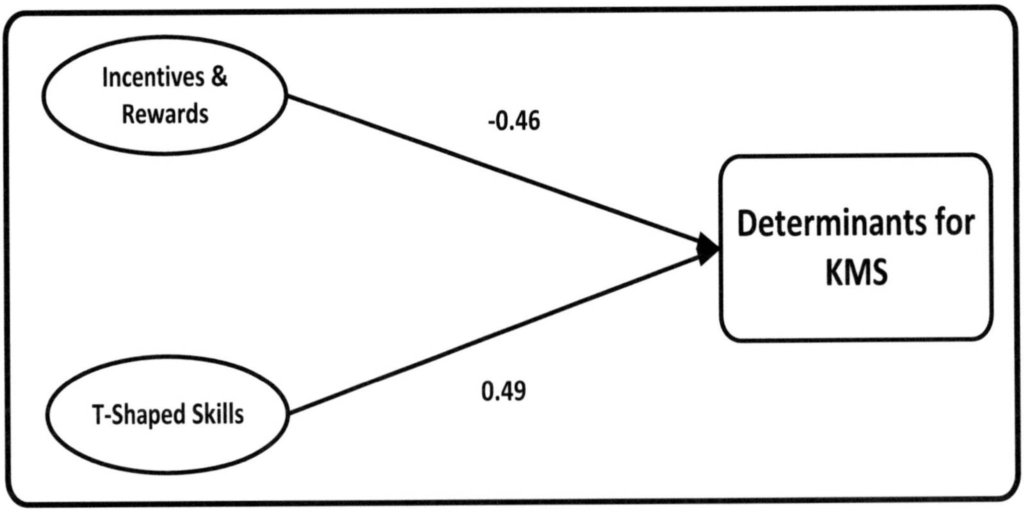

Fig. 2. Summary of direct effect on determinants of KMS

The above analysis showed that Indian business environment determinants such as 'Incentive Rewards' and 'T-Shape Skills' were considered critical variables in determining the process of sharing knowledge. However, other variables such as Collaboration, Mutual Trust, Learning, Leadership, Centralisation, and ICT were not considered important contributors to the sharing of knowledge in the Indian business environment. This aspect of the Indian executive is yet to be further researched to understand the phenomena behind this philosophy.

The multiple regression analyses conducted above clearly showed only two variables, 'Incentive Rewards' and 'T-Shaped Skills' that directly contributed towards the knowledge management enablers. However, there is a real possibility that the remaining seven variables might have indirectly contributed towards determining the enablers of the knowledge management. The multiple regression analyses has this limitation and is unable to reveal the interrelationship among the independent variables. To understand this, structural equation modelling was conducted to explore such a relationship (see Figure 2 below). Researchers used the AMOS 18 software application to complete the structure equation modelling.

Figure 3 shows the fit indices for the data and the interrelationship of the variables through good fit and the proposed model for the production of the 'KM Enabler' through the KM determinants. The above SEM model was the output produced by Amos and the entire path, in terms of interrelationship among the variables, was found to be significant ($p < .05$). The analysis of various indices associated with the model also showed a fit between the data and the model for each of the variables. For example, the indices of the above model are summarised as follows:

NO	Indices	Value
1	CMIN/DF	1.9
2	P Value	.004
3	RMR	.004
4	GFI	.92
5	IFI	.99
6	TLI	.98
7	CFI	.99
8	NFI	.98
9	RFI	.96
10	REMSEA	.095

Table 2. Summary of Indices

The above table shows various indices. The indices 'Goodness of Fit' (GFI) value is higher than the acceptable value espoused in the literature (≥0.9)(Hair et al., 2006; Joreskog & Sorbom, 1993). Furthermore, the value of 'Root Mean square Residual' (RMR) (0.004) in the above table is above the benchmark recommended by literature (≤ 0.05),(Hair et al., 2006; Wu et al., 2008; Wu et al., 2007; Hu & Bentler, 1995). The above table and the value of indices

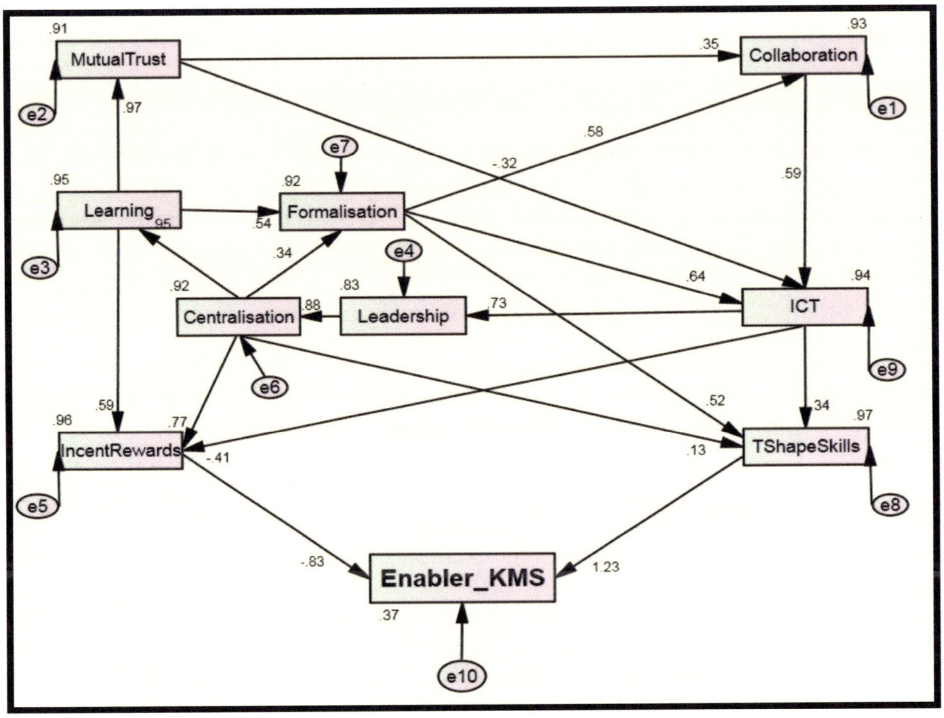

Fig. 3. SEM model through AMOS

show that the final model depicted in Figure 2 has the ability to facilitate a KMS environment in the Indian business environment. The composite variables 'Incentive Rewards and T-Shaped Skill' have a direct effect on KM due to their ability to facilitate the implementation of a knowledge sharing environment as enablers of KM. Therefore, it can be summarised from Table 2 that various indices such as the GFI, RMA, RMSEA and Chi-Square values were not only significant, but their values were also within the acceptable range. Such a model is not only able to predict the interrelationship among the variables but is also able to provide information about the strength of that relationship. Such information provides valuable insight for managers and individuals responsible for the development and implementation of a knowledge sharing culture in the Indian business environment. All the paths in the path diagram, Figure 2, were statically significant ($p < 0.05$), even though some of them were not directly influencing the variable 'Enabler of KM'. Data analysis and the discussions presented above not only help researchers understand the knowledge economy in the Indian business environment, but also provide an initial insight role of various determinants of knowledge management and their association in promoting a knowledge sharing environment.

4. Conclusion and limitations

This research study is the first of its kind to explore the knowledge management philosophy in the Indian business environment. The findings of this study also highlight the perceptions of the Indian business community towards knowledge management and knowledge sharing. The findings of this study indicate that variables such as 'Incentive Rewards' and 'T-Shaped Skills' are directly related to the enablers of knowledge management. It also provides evidence that in the Indian business environment, all the variable are significant; however, the variables 'Incentive Rewards' and 'T-Shaped Skills' have a direct effect on the environment of knowledge sharing and knowledge building. Nonetheless, there is a need to conduct further research in this domain before generalising the findings of the study, as the data collected in this project was limited to only four cities in India.

5. Acknowledgement

The authors would like to thank Mr. Gerald Gan for his previous work and contribution on sections of the literature review and survey instruments.

6. References

2009. India [Online]. Available: http://en.wikipedia.org/wiki/India [Accessed 2 October 2009].

Abdullah, R., Selamat, M. H., Sahibudin, S. & Alias, R. A. 2005. A framework for knowledge management system implementation in collaborative environment for higher learning institution. Journal of Knowledge Management Practice, 6.

Al-Hawamdeh, S. 2002. Knowledge management: re-thinking information management and facing the challenge of managing tacit knowledge. Information Research, 8.

Alavi, M. & Leidner, D. E. 2001. Review: knowledge management and knowledge management systems: conceptual foundations and research issues. MIS Quarterly, 25, 107-136.

Bock, G.-W., Zmud, R. W. & Kim, Y.-G. 2005. Behavioral intention formation in knowledge sharing: Examining the roles of extrinsic motivators, social-psychological forces, and organisational climate. MIS Quarterly, 29, 87-111.

Chaudry, A. Year. Knowledge sharing practices in Asian institutions: a multi-cultural perspective from Singapore. In: World Library and Information Congress 71st IFLA General Conference and Council, 2005 Oslo, Norway.

Constant, D., Kiesier, S. & Sproull, L. 1996. The kindness of strangers. Organization Science, 7, 119-135.

Cortada, J. & Woods, J. 1999. The Knowledge Management Yearbook 1999-2000, Oxford, Butterworth-Heinmann.

Cowie, J., Cairns, D., Blunn, M., Clarewilson, Pollard, E. & Davidson, D. 2009. A mobile knowledge management and decision support tool for soil analysis. International Journal of Information Management 29, 397-406.

Davenport, T. H. & Prusak, L. 1998. Working knowledge, Boston, Harvard Business School Press.

Davvy, C. 2006. Recipients: the key to information transfer. Knowledge Management Research and Practice, 4, 17-25.

Emelo, R. 2009. The future of knowledge management. Chief Learning Officer.

ERS. 2009. India [Online]. Economic Research Service, Department of Agriculture, United States. Available: http://www.ers.usda.gov/Briefing/India/ [Accessed 2 October 2009].

Ford, D. & Staples, D. 2006. Perceived value of knowledge: the potential informer's perception. Knowledge Management Research and Practice, 4, 3-16.

Frazier, G. L. 2009. Physical distribution and channel management: a knowledge and capabilities perspective. Journal of Supply Chain Management, 45, 23-36.

Gan, G. G. G. 2006. Knowledge management practices in multimedia super corridor status companies in Malaysia. Master of Business Information Technology, University of Southern Queensland.

Hair, J. F., Black, W. C., Babin, B. J., Anderson, R. E. & Tatham, R. L. 2006. Multivariate data analysis, Upper Saddle River, NJ, Pearson Education Inc.

Heisig, P. 2009. Harmonisation of knowledge management—comparing 160 KM frameworks around the globe. Journal of Knowledge Management, 13, 4-31.

Holsapple, C. 2005. The inseparability of modern knowledge management and computer-based technology. Journal of Knowledge Management, 9, 45-52.

Hu, L. & Bentler, P. M. 1995. Evaluating model fit. In R. H. Hoyle, Ed. Structural equation modeling: Concepts, issues and applications, Thousand Oaks: Sage.

Huber, G. P. 2001. Transfer of knowledge in knowledge management systems: unexplored issues and suggested studies. European Journal of Information Systems, 10, 72-79.

Iansiti, M. 1993. Real-world R&D: jumping the product generation gap. Harvard Business Review, 138-147.

Joreskog, K. G. & Sorbom, D. 1993. Lisrel 8: Structural equaction modeling with the SIMPLIS command language. Chicago: Scientific Software International.

Khalifa, M. & Liu, V. 2003. Determinants of sccessful knowledge management programs. Electronic Journal of Knowledge Management, 1, 103-112.

Km, W. 1997. Knowledge Management: An Introduction and Perspective. Journal of Knowledge Management, 1, 6-14.

Lamont, J. 2009. Knowledge management: naturally green. KM World.

Lee, H. & Choi, B. 2003. Knowledge management enablers, processes and organisational knowledge: an integrative view and empirical investigation. Journal of Management Information Systems, 20, 179-228.

Leonard-Barton, D. 1995. Wellsprings of Knowledge: Building and Sustaining the Sources of Innovation, Boston, Harvard Business School Press.

Li, S. T. & Tsai, F. C. 2009. Concept-guided query expansion for knowledge management with semi-automatic knowledge capturing. Journal of Computer Information Systems, Summer 2009, 53-65.

North, K., Reinhardt, R. & Schmidt, A. Year. The benefits of knowledge management: some empirical evidence. In: The Fifth European Conference on Organisational Knowledge Learning and Capabilities, 2004 Innsbruck, Austria. 2-3.

Okunoye, A. & Karsten, H. Year. ITI as a Enabler of Knowledge Management: Empirical Perspective from Research Organisations in sub-Saharan Africa. In: 35th Hawaii International Conference on System Sciences, 2002 Hawaii, USA.

Oldenburg, P. 2007. India history: Microsoft Encarta online encyclopedia. Microsoft Corporation.

Probst, G., Raub, S. & Romhardt, K. 2000. Managing Knowledge - Building Blocks for Success, UK, John Wiley & Sons.

Prusak, L. (ed.) 1997. Knowledge in organizations, Boston: Buttcrworth-Hcincmann.

Robbins, S., Millett, B. & Cacioppe, R. 2001. Organisational behaviour: leading and managing in Australia and New Zealand, Malaysia, Prentice Hall.

Smith, P. 2004. Knowledge management: people are important. Journal of Knowledge Management Practice.

Song, S. W. 2002. An internet knowledge sharing system. Journal of Computer Information Systems, 42, 25-30.

Srinivas, N. 2009. Mimicry and revival: the transfer and transformation of management knowledge to India 1959–1990. International Studies of Management and Organisation, 38, 38-57.

Stewart, K., Baskerville, R., Storey, V., Senn, J., Raven, A. & Long, C. 2000. Confronting the assumptions underlying the management of knowledge: an agenda for understanding and investigating knowledge management. The Data Base for Advances in Information Systems, 31, 41-53.

Stewart, T. 1997. Intellectual Capital, London, Nicholas Brealey Publishing.

Sveiby, K. 1997. The new organisational wealth: managing and measuring knowledge-based assets, San Francisco, Berret-Koehler Publishers.

Szulanski, G. & Jensen, R. 2006. Presumptive adaptation and the effectiveness of knowledge transfer. Strategic Management Journal, 27, 10-29.

Weber, R., Aha, D. W. & Becerra-Fernandez, I. 2001. Intelligent lessons learned systems. Expert Systems with Applications, 20, 17-34.

Wong, K. Y. & Aspirwall, E. 2006. Development of a knowledge management initiative and system: a case study. Expert Systems with Applications, 30, 633-641.

Wood, J., Wallace, J., Zeffane, R., Schermerhorn, J., HUNT, J. & OSBORN, R. 1998. Organisational Behaviour: An Asia-Pacfic Perspective, Australia, John Wiley.

Wu, J.-H., Shen, W.-S., Lin, L.-M., Greenes, R. A. & Bates, D. W. 2008. Testing the technology acceptance model for evaluating healthcare professionals' intention to use an adverse event reporting system. International Journal for Quality in Health Care, 20, 123-129.

Wu, J.-H., Wang, S.-C. & Lin, L.-M. 2007. Mobile computing acceptance factors in the healthcare industry: A structural equaction model. International Journal of Medical Informatics, 76, 66-77.

Yelden, E. & Albers, J. 2004. The case for knowledge management. Journal of Knowledge Management Practice.

Yu, S.-H., Kim, Y.-G. & Kim, M.-Y. Year. Linking Organisational Knowledge Management Drivers to Knowledge Management Performance: An exploratory study. In: 37th Hawaii International Conference on System Sciences, 2004 Hawaii, USA.

8

Building Information Systems – Extended Building-Related Information Systems Based on Geospatial Standards

Jörg Blankenbach and Catia Real Ehrlich
Technische Universität Darmstadt,
Germany

1. Introduction

In the context of facility management, specific building information systems or so called Computer Aided Facility Management (CAFM) systems are often utilised. Similar to geo information systems, these systems use geometric and graphical data (e.g. CAD floor plans) for space management inside buildings. By the use of current trends in geo information science (e.g. 3D interior room models) these systems could be extended considerably. Moving to real-time data exchange and interoperability across several systems; geo standards and geo web services can be used for the description and provision of building objects with all their information. Thus, new web or mobile applications based on building information systems will become possible where geo information plays a crucial role. The applications, which could benefit from such extended building information systems, reaches from services for improved facility management (e.g. inspection and maintenance) to mobile navigation for pedestrians and emergency staff (e.g. fire fighters).

This chapter introduces CAFM-systems. Modern geo information standards like CityGML and geo web services are described (Section 3), which could be used to extend these systems. Workflow and software architecture for utilising these standards for building information systems will be outlined (Section 4). In conclusion, application examples which could benefit from these new building information systems are demonstrated (Section 5).

2. Motivation and subjective

In general, Geo Information Systems (GIS) are tools for the capture, storage, management, visualisation, and presentation of spatial related data. In addition, this spatial data can be queried, analysed, evaluated, or simulated in real time. Usually geo information systems are used for outdoor issues (i.e. urban planning), but buildings, their interior components, and assemblies are also spatially referenced and can be implemented with a GIS. For the management and provision of (spatial and non-spatial) building data, Building Information Systems (BIS) can be applied. With Computer Aided Facility Management (CAFM) systems, a type of GIS for buildings already exists supporting in particular the facility management. Specifically the space management in CAFM systems i.e. for cleaning, occupancy, or lease issues are done with geometric data of the building quite similar to GIS. Most CAFM systems, however, are using 2D data such as floor plans or 2D CAD drawings. The user interface of these systems are normally desktop or browser (web) clients (Figure 16).

With the third dimension an enhanced description of the building is possible. Details of a building such as installations and equipment can be described more realistically and viewed in each possible perspective. The observer stands in the centre of the 3D building and can move on his own axis or change the line of sight in this scene. Materials, textures, lights, and other effects make the 3D interior building model more realistic. The observer in virtual reality can examine and analyse the building without being on-site. When on-site the user, equipped with a mobile device, can find his/her way through the building without cumbersome plans in his/her hands and can demand and display building attributes (e.g. building services). A plethora of questions and problems may be solved and are suitable for many business applications.

The deployment of a geo information system on the basis of three-dimensional interior building models requires the correct modelling of geometry, semantics, and topology as well as the provision of this data via standardised web based interfaces.

3. Basic technologies

Standardisation plays an important role in the multifunctional use and profitability of a building information system. Web standards ensure that information can be accessed by all users and applications (interoperability).

The next sections describe the important basic technologies which will support the developed building information system.

3.1 CityGML

CityGML is an interoperable data model of the Open Geospatial Consortium (OGC) for virtual 3D models of a city and can be used to describe, exchange geometric and topological, as well as semantic properties of buildings. This standard is based on XML (Extensible Markup Language), an expandable, text based, and standardised format for the representation of any information (e.g. documents, data, configuration, or transaction).

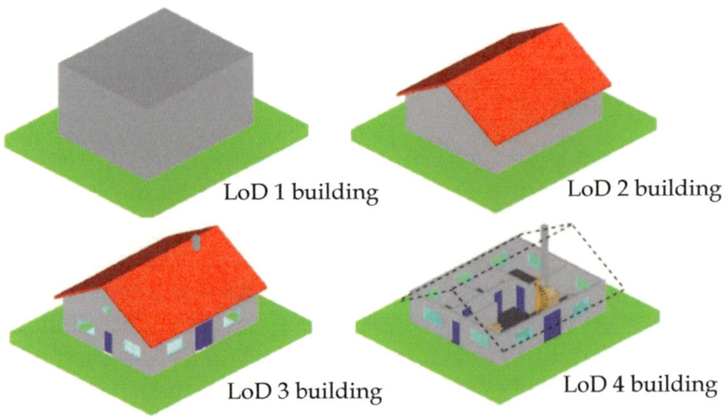

Fig. 1. Building model in LoD 1 to LoD 4 (Gröger et al., 2008)

CityGML differentiates between four Levels of Detail (LoD 0-4). For example, a building can be described geometrically as block model in level 1 or as an interior room model in level 4 (see Fig. 1). With increasing level, more details about the building will be depicted and the building model gains clarity and expressiveness. The following table describes the correspondence of the different building objects to LoDs. (Bleifuss, 2009; Gröger et al., 2008)

Building features	LoD 1	LoD 2	LoD 3	LoD 4
Building shell	x	x	x	x
Outer boundary surfaces (outer wall, roof, ground)		x	x	x
Outer building installations		x	x	x
Openings (Door, Window)			x	x
Rooms				x
Interior boundary surfaces (ceiling, floor, interior wall, closure surface)				x
Interior building installations				x
Building furniture				x

Table 1. Building features with their Levels of Detail (in according to Gröger et al., 2008)

CityGML includes a geometric, topological, and a semantic model. All models can be linked together and used for the execution of thematic queries, analyses, and simulations. The semantic model defines real objects in the form of classes, which represent the meaning and classification of objects. These objects (e.g. buildings, outer walls, windows, or rooms) are referred to as *features*. The geometric model allows the definition of geometric properties of three-dimensional spatial objects. For this, the position and form of the CityGML-feature is described uniformly as GML-geometry. GML (Geography Markup Language) is a XML-based, international standard for the exchange of geo data. It allows the modelling of 0-3-dimensional objects. For the relations between features, CityGML offers a topological model. The relationship is implemented through references. Multiple Features can refer to the same feature or geometry object. (Gröger et al., 2008)

Figure 2 illustrates a part of CityGML document. Every building component can be modelled with CityGML building features. In addition to the description of the building with attributes (e.g. class, function, usage, year of construction, year of demolition, roof type, measured height, ...), a wall surface for the presentation of a building in LoD 4 is defined. The wall surface is combined by multiple GML surfaces (*gml:MultiSurface*), which in turn is described with GML polygons (*gml:Polygon*). Subsequently rooms, outer building installations, room installations, and building furniture can be modelled.

The CityGML document can be viewed with dedicated software. For example, LandXplorer CityGML Viewer from Autodesk (available from http://www.citygml.org) is a visualisation program which allows the simultaneous display of geometric and semantic properties of buildings.

```
<?xml version="1.0" encoding="UTF-8"?>
<CityModel
...
xmlns:citygml="http://www.citygml.org/citygml/1/0/0"
xmlns:bldg="http://www.opengis.net/citygml/building/1.0"
xmlns:gml="http://www.opengis.net/gml"
xmlns="http://www.opengis.net/citygml/1.0">
  <cityObjectMember>
    <bldg:Building gml:id="BUILDING_1">
      <bldg:class> schools, education, research </bldg:class>
      <bldg:function>kindergarten or nursery </bldg:function>
      <bldg:usage>kindergarten or nursery</bldg:usage>
      <bldg:roofType>combination of roof forms </bldg:roofType>
      <bldg:storeysAboveGround>3</bldg:storeysAboveGround>
      <bldg:storeysBelowGround>1</bldg:storeysBelowGround>
      ...
      <bldg:boundedBy>
        <bldg:WallSurface gml:id="SURFACE_1">
          <bldg:lod4MultiSurface>
            <gml:MultiSurface>
              <gml:surfaceMember>
                <gml:Polygon>
                  <gml:exterior>
                    <gml:LinearRing>
                      <gml:posList count="5" srsDimension="3">
                        7.196 2.719 -4.294
                        6.623 2.713 -4.294
                        6.556 10.749 -4.294
                        7.123 10.752 -4.294
                        7.196 2.719 -4.294
                      </gml:posList>
                    </gml:LinearRing>
                ...
            </gml:MultiSurface>
            <gml:MultiSurface>
              ...
            </gml:MultiSurface>
          </bldg:lod4MultiSurface>
          <bldg:opening>
            ...
          </bldg:opening>
        </bldg:WallSurface>
      </bldg:boundedBy>
      ... outerBuildingInstallation, roomInstallation, interiorFurniture
    </bldg:Building>
  </cityObjectMember>
</CityModel>
```

Fig. 2. Part of a CityGML document

3.2 Geo Web Services

Web services represent a modern model for Internet based applications following the paradigm of Service Oriented Architectures (SOA). This architecture bases on components (i.e. services) that can be plugged together to build larger more comprehensive services. Each service is self-describing and provides standardised interfaces. Geo Web Services are specialised web services following the standards of the OGC as framework for online geospatial services such as mapping, geo data providing, or geo processing services. These services, also called OGC Web Services (OWS), allow distributed geo processing systems to communicate with each other across the Web using familiar technologies such as XML and HTTP. The following subchapters detail several OWS which support three-dimensional geo data.

3.2.1 Web Feature Service

The Web Feature Service (WFS) is one of the basic OGC Web Service for the access and manipulation of geo information at any time and place. For the exchange of geo data, GML is used, which allow the storing, editing, and transformation of spatial information in vector format.

The communication is carried out by a software client (e.g. Web browser). In this process, the WFS receives the client-request and sends back a response to the client (see Fig. 3). The service will be available via a fixed address (Uniform Resource Locator, URL). (Vretanos, 2005)

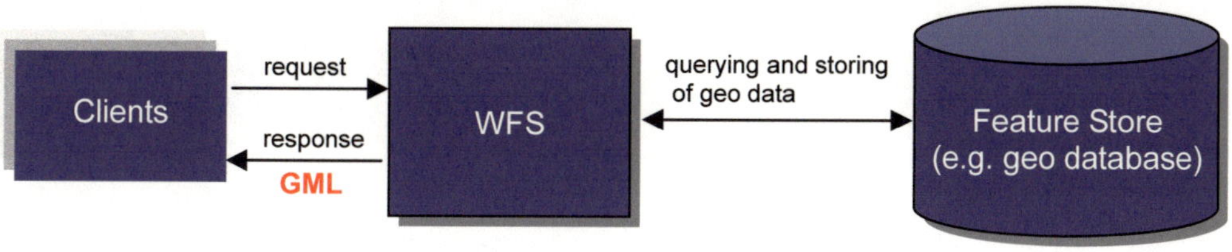

Fig. 3. Interaction of a WFS

According to the OGC-specification, the WFS provided up to six request operations (Vretanos, 2005):

- *GetCapabilities*
- *GetFeature*
- *DescribeFeatureType*
- *Transaction*
- *GetGMLObject*
- *LockFeature*

For the query of all or individual feature instances, the *GetFeature* operation can be used.

3.2.2 Web 3D Service

At the moment, OGC develops several services for the visualisation of three-dimensional geo data (http://www.opengeospatial.org/standards/dp). Examples include the Web Terrain Service (WTS), the Web View Service (WVS) and the Web 3D Service (W3DS). The WTS and WVS provide the internet user a rendered picture (JPEG, PNG, etc.) of 3D geo data. The selection, displaying, and rendering of geo features is executed by the server (Thick Server), refer Figure 4. The advantages of thick-server-models are that clients do not need specially hardware and software updates. Technical changes are installed on the server. Disadvantages are severely limited interaction of the client site and potential server overload. For every interaction of the user new rendered pictures must be sent to the client, meaning the geo data must be again selected, viewed, and rendered by the server. If too many clients queries at the same time, it may lead to delays and the client is waiting for an answer. In the worst case scenario it could lead to a breakdown of the server.

The Web 3D Service (W3DS) allows also the visualisation and navigation of 3D geo data on the web. In contrast to the other services, the W3DS transfers a 3D graphic format to the

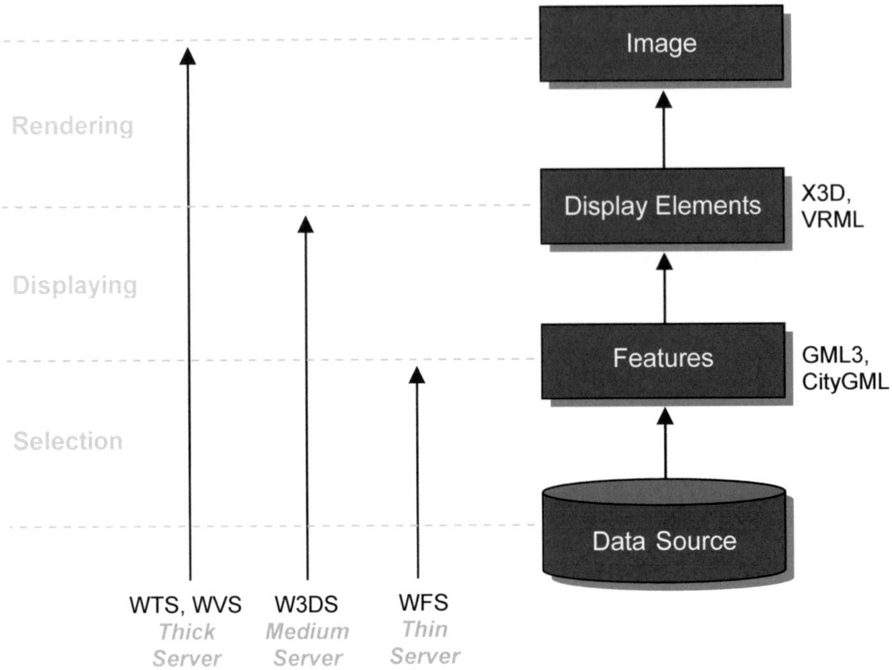

Fig. 4. Several 3D web services (in according to Schilling et al., 2010)

client, which contains a 3D scene. The 3D scene can be viewed interactively in the web browser with 3D plug-ins or in a visualisation software (Medium Server). Through the use of standards and plug-ins, a simple operation of the visualisation of 3D geo data in the web is possible. (Schilling et al., 2010)

For the visualisation of geo data in the web the W3DS supports several 3D graphic formats, for example X3D (Extensible 3D) or VRML (Virtual Reality Modeling Language). VRML is a text based format and is used as description and visualisation of 3D scenes in the web. X3D is a XML based standard for three-dimensional graphics in the web. In view of high complexity, inability to expand, and the large data volumes of the VRML standard this standard will be replaced by X3D. With X3D it is possible to create and visualise complex geometry objects. The structure of X3D is divided into header and scene (see Fig. 5). The header include the metadata (title, creator, description, created, version, ...) for the specification of the document. The scene contains the description of the 3D world with lights, background, navigation, viewpoint, and shapes. The element shape defines the geometry and appearance of the geometry object. In addition to the basic geometric forms (box, cone, cylinder, and sphere) it allows to describe objects with coordinates (IndexFaceSet), extrusion of 2D geometries (Extrusion) and elevation grid (ElevationGrid). (Pomaska, 2007)

A W3DS enables the visualisation of 3D scenes in the X3D format. The service provides five operations, which could be accessed by the user. The *GetScene* operation provides a scene in X3D or VRML format and can be viewed in a internet browser.

- *GetCapabilities*
- *GetScene*
- *GetFeatureInfo*
- *GetTile*
- *GetLayerInfo*

The W3DS is presently an OGC discussion paper but it will, in all probability, become an OGC standard. (Schilling et al., 2010)


```
<?xml version="1.0" encoding="UTF-8"?>
<X3D
xmlns:xsd="http://www.w3.org/2001/XMLSchema-instance"
xsd:noNamespaceSchemaLocation="http://www.web3d.org/specifications/x3d-3.0.xsd"
profile="Interchange" version="3.0">
  <head>
    <meta name="title" content="building"/>
    <meta name="description" content="X3D-Model of a Building"/>
    <meta name="created" content="08.12.2010"/>
    <meta name="modified" content="08.12.2010"/>
    <meta name="generator" content="transformation.CityGMLToX3D"/>
  </head>
  <Scene>
    <Background groundColor=".1 .4 .1" skyColor=".8 .8 1"/>
    <Shape>
      <IndexedFaceSet convex="false" solid="false" coordIndex=" 5  6  7 -1  4  5  7
-1  4  7  8 -1  4  8  9 -1  3  4  9 -1  3  9  0 -1  3  0  1 -1  3  1  2 -1">
        <Coordinate point="2.0 6.613 -3.221, 2.558 6.613 -3.224, 4.794 9.419 -3.236,
4.794 9.489 -3.236, 8.023 9.489 -3.254, 8.023 9.151 -3.254, 9.985 6.613 -3.264,
10.543 6.613 -3.264, 7.666 10.009 -3.252, 5.019 10.046 -3.238, "/>
      </IndexedFaceSet>
      <Appearance>
        <Material diffuseColor="0.5 0.1 0.1" transparency="0.0"/>
      </Appearance>
    </Shape>
    <Shape>
      ...
    </Shape>
    ...
  </Scene>
</X3D>
```


Fig. 5. Part of a X3D document

4. Workflow and architecture

The development of a building geo information system by the use of CityGML and Geo Web Services require some important steps; capture, storage, management, provision, visualisation, and analysis of building-related geo data. A brief overview of these consecutive steps is described below.

4.1 Capture

For measuring as the basis for the building data capturing various techniques like hand measurements, laser scanning, photogrammetry, or tachymetry can be employed.

Hand measurements

For the acquisition of simple geometries, measuring tapes, folding rules, and laser distance meters can be used. If the room is not rectilinear and complex, the method reaches its limits. This technique is mostly consulted as extended method for the building survey.

Tachymetry

With electro-optical distance measuring, a tachymeter determines contactless the position of points (polar point determination). In addition to the measuring of horizontal and vertical angles the total station is able to measure distances very precisely.

Photogrammetry

An additional possible process is photogrammetry. The 3D object is recorded by a camera. Before 3D measurements can be made on the recording photos all pictures have to be analysed (determination of camera parameters, etc.). Contact with the object is not necessary.

Laser scanning

With a laser scanning the room can be scanned automatically in a raster. In short periods of time, a great number of points with x,y,z-coordinates (also called 3D point cloud) is available (polar point determination). From this 3D point cloud a CAD model can be obtained.

The choice of a suitable capturing method depends on the recorded object (interior building structure, lighting, size, usage, etc.), on the completeness, accuracy, speed, and efficiency required. The table below compares various methods.

	Hand measurement	Tachymetry	Photo-grammetry	Laser scanning
Expenditure of time in capturing	-	+	+ +	+ +
Accuracy of individual measurement	+	+ +	+ +	+ +
Expenditure of time in object modelling	-	+	-	- -
Topology	+	+	-	-
Semantic	-	+ +	+	- -

Table 2. Capturing methods by comparison (+: good, -: bad)

Tachymetry utilises a total station enabling the precise determination of individual points of space on the basis of electro-optical distance measuring. It can be equipped with a laser range finder to measure reflectorless. Horizontal directions, vertical angles, and slope distances are registered simultaneously and stored digitally.

If the total station is connected to a computer (e.g. notebook, handheld), the evaluation or construction of the data can be done on-site (see Fig. 6). In this process the measurement data is sent from the instrument to the computer. At the computer the data is processed and

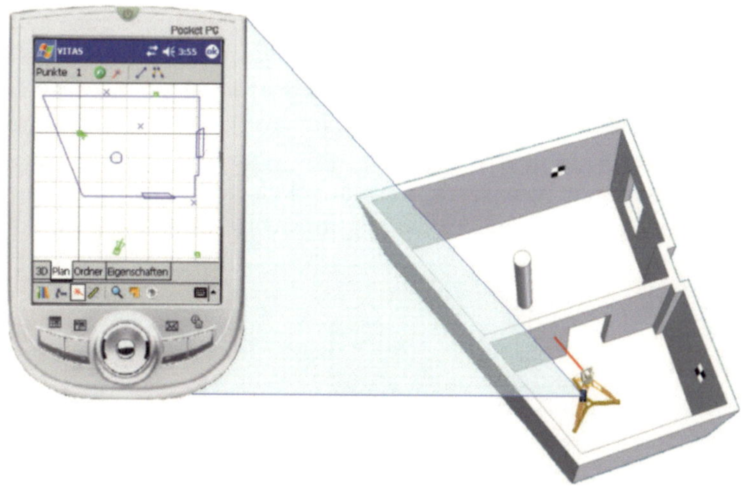

Fig. 6. Building survey with a total station combined with a computer (http://www.vitruvius.de/software/index.html)

transformed to a geometry model using dedicated measurement software. Building data (including semantics and attribute data), are captured and constructed simultaneously. Additionally, the graphical output of the software allows an easy visual controlling of the measurement.

4.2 Post processing

The measurement software used for data capturing generally creates automatically a three-dimensional wireframe graphic. For the correct processing of geometric, semantic, and topological building data a 3D volume model of the building is necessary. With a built-in export tool the drawing can be exported directly into CAD (Computer Aided Design) software and converted into a 3D volume model. With the constructive functions of the CAD program 3D geo data can be generated, modified, and visualised.

4.3 Storage and management in a geometrical-topological data model

In a CAD system, data is stored usually in CAD formats (e.g. dxf, dgn, dwg). CAD formats show the disadvantage of restricted further processing. Only single user access to the building model data is possible. Furthermore, CAD systems are not compatible with each other. In the exchange of data information cannot be read and may be lost. In addition, CAD formats generally do not support thematic or topological information for analysis and simulations. For this reason the building data is to be stored in an object-relational geo database where all building information (including geometry and semantic) can be organised and managed. AutoCAD Map 3D from Autodesk (http://usa.autodesk.com-/autocad-map-3d/) is an example of CAD software allowing connection to a geo database system. This makes it feasible to create, visualise, and save building information in a database contemporaneously. For the external storage and management of spatial data, AutoCAD Map 3D use open source technology FDO (Feature Data Object), which allows direct access to several data formats and databases.

Oracle is a widespread database management system used for the storage and management of different information types. Additionally, Oracle provides a spatial extension *Oracle Spatial,* which offers tools for the storage of three-dimensional geometries (Brinkhoff, 2005; Oracle, 2009). In this case the building elements are stored by use of the special geometry data type from Oracle Spatial. However this geometry data type, also called *SDO_GEOMETRY,* does not include the spatial relationships to other elements. Shared points, lines, surfaces, and solids which belong to several objects are stored multiply, see picture 7.

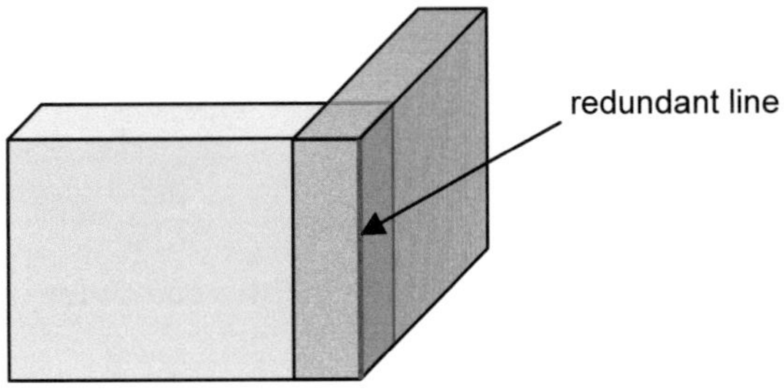

Fig. 7. Redundancy

This leads to redundant data storage, raising the data volume, and the risk of inconsistencies in stored data. SDO_GEOMETRY possesses no topographical information. Neighbourhood analyses are thus possible only with time consuming calculations. As a result, an extended geometrical-topological data model is developed which saves the geometry, semantic, and topology efficiently and allows the export into the CityGML data format (refer Subchapters 4.3.1 and 4.3.2). With the help of Java, the stored CAD data can be converted into the extended CityGML data model. For this, the Java application establish a connection to the database (e.g. about Java Database Connectivity, JDBC), queries the corresponding data, divides the Oracle geometry type in his topological primitives, and stores all in the extended CityGML data model.

4.3.1 Semantic data model

The semantic data model based on the CityGML building schemata (see Fig. 8) is to ensure the output of the building data in CityGML format. All building features as such as rooms, building installation, building furniture, and building properties are realised as tables and attributes. Database relationships describe the link between the features.

4.3.2 Geometric-topological data model

The semantic data model will be supplemented with a geometric-topological data model. This geometric-topological model is based on the concept of Boundary Representation (B-Rep). B-Rep is a description method for vector data and describes three-dimensional solids with topological primitives (see Fig. 9). A solid consists of limiting faces. The face, in turn, is bonded with edges and an edge is defined through two vertices which carry the geometrical information in the form of Cartesian coordinates (x,y,z).

Oracle provides a tool for the storing of topological data (*SDO_TOPO*), but it works in current version 11g only with two dimensional objects and cannot be used in a 3D geo information system. In this case, the topological primitives (solid, face, edge, node) are realised as tables and linked together with relationships. With these database relationships, neighbourhood relations between building objects can be detected, because adjacent building objects refer to the same primitives.

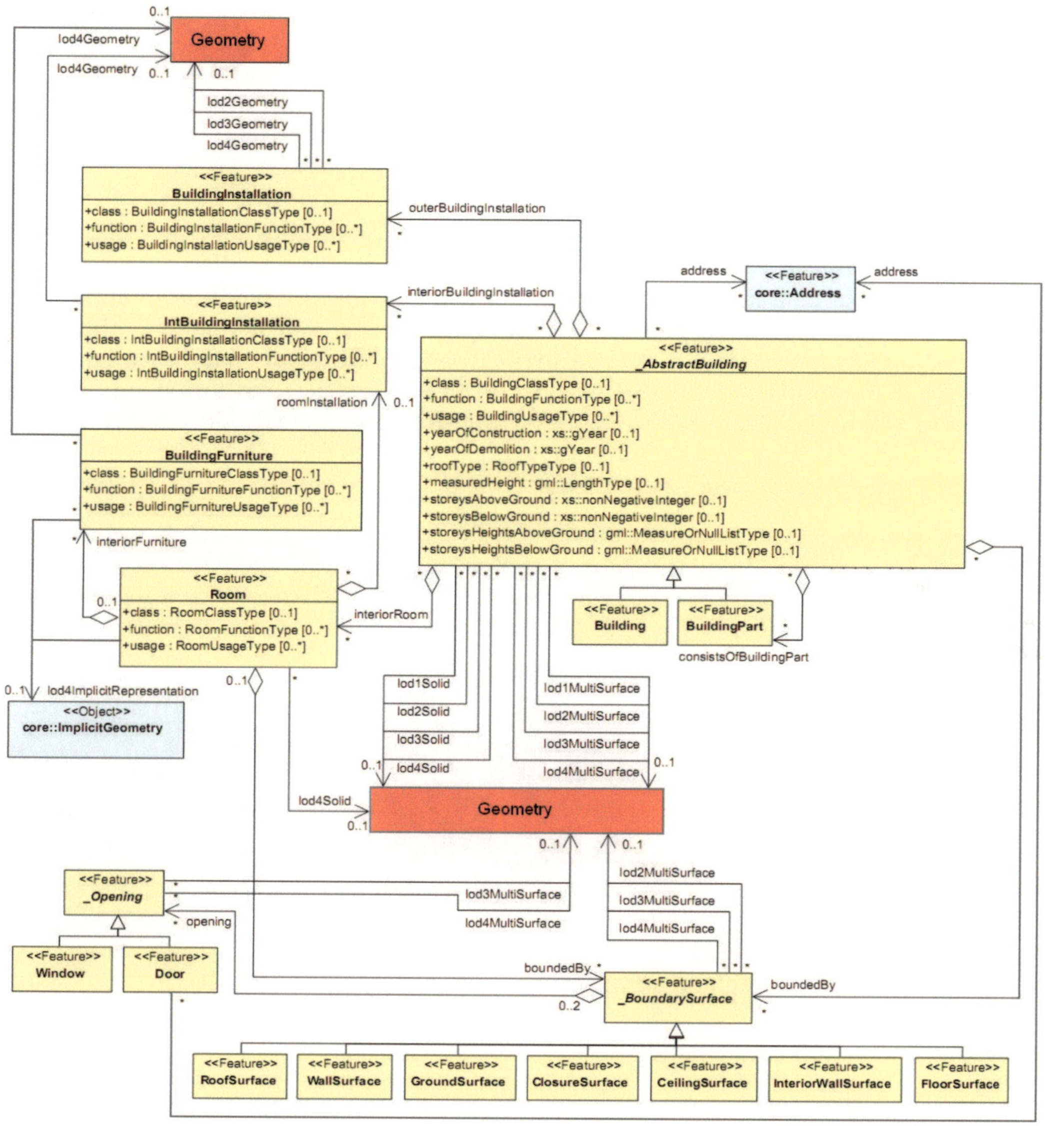

Fig. 8. Extended CityGML-Database-schema (in according to Gröger et al., 2008)

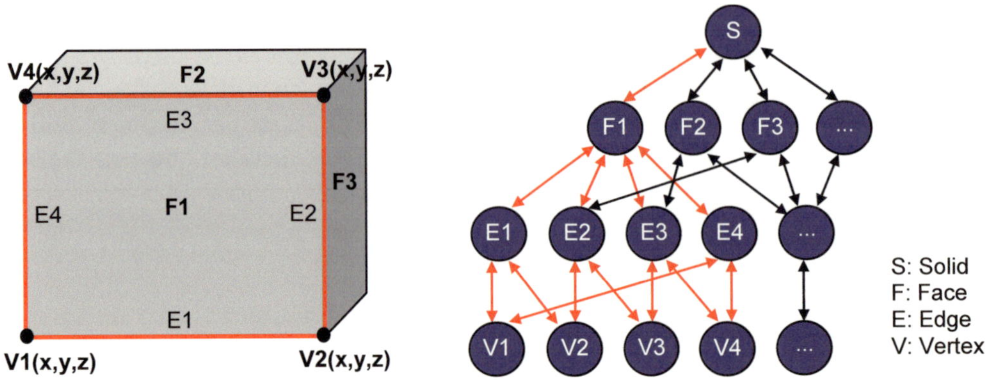

Fig. 9. Concept of Boundary Representation

4.4 Provision

For the provision of the building data at any time, a Web Feature Service (WFS) which supports CityGML can be used. A Web Feature Service is an OGC Web Service for the provision of vector data in GML format (see Subchapter 3.2.1). CityGML is an application schema of GML. With an Extensible Stylesheet Language Transformation (XSLT) the generated XML output can be converted into CityGML. XSLT is a XML-based language, defined by the World Wide Web Consortium (W3C) for the transformation of XML documents (Tidwell, 2002). With this XSL transformation, XML documents can be transformed in each other format, for example HTML (Hyper Text Markup Language), and ensures the data exchange of several systems.

The Web Feature Service was extended by such a XSL transformation that allows the exporting of the stored building data in a conforming CityGML document or in another format such as IFC (Industry Foundation Classes) for the data change of buildings between different architecture software (Coors & Zipf, 2005), see Fig. 10.

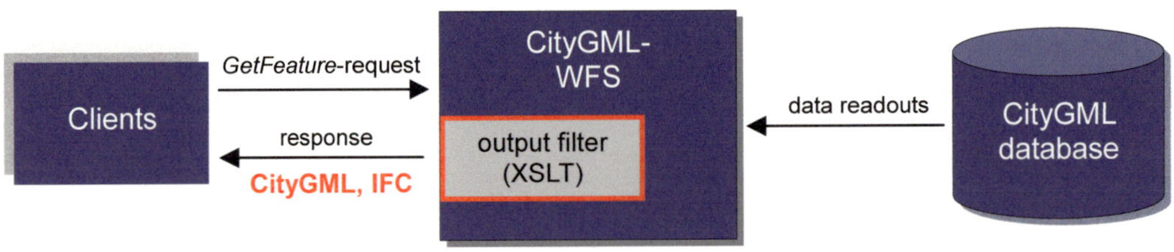

Fig. 10. Communication between client and the database about a Web Feature Service

For the access to the geometrical- topological data model, multiple PL/SQL-scripts are used, which transforms the topological elements into WFS readable geometry objects.

4.5 Visualisation and analysis

The CityGML document can now be visualised and analysed with special viewing software (e.g. LandXplorer). For example, attribute data of each building object (e.g. walls) can be queried for the determination of the energy balance of a building (see example application in Chapter 5). But CityGML is not an efficient graphic format. For the visualisation of 3D interior building models with less effort formats such as X3D or VRML can be used. In contrast to CityGML, X3D is developed for the visual appearance and performance of the transmittal and display of 3D objects.

With a visualisation service the generated CityGML document can be converted into the X3D format. OGC has developed a series of services which allow a visualisation of three-dimensional geo data. The Web 3D Service (W3DS), see Chapter 3.2.2, is such a visualisation service and able to read and visualise CityGML data in the web when the service contains a CityGML-X3D-converter. At present this service is not OGC standard but an OGC Discussion Paper (see http://www.opengeospatial.org/standards/dp). As a result, a bespoke web service as Java EE (Java Enterprise Edition) web application simulating W3DS was developed generating the desired output formats (see Fig. 11).

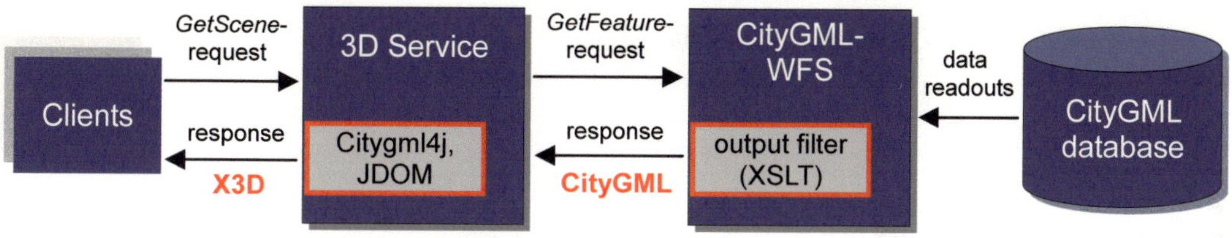

Fig. 11. Transformation from CityGML to X3D

The 3D web service, realised as servlet, requests the CityGML data via the Web Feature Service and transforms this data into the structure of X3D. A servlet is a Java program running in a servlet container (e.g. Tomcat). It receives and answers inquiries from users about HTTP (Hypertext Transfer Protocol). The *GetScene*-parameters of this service has been adapted to the OGC standard. In addition to the parameters *Service, Request, Layer, Version,* and *Format* are offered a *Viewpoint*. This allows the user to specify his/her position and view angle in the 3D scene. Via that viewpoint it is possible to load only visible objects in order to reduce the data volume and response time.

The transformation from CityGML to X3D is realised with the help of Citygml4j and JDOM (Java Document Object Model). Citygml4j is an open source Java application from the Institute for Geodesy and Geoinformation Science of the technical university Berlin (http://opportunity.bv.tu-berlin.de) for handling with CityGML documents. JDOM (http://www.jdom.org/) creates a tree structure from a XML document in Java and allows the building and manipulation of XML objects. With these two tools, the CityGML building data can be easily read and transformed in X3D with Java.

The generated X3D scene can be saved and visualised with a viewer (e.g. InstantPlayer, Octaga Viewer) or displayed directly in a web browser.

The use of digital information remotely has become matter of fact. Building information can be queried and displayed on-site with mobile devices such as handhelds or mobile phones. A special viewer is necessary given the limited display area, relatively poor graphic performance, and restricted transmission capacity. For that purpose a JavaME (Java Micro Edition) viewer was developed allowing the visualisation of X3D data. JavaME is tailored to the limited scope of functions. For the implementation of 3D applications on mobile devices the Mobile 3D Graphics API (M3G) from JavaME is used. It allows the creation and visualisation of 3D scenes. (Breymann & Mosemann, 2008)

In this process the JavaME application reads and parses the X3D file, creates M3G-objects, renders, and draws directly the 3D scene (Fig. 12). Moreover, it is possible to define additional cameras, lights, and background features for lifelike three-dimensional objects.

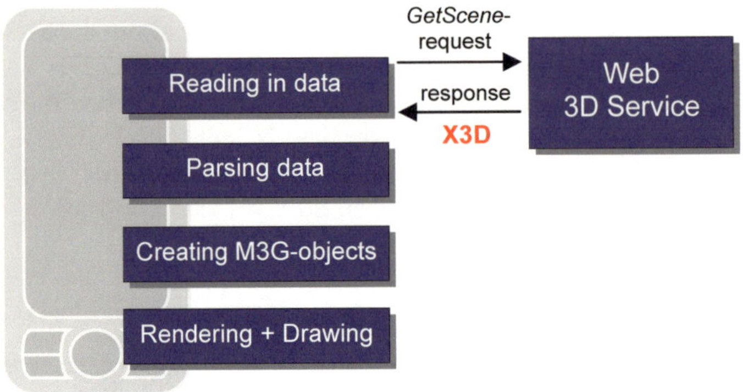

Fig. 12. Mobile devices application with JavaME

5. Application example

The three-dimensional building data may be integrated in several applications. The determination of energy balance for buildings in case of restorations or the navigation in a building for rescue teams in case of fire are two examples. In the next chapters, there two example applications describe how the implemented building information system can be used.

5.1 Building Information System for energy balances

The German Federal Ministry of Education and Research (BMBF) finances the project "PokIm". PokIm (Portfoliostrategien für kommunale Immobilien, Portfolio Strategies for Municipal Estates) develops strategies for eliminating deficiencies of real estate management. The aim is to save costs, preserve, and build up public real estate. A possible approach is through the improvement of buildings. With the help of renovations, the energy consumption of buildings and corresponding costs (e.g. heating) can be reduced. In order to be able to renovate in the best way possible an energy balance is needed. With energy balances, measures and their effects can be checked. Thus suitable energy and cost savings may be found. For this purpose an geo information system with an accurate building model is needed. This would include information about the internal structure of the building and the building basic fabric (material, heat transfer coefficient, etc.). The developed concept can be used and extended. For the energy balance, properties about building components, how material characteristics, and thermal conductivity are added in the developed model as attributes (see Fig. 13).

The building geo information system was implemented and tested on a building (a villa used as kindergarten). All geometric, topological, and semantic properties were recorded, modelled, and saved. They can be used for the energy balance of this building (see Fig. 14).

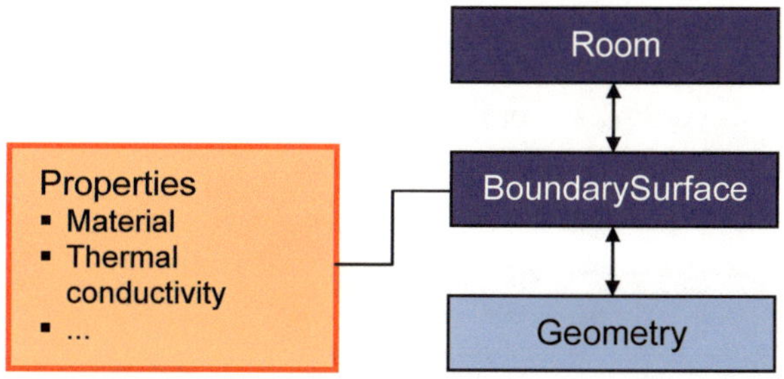

Fig. 13. The expansion of the data model

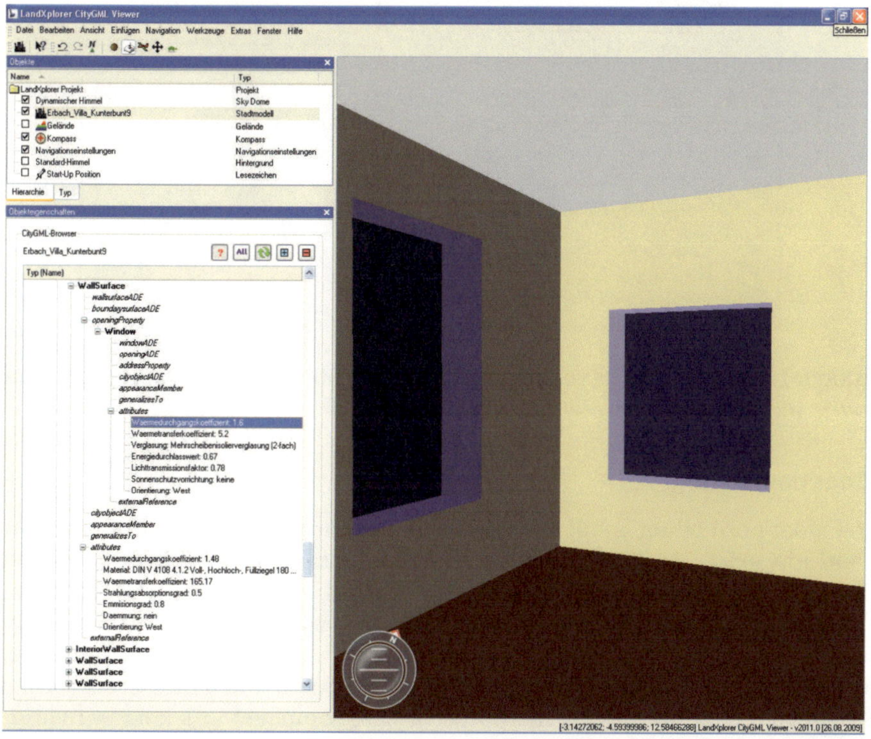

Fig. 14. Simultaneous display of building attribute data and geometry for the determination of the energy balance of a building in Autodesk LandXplorer Software

5.2 Distributed Building Information Systems and Indoor Location Services

The availability of semantic 3D building models and the use of open geo standards (CityGML, WFS, W3DS etc.) previously described allows the interoperable access to building information at every time. Thus, modern web-based and distributed building information systems may grow up from which many applications may benefit from. A selection of possible applications is already mentioned in Section 1.

Interesting kinds of applications in this context are mobile applications which allow the providing of building information on mobile devices (e.g. smartphones) at any time or place. Combining these mobile applications with localisation technology for determining the users geolocation inside the building automatically (Indoor Positioning), Location-based services or, expressed more precisely, *Indoor Location Services* could be developed (Fig. 15). Indoor location services are meant in this context as applications which provide information or other services based on a position determination in indoor environments. Generally indoor location services address mobile applications using portable devices like handhelds or smartphones.

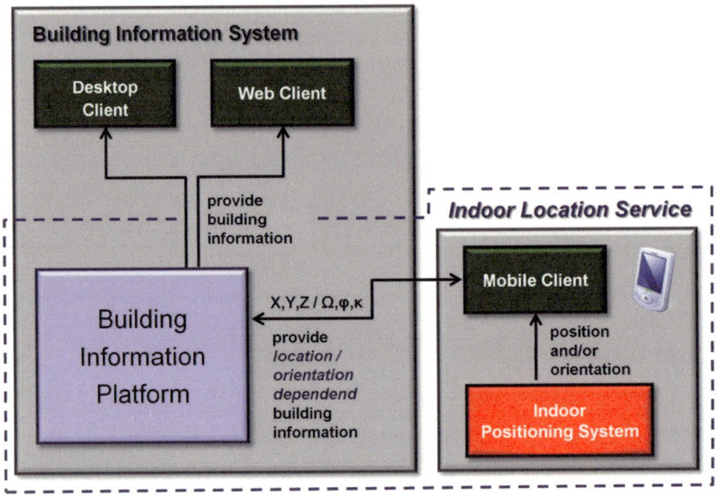

Fig. 15. Indoor Location Services resulting from the combination of building information systems with indoor positioning systems

5.2.1 Indoor positioning

Although indoor positioning is still a young field of research many localisation prototypes and systems already exists. Many of those systems utilises a permanent installed localisation infrastructure like reference stations or beacons inside the building and apply radio waves (e.g. WLAN, RFID) or ultrasound for localisation of a mobile station. Autonomous systems in turn detect existing physical forces respectively fields and utilise low-cost sensors (e.g. inertial sensor units, electronic compasses, barometer) often embedded in a mobile sensor module for position estimation. Occasionally both approaches are combined in a kind of hybrid position system. An overview of indoor positioning techniques and system can be found at Bensky (2008), Kolodziej & Helm (2006), Koyuncu & Yang (2010) and Liu et al. (2007).

In the following a software architecture design for indoor location-based applications is described using the developed concept of a building information system. An augmented reality prototype as one application of the developed concept is then introduced.

5.2.2 Architecture for Indoor Location Services

The software architecture of indoor location services resembles commonly used web applications as a distributed software system. Following the concept described in Sections 4.4 and 4.5 a three tier web application was conceived.

The server side of the developed architecture contains the *web* and *data tier* bundled to the building information platform (Fig. 16). The web tier is composed of some chained geo web

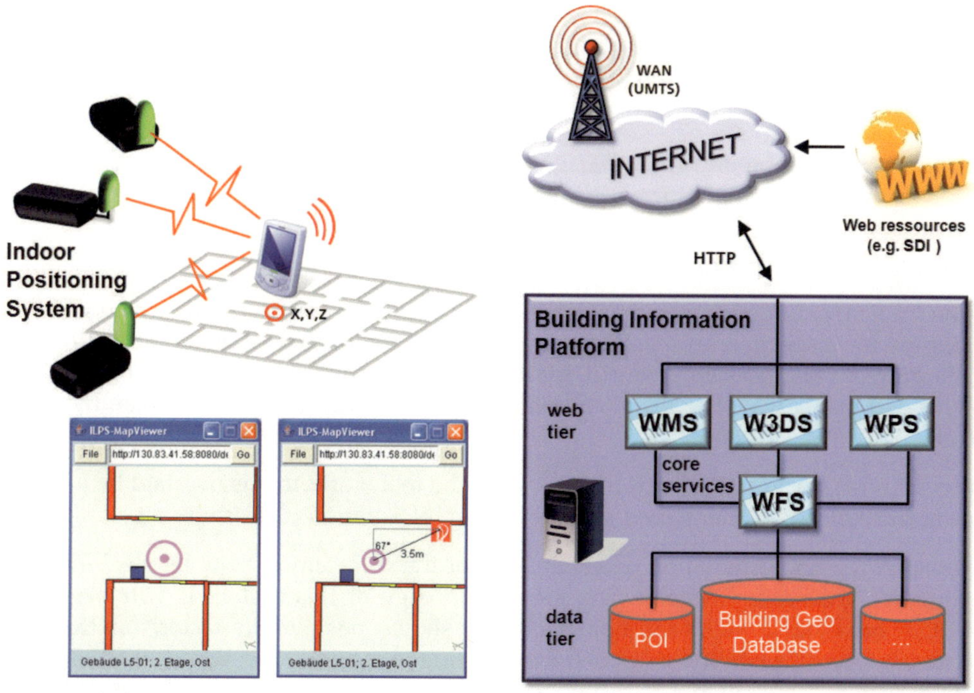

Fig. 16. Software architecture for indoor location services based on geo web services and building geo databases

services like a WMS for the dynamic generation of 2D floor maps, a WFS providing all building and POI data in GML format and a W3DS for the delivery of 3D visualisation models. In addition, a Web Processing Service (WPS), an additional OGC geo web service is embedded and able to offer any geospatial processing task. These core services of the architecture design represent the server side application logic. An additional feature of this concept is the service chaining meaning that WMS, W3DS and WPS access the WFS as a client for querying all desired building data.

The data tier contains the geo databases for all information needed; the building data stored in geometric-topolocigal datamodel (cf. Section 4.3), the point of interest as well as all further required information.

It is conceivable that more and more building data and services will be available over standardised web interfaces. These web resources may also be accessed by an indoor location service over the building information platform.

The client side of the system is a software interface running on handheld, laptop, or any other kind of (typically mobile) device equipped with a wireless communication interface for establishing an internet connection and access to the building information platform.

The software architecture design described was implemented for location services in a building on the university campus. The client side was implemented as a software application for a handheld device developed with JavaME with interfaces to the core services of the building information platform. The main component of the client is the map viewer (Fig. 16) for

- rendering 2D floor plans derived from the WMS
- visualisation of the user's position determined with the indoor positioning system
- display the POIs requested form the WFS and their relative position derived from the WPS.

For further information and more detailed description of possible mobile user scenarios of the building information platform see Blankenbach & Norrdine (2010).

5.2.3 Indoor augmented reality

As one implementation of an indoor location services a prototype of an augmented reality application for inspection and maintenance tasks was developed. Augmented reality means the merging of real and virtual world, for example by displaying virtual objects (e.g. power lines located inside walls) or texts (e.g. names, descriptions) in a picture taken by a digital camera.

Here a calibrated web cam is used for capturing the real world that is overlaid by a rendered scene of the building model stored in the building information platform.

The positioning and orientation determination of the web cam is done by a self-developed indoor local positioning system. The basic technology of this system is Ultra Wide Band (UWB), a broadband radio technology which shows positive characteristics for indoor positioning (e.g. the ability to penetrate building materials like walls). The developed position system - so called UWB-ILPS - allows the precise position determination of a mobile station equipped with UWB inside a building. Therefore UWB reference stations with known coordinates are placed indoor. By measuring the time of flight of UWB signals exchanged between the reference stations and the mobile station, the unknown position can be determined by means of lateration. More detailed information about UWB-ILPS can be found at Blankenbach et al. (2009) and Blankenbach & Norrdine (2010).

For the determination of the 3D position and orientation (pose) of the web cam the measurement system shown in Figure 17 was used. A UWB mobile station was equipped

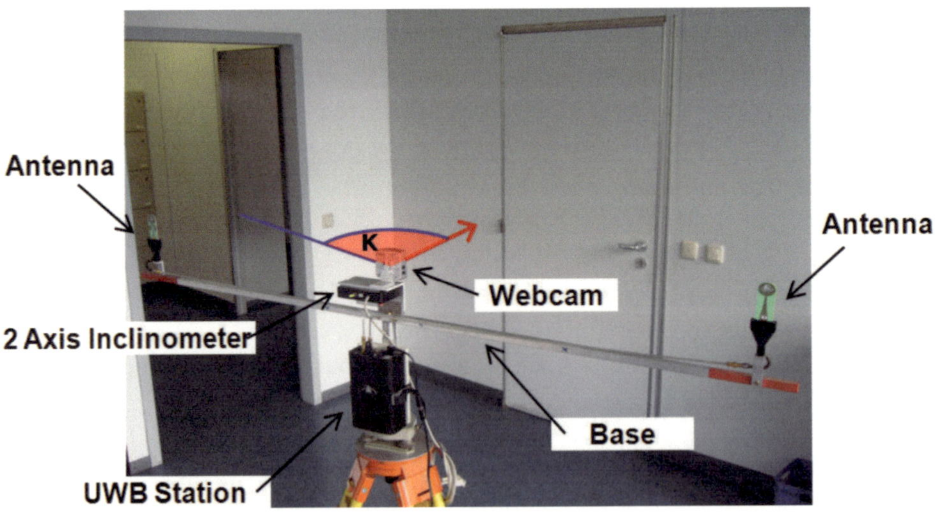

Fig. 17. Prototype of indoor augmented reality measurement system

with a base in the middle on which the web cam was adapted. At the ends of the base two antennas connected to the UWB mobile station were mounted. By determining the 3D position of the two antennas the 3D position and the yaw angle of the camera can be determined directly. To find out the two missing degrees of freedom (roll and pitch angle) an inclinometer as additional sensor is used.

For the control of the augmented reality application a software module with an interface to the UWB-ILPS system was implemented. The pose estimation of the camera is done continuously and for every new estimation the W3DS of the building information platform is queried by sending an http request with the pose as parameters. As result, a 3D scene in VRML format (Fig. 18, left) is received and overlaid with the taken web cam picture (Fig. 18, right) by the developed software client.

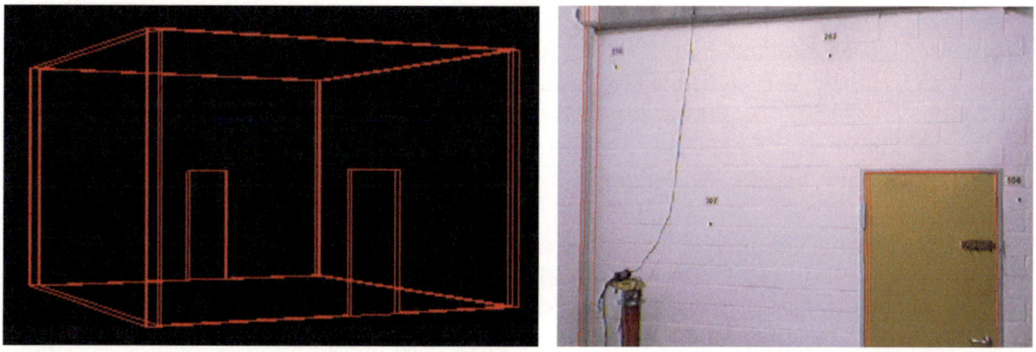

Fig. 18. Augmented Reality based on CityGML building models: Simplified interior room model (left); By a precise indoor positioning system oriented web cam picture overlaid with the room model

6. Conclusion

With this closed concept three-dimensional building models can be managed and provided efficiently. Furthermore, with the involvement and combination of additional information, the system can be used for analysis, planning, and control of building processes.

Utilising mobile information technology the building data can be queried anywhere using World Wide Web combined with mobile devices. These allow the user to access information about the building in real time and also on-site.

The advantage of this implementation of a building GIS has optional expandability. It can be realised in other data formats and the system can be linked with modern web services. The data model can be extended with additional data to accomplish a series of tasks like improved documentation and analysis for facility management (e.g. energy balance Fig. 14), inspection, maintenance issues, or logistics. If it is possible to obtain the location within the building (indoor positioning), a variety of new applications can be realised that were not feasible previously (e.g. pedestrian navigation, indoor location services, augmented reality Fig. 18).

7. References

Bensky, A. (2008): *Wireless Positioning - Technologies and Applications*, Artech House, Norwood, Massachusetts, USA

Blankenbach, J. & Norrdine, A. (2010): *Building Information Systems based on Precise Indoor Positioning*. Journal of Location Based Services, Volume 5, Issue 1, Taylor & Francis, London, pp. 22-37. Available at http://www.tandfonline.com

Blankenbach, J.; Norrdine, A. & Willert, V. (2009): *Ultra Wideband Based Indoor Positioning – A Localization Prototype for Precise 3d Positioning and Orientation*. Grün/Kahmen (Eds.): Optical 3-D Measurement Techniques Ix, Volume Ii, 2009, Pp. 179-188, Self-Published, Vienna, Austria

Bleifuss, R. (2009). *3D-Innenraummodellierung, Entwicklung und Test einer CityGML-Erweiterung für das Facility Management*, Technische Universität München, Institut für Geodäsie, GIS und Landmanagement, Fachgebiet Geoinformationssysteme, Diplomarbeit, unpublished

Breymann, U. & Mosemann, H. (2008). *JavaME, Anwendungsentwicklung für Handys, PDA und CO*, Hanser Verlag, München, Germany

Brinkhoff, T. (2005). *Geodatenbanksysteme in der Theorie und Praxis - Einführung in objektrelationale Geodatenbanken unter besonderer Berücksichtigung von Oracle Spatial*, Wichmann Verlag, Heidelberg, Germany

Coors, V. & Zipf, A. (2005). *3D-Geoinformationssysteme - Grundlagen und Anwendung*, Wichmann Verlag, Heidelberg, Germany

Gröger, G.; Kolbe, T. H.; Czetwinski, A. & Nagel, C. (2008). *OpenGIS® City Geography Markup Language (CityGML) Encoding Standard*, Version 1.0.0, Doc. No. OGC 08-007r1, 16.08.2011, Available at http://www.opengeospatial.org/standards/citygml

Liu, H.; Darabi, H.; Banerjee, P. & Liu, J. (2007): *Survey of Wireless Indoor Positioning Techniques and Systems*. IEEE Transactions on Systems, Man and Cybernetics, Part C: *Applications and Reviews*, Vol. 37, No. 6, (Nov. 2007)

Kolodziej, K. & HJelm, J. (2006): *Local Positioning Systems – LBS Applications and Services*. Taylor & Francis

Koyuncu, H. & Yang, S.H. (2010): *A Survey of Indoor Positioning and Object Locating Systems*. IJCSNS International Journal of Computer Science and Network Security, Vol.10 No.5, (May 2010)

Pomaska, G. (2007). *Web-Visualisierungen mit Open Source - Vom CAD-Modell zur Real-Time-Animation*, Wichmann Verlag, Heidelberg, Germany

Oracle (2009). *Oracle Spatial Developer's Guide, 11g Release 1 (11.1)*, part Number B28400-05, 23.09.2011, Available at http://download.oracle.com/docs/cd/B28359_01/appdev.111/b28400/toc.htm;

Schilling, A. & Kolbe, T. H. (2010). *Draft for Candidate OpenGIS Web 3D Service Interface Standard*, OpenGIS Discussion Paper, Version 0.4.0, Doc. No. OGC 09-104r1, 17.10.2011, Available at http://www.opengeospatial. org/standards/dp

Tidwell, D. (2002). *XSLT*, O'Reilly Verlag, Köln, Germany

Vretanos, P. A. (2005). *Web Feature Service Implementation Specification*, Version 1.1.0, Doc. No. OGC 04-094, 18.08.2010, Available at http://www.opengeospatial.org/standards/wfs/